Quality Circles Handbook

Quality Circles Handbook

David Hutchins

David Hutchins Associates Limited,
Ascot

Pitman

PITMAN PUBLISHING LIMITED
128 Long Acre, London WC2E 9AN

A Longman Group Company

© David Hutchins 1985

First published in Great Britain 1985
Reprinted 1985, 1986

British Library Cataloguing in Publication Data
Hutchins, David
　Quality circles handbook.
　1. Quality circles
　I. Title
　658.4　　　HD66

ISBN 0-273-02644-5

All rights reserved. No part of this publication may be reproduced,
stored in a retrieval system, or transmitted, in any form or by any
means, electronic, mechanical, photocopying, recording and/or otherwise,
without the prior written permission of the publishers. This book may
not be lent, resold, hired out or otherwise disposed of by way of trade
in any form of binding or cover other than that in which it is published,
without the prior consent of the publishers.

Typeset and printed in Great Britain
at The Bath Press, Avon

To
MARGARET, CAROLINE and MICHAEL

Contents

Preface ix

1 Introduction 1

Part I—What are Quality Circles?
Preface 7

2 Quality Circles in context 8
3 Development of a people-based philosophy 15
4 Quality Circles—what they are 29
Summary of Part I 39

Part II—How Quality Circles work
Preface 43

5 The basic tools 44
6 Quality Circle data gathering and analysis 59
7 Case studies of Quality Circles 70
Summary of Part II 115

Part III—Preparation and Introduction
Preface 119

8 Organisational development 120
9 The role of top management 128
10 The role of middle management 135
11 The supervisor as Circle leader 145
12 The trade unions and Quality Circles 154
13 Quality Circles—the specialists and non-Circle members 164
14 The steering committee 170
15 The facilitator 182
Summary of Part III 190

Part IV—Supporting the programme
Preface 193

16 Circle rewards—dividing the spoils 195

17 Vitalising and developing Quality Circle programmes 202
18 Answers to the 152 questions most frequently asked about Quality Circles 210

Summary of Part IV 242

Part V—The history of Quality Circles

Preface 245

19 Quality Circles in Japan and America 246
20 Developments in the UK and continental Europe
—a personal view 252

Summary of Part V 256

Highlights of the Quality Circle movement 257

Bibliography 260

Index 268

Preface

In the late 1960s America's Dr J. M. Juran commented: 'The Quality Control Circle movement is a tremendous one which no other country seems able to imitate. Through the development of this movement Japan will be swept to world leadership in Quality'.

In June 1966 the European Organisation for Quality Control held an extended conference session at its conference in Stockholm to discuss the phenomenon of QC Circles, and by that time the majority of Western leaders in the field of Quality Control were aware of the concept. I know I was aware of Circles as long ago as 1969 because I have an examination paper that I prepared in that year with a question asking students to compare Quality Circles with zero defects—a concept quite popular in the West at that time. However, my impression of Circles then was little different from that of others acquainted with the concept. Quality Circles were Japanese, and all I then knew of the Japanese was that they supposedly sang the Company Song each morning, participated in physical jerks at intervals during the day and punched effigies of their bosses at break times. It never occurred either to me or to others that there was anything the Japanese were doing that could be practically transferred to our society and culture. However, as we came into and through the 1970s I became increasingly concerned about two major problems in our industrial society, both of which prompted me to take a closer look at Quality Circles.

1 I formed the belief that Western approaches to Quality Control based entirely on Quality Assurance were fundamentally wrong and
2 Whilst there has been a widespread awareness of the need for greater worker involvement or participation, we have never been able to find a satisfactory vehicle that is attractive to all levels and groups within an organisation, and to society in general.

By the mid 1970s my concern for both of these problems, combined with a greater understanding of the Quality Circle concept, led me to believe that, first of all there was nothing inherently Japanese in Quality Circles at all; it simply represented another way of treating people. Secondly, it provided a form of worker involvement which could not only overcome my misgivings about Western Quality Control, but if properly understood would be extremely attractive, both to management and workpeople alike.

At that time, unfortunately, I lacked a suitable platform to convey my ideas to others in a position to accept the challenge that such an approach offered. But, later, when speaking to Tony Shaw of Ashridge Management College in 1977, I commented that if only I could bring a prominent Japanese specialist to the UK to explain this concept, perhaps we could encourage a number of companies to start these activities. Tony Shaw replied: 'Professor Sasaki from Sophia University in Tokyo comes here regularly, perhaps you would like to discuss your ideas with him'. Professor Sasaki then put me in touch with Professor Ishikawa, the father figure of Quality Circles in Japan. Apart from sending me a considerable quantity of material on the subject, Professor Ishikawa offered to come to the UK. I then organised a three-day conference in London at the Institute of Directors in September 1979 and Professor Ishikawa spoke for the whole of the first day.

Whilst organising the conference I learned that Rolls Royce at Derby had already started a similar programme which they referred to as 'Quality Control Groups'. Frank Nixon, a Director of Rolls Royce, had been to Japan in 1969 with Harry Drew, Director General of the Defence Quality Assurance Board, and returned with a quantity of training material which was subsequently adapted. The programme at Rolls Royce was organised by Jim Rooney, who has since become very well known in the field. I asked Rolls Royce if Jim Rooney could participate in the conference, to which they agreed. I shall be eternally grateful both to Rolls Royce and to Jim Rooney for that co-operation. The fact that we were able to show a well-known British company already established with an adaptation of Quality Circles must have given considerable confidence to the 120 participants. Professor Ishikawa said to me at the conference: 'Don't expect too much. If you are able to encourage just two companies to take up the concept within a year, you will be doing very well.' Twelve months later, having established my own training company, I had in fact trained over fifteen companies, and at the time of writing (1984) the number has grown to over one hundred firms trained in the UK, besides others in Belgium, France, Ireland, Switzerland, Hungary and Germany. I have also been to and lectured several times in Japan, have visited over 40 Japanese companies and met many Japanese visitors to the UK.

This book is based upon these experiences and those of my friends and colleagues with whom it has been a pleasure to work. Whilst there are far too many to mention by name, I am particularly grateful to my Japanese friends, especially Professor Ishikawa, President of JUSE, Mr Jongi Noguchi, General Manager of JUSE, my good friend Naoto Sasaki of Sophia University, Mr Miyauchi and many directors and managers of Japanese companies who have been so helpful in my acquisition of knowledge. I should also like to give special thanks to Dr W. R. Thoday, a past President of the European Organisation for Quality Control who has given me great help and encouragement over many years. Jeff Beardsley of Beardsley & Associates Inc., whose advice, based upon practical experience in the implementation of Quality Circles in the USA, has proved invaluable, as has also his friendship. I am likewise greatly indebted to the many facilitators from companies trained by David Hutchins Associates, and especially to Dick Fletcher from Wedgwood, who is doing so much to further the Circle Movement through the National Society for Quality Circles, and to Frank Glenister, Ted Jowett and Brian Tilley of David Hutchins Associates who have all contributed materially from their own experiences to this book. Most of all, I owe a great debt of gratitude to my wife Margaret, without whose steadfast support I could never have had the opportunity to develop my work.

This book is written in the hope that in its own small way it will add a further dimension to this most exciting new concept, which I am sure will soon affect the lives of us all.

David Hutchins

1 Introduction

A Quality Circle is:

> 'A small group of between three and twelve people who do the same or similar work, voluntarily meeting together regularly for about an hour per week in paid time, usually under the leadership of their own supervisor, and trained to identify, analyse, and solve some of the problems in their work, presenting solutions to management, and where possible, implementing the solutions themselves.'

Originating in Japan in 1962, this seemingly simple concept has now spread with mixed fortunes to every industrialised country in the world.

Whilst appearing simple, in fact the Quality Circles concept is anything but simple. Indeed, it is the apparent simplicity which is currently fooling many people and leading to considerable disappointment. It is the author's opinion that many so-called Circle programmes, as adapted in Western countries, are very far removed in fact from the true nature of the concept as it appears in Japan, and these adaptations are mostly doomed to failure. This is not because of the cultural differences. Mostly it is due to a lack of a proper understanding of the underlying philosophy of Circles, Circle infrastructure, and the fundamental reasons for their existence in the first place. Many programmes have been started, based upon nothing more than a one-off lightning visit to Japan, a superficial look at the idea, and the return home as an 'expert'. Consequently, much of the essential background is overlooked, and the intricate subtleties are never discovered. All too frequently such ill-conceived programmes are copied by others, and their subsequent failure attributed to weaknesses in the concept rather than to an inadequate approach.

This book is intended in part to highlight the important features of true Quality Circles in order in some small way to help others to make the same achievements currently being experienced by Japanese companies and to build a better future for those who work. It is based upon over 15 years of study and research into the basic philosophies and concepts, and considerable practical experience in the establishment of Circles in Britain and other parts of Western Europe.

It has been claimed in Japan that the management philosophy which supports Quality Circles is responsible for some 16% of the total profit of Japanese industry, and in one large company it is claimed that Quality Circle successes contribute 25% of the profits. Any concept which has this potential deserves the most detailed study.

Quality Circles are the most exciting and profound approach to management to have become established in the world since the advent of 'scientific management' at the turn of the last century. Properly introduced, they represent an opportunity to create a totally new kind of industrial environment from any alternative within the experience of those living in a non-Japanese society. If the current progress of those properly trained in Quality Circles continues, then within a few years, the relationships between management and workers, managers and unions, will have been changed completely and hopefully irrevocably. Of course, any management approach which has the potential for bringing about such a change cannot be simple. Our current industrial environment has evolved over a very long time, much longer than the lifetime of anyone currently in employment. Those who have lived and worked in the more hostile extremes of that environment have developed entrenched attitudes that cannot be changed overnight, but we must sympathise with the basis for their feelings. A concept which aims to change these attitudes is bound to be greeted with more than a little scepticism, and is certain to be regarded as a potential threat to the security of those who have learned to survive and even take opportunities from conflict management. To be successful, Quality Circles must take account of all of these factors, and that is what this book is about. Each chapter is designed to cover a specific aspect of these factors.

Quality Circles are not a slick cure-all, a sprinkling of magic dust. At face value, they may appear to be such, but that is yet another of the problems facing those who are endeavouring to develop them in their own organisations. This book is intended to help these people, and to provide a sound basis for development. It is also intended as a reference work. Hopefully, some comment on any particular point may be easily found in the text.

Essentially, the book is organised in four distinct sections:

PART I *What are Quality Circles?*
The philosophy and supporting style of management necessary for success.

PART II *How Quality Circles work*
An explanation of the techniques and case studies from various countries and industries.

PART III *Preparation and introduction*
A discussion of the implications of Quality Circles for all levels of employee within an organisation and the structure necessary for their support.

PART IV *Supporting the programme*
A look at the means by which the full benefits of QC style management can be achieved and developed as part of the corporate plan.

The book is not intended as a substitute either for Quality Circle training or for training materials. It is supportive of both.

It is both the opinion of the author, and of the many successful companies with established Quality Circles, that there can be no substitute for initial training by a thoroughly experienced Quality Circle training specialist with a sound industrial background. Almost all programmes which have been started on a self-help basis, or by the purchase of a pack of training materials or by incompetent trainers, have been disappointing failures or at best pale imitations of the real thing. There are no short cuts. Introducing Quality Circles is not easy, but neither is it necessarily difficult. It only requires careful and patient planning and a commitment to accept the entire philosophy. An awareness of the pitfalls, qualified advice, good training materials, and a good sound reference book easily read by those involved or affected by the programme are essential supportive requirements. Hopefully, this book will meet the requirements of the latter.

There may be some confusion whether Quality Circles are the same thing as Quality Control Circles (QCC's). Quality Control Circles is the original name of the concept, and is the term used to describe it in most Japanese companies. Most Western countries prefer to avoid using the word 'Control' hence 'Quality Circles'. This is mainly because most Western managers associate 'Quality Control' with a police force style approach, and there is some alienation as a result. In Japan Quality Control is part of everyone's job and it therefore has different connotations. Even in Japan, there is some variation. For example, in the steel industry, these small groups are referred to as 'Jishu Kanri' activities, which roughly translates to 'workshop enlightenment groups'. In all other respects the concepts are identical and the term 'Quality Circles' will be used in this text unless referring directly to specific Japanese examples.

PART I What are Quality Circles?

Preface

Quality Circles are thought by many to be an appendage of the normal everyday activities in the work environment. This is not so. To be successful with Quality Circles it is important to recognise that the concept will have a revolutionary effect on the entire organisation and that everyone from chairman down to cleaning staff will eventually become involved.

It is not only important to understand the nature of this change in organisation as it takes place; it is equally important to plan for it, if the full potential of the concept is to be realised.

This first part of the book is intended to identify the important aspects of management philosophy that underlie Quality Circles and are essential to success.

This section must be thoroughly understood and the philosophy accepted by all levels of management and employee representatives before any attempt is made to introduce Circles into any organisation.

2 Quality Circles in context

The importance of 'Quality'

This chapter is intended to explain the basic organisational objectives upon which Quality Circles are based. These objectives are the foundation upon which a successful programme of Quality Circles is built. Whilst there is no cultural basis in Quality Circles, they are, nevertheless part, and only part, of a new philosophy of management which is an essential ingredient if the full potential of the concept is to be realised. This philosophy is outside the experience of most people in industry and commerce anywhere in the world except Japan. The details of this philosophy should be studied carefully and brought to the attention of all levels of employee before Quality Circles are even attempted. A successful Quality Circle programme will create a new culture within an organisation and it is essential that top plant management has both the desire and will to enable it to develop.

If the principles outlined in this chapter are properly understood and heeded during the introduction and development of Quality Circles, then within a few years the whole culture of that organisation will have been changed fundamentally and irrevocably. If the principles continue to grow and develop throughout society, we shall soon have created a totally new industrial culture which will alter the relationships between everyone in society, both inside and outside the working environment.

At first sight, Quality Circles may appear to be a simple idea, but nothing which has this potential could possibly be that simple. In this chapter we shall also look at the reason for calling the groups 'Quality Circles', rather than some of the alternatives that may be suggested. We also include a discussion of the overall corporate objectives for introducing the concept into an organisation.

Why 'Quality' Circles?

The motives of a commercial organisation must always be to increase its competitiveness in the market place. Basically, a commercial organisation exists to make a profit for its backers and to provide employment for those involved. It aims to achieve this through success in the market place. In other words, it must optimise the twin factors of selling price and demand. Selling price is determined by the utility of the product or service in relation to alternative choices available to the consumer. The attractiveness of the service itself is determined by the combined ability, talent and attitudes of the employees. These same factors influence the production cost and hence the pricing flexibility and therefore profit margin of each unit of sale. In order to achieve the optimum for each of these requirements, two basic factors emerge: systems and people.

SYSTEMS	PEOPLE

At corporate level, goals and objectives must be established for the organisation as a whole. To achieve these goals, it is necessary to establish systems and procedures for each department or function: a system for quality control, production control, inventory control, budgetary control, and so on. Many UK and Western companies have been particularly good at this, probably as good as anyone in the world. But systems do not motivate people and it is the management of people which has presented the most problems. If people do not really care, if they just do their jobs according to instructions, then no amount of system is going to make any difference. Unfortunately, it is this side of quality, the motivational and involvement side, which has proved to be the most difficult for most managements to comprehend. The reason for this failure is that very few managements have ever challenged the fundamentals of the system of management they operate. Most developments have only involved cosmetic changes which, because they lack substance, have been difficult to sustain.

The reason why Quality Circles emerged in Japan was largely due to the fact that during the early stages of their post-war reconstruction, the Japanese found themselves confronted with precisely the same industrial problems that the rest of the world is still faced with today: labour alienation, worker indifference, strikes, absenteeism, excessive sick leave and grievances. It was as much a result of the way they addressed themselves to these problems that led them eventually to Quality Circles, as it was their awareness of a much broader perception of the meaning of the word 'quality'.

Many people are frequently puzzled by the use of the word 'quality' in connection with the concept of Quality Circles. They say that many of the problems tackled by Circles are not 'quality' problems! This is because they do not realise that the word 'quality' has different connotations to different people, and this difference is quite important to a proper understanding of the philosophy.

Most people have too narrow a perspective of the meaning of the word 'quality'. They associate it with defects in products: scratches, cracks, missing parts and so forth, but quality is much more than that. Quality is everything that an organisation does, in the eyes of its customers, which will encourage them to regard that organisation as one of the best, if not *the* best, in its particular field of operation. In other words, quality is a measure of the achievement of customer satisfaction.

For example, we do not give customer satisfaction if our staff are unfriendly or unhelpful when dealing with a customer. This would be regarded as 'poor quality service'. Neither do we achieve customer satisfaction if our telephone operator is untrained and does not sound very efficient, or unplugs the call in the middle of a conversation, or is a long time answering. The customer would also be unimpressed if he were invoiced for the wrong amount, or the products were sent to the wrong destination. These items would relate to 'poor quality organisation'.

Customer satisfaction has several dimensions, for example:

Fitness for use
Reliability—the life aspect of quality
Value for money
After sales service and support
Packaging
Customer information and training
Maintainability
Variety
Speed of service
Civility of service at all levels
Image of the company and customer confidence in the organisation.

All these factors added together form an image of the organisation in the eyes of the customer. This image may be good or bad. The confidence of the customer will be determined by it, and that will be a major influence on the company's share of the market. The company is just as much affected by the attitudes of employees who are in contact with the customer as it is by its own products or services.

An American, Phil Crosby, once said that 'quality' is buying from the same place twice!

In the Western world there persists a widely held view that the requirements of quality and productivity are in conflict with each other, and that one is achieved at the expense of the other. This is, in fact, a fallacy. Productivity is a measure of the effective use of resources. If people work twice as quickly, they do not increase their productivity, but only their production. They only increase their productivity if they can produce more for the same effort. Productivity therefore is a measure of efficiency. In a manufacturing organisation, productivity is reduced by scrapped, reworked or repaired items, wastage of materials, time loss, machine delays and breakdowns, items not in the right place at the right time, excessive energy consumption, disputes and low motivation. They are all quality-related in one form or another, and in different ways each can be described as a quality problem. But not in the way that Western people would normally define quality. If one could regard all these as quality items, then rather than seeing a conflict between productivity and quality one would argue that if everything is concentrated on quality, productivity would look after itself. This is why the word 'quality' is used in connection with Quality Circles, and hopefully, the concept of Quality Circles will, in the course of time, broaden the general perspective of the meaning of the word 'quality' around the world.

Quality is dynamic

Perhaps the most dangerous misconception about quality is the apparent belief that it has some kind of absolute value. People sometimes say, 'What happens when we have solved all our quality problems?' The question itself proclaims a failure to understand what quality really means. In a competitive world, it is impossible for an organisation to solve all its quality problems, because with the solution of each individual problem, the organisation, by improving its performance, has improved its competitiveness in the market place, at the expense of its competitor. If the improvement continues, there will come a time when, if the competitor fails to react, he will be forced out of business, and this may happen in some cases. However, not all competitors will ignore this changing balance, and some will develop their own counter-strategy. Ultimately, only those organisations that are capable of this form of continuous improvement, and at a pace at least equal to that of their competitor, will survive.

Quality therefore is not an absolute entity but a relative one. The quality standard of a product or service is judged by the consumer, but is set by the best performer. If there be any ultimate quality goal, it can only be perfection: a perfect product, perfect service, perfect packaging, perfect instructions, perfect organisation, perfect staff and so on. Of course, perfection is impossible, but it does mean that it is always possible for one organisation to be better than another, and for improvement to be continuous and unlimited.

If we are the best, in the eyes of the customer, and we can sell our products cheaply, at low cost, then we are successful. If we are second best, then we are in trouble. As soon as we become the best, the pressure is to remain there. Others will be all too anxious to remove our crown.

As organisations become more competitive, the tensions in the market-place become more severe. Quality, therefore, is a dynamic process, which enables the good to survive. To be successful, it is necessary to attempt to be better than the competitor across the entire spectrum of the organisation's activities and at all levels. It is just as important for a truck driver wearing the company's overalls to be civil to someone obstructing the traffic, because at that moment he represents the organisation, as it is for the marketing director to 'pull off' a good deal!

In the future, as competition globally becomes more and more intense, it is no longer good enough to rely upon the past reputation of a good product. It is necessary to galvanise the resources of all our people to work towards making our organisation the best in its particular field. 'Our' people must project an image both at work and in their private lives, of pride in the organisation of which they are a part. This can only be achieved if 'our' people think that their organisation is better for their being there, and that they are recognised for their contribution. This recognition comes in the form of being listened to, being given an opportunity to participate. It is impossible to achieve these objectives under the system of management operating in our society at present. To achieve even partial success it is necessary to change fundamentally the system of management operating currently across all sectors of industry. The quality of working life is at least equal in importance to the quality of the product or service. Ultimately, quality is the basis of everything. Again this qualifies the term 'Quality Circles'.

Perhaps a more negative reason for using the word quality is the fact that it is difficult to think of a better one. Terms such as Productivity Groups, Efficiency Committees etc., all have IR connotations and are likely to appear in the bargaining arena. The word 'quality' on the other hand does not suffer from these disadvantages; additionally most normal people would claim to want to do a good quality job given the right opportunities.

Perhaps the best illustration of the fundamental difference between the Japanese impression of the importance and meaning of quality underlying their recent success can be made from a study of their definition of Quality Control compared with that of the European Organisation for Quality Control (EOQC).

EOQC definition (fifth edition, 1981)

'Quality Control
The operational techniques and activities which sustain a quality of product or service that will satisfy given needs; also the use of such techniques and activities.

Note 1: The aim of Quality Control is to provide quality that is satisfactory (e.g. safe, adequate, dependable and economical). The overall system involves integrating the quality aspects of several related steps including the proper specification of what is wanted; design of the product or service to meet the requirements; production or installation to meet the full extent of the specification; inspection to determine whether the resulting product or service conforms to the applicable specification; and review of usage to provide for revision of specification. Effective utilisation of these technologies and activities is an essential element in the economic control of quality.

Note 2: When Quality Control is used in the total system sense, as it normally is without a restrictive adjective, it has to do with making quality what it should be. When used in a more restrictive sense for a particular phase or function within the total Quality Control system, the phrase 'Quality Control' is modified by an adjective or used as an adjective to restrict some other operation. For example: process Quality Control; manufacturing Quality Control; design Quality Control etc., in the same sense, it is often used as an adjective to restrict other operations to that part which belongs within the Quality Control system, as, for example, Quality Control inspection; Quality Control testing, etc.'

This definition makes no reference to the involvement of people or specifically, the buyer.

Japanese definition (JIS* Z8101)

'A system of means for economical production of commodities or services of the quality that meets the buyers' demands.

Quality Control is often abbreviated to QC. Also, since modern control employs statistical approaches, it is sometimes specifically referred to as Statistical Quality Control (abbreviated to SQC).

To effectively execute Quality Control, participation by and co-operation of all members of the enterprise, including the owners, managers, supervisors and operators, are necessary in all stages of enterprise activities covering market research, research and development, production planning, designing, production preparations, purchasing and sub-contracting, manufacturing, inspection, sales and after sales service, as well as finance, personnel and education. Quality Control thus executed is called Company-Wide Quality Control (abbreviated to CWQC) or Total Quality Control (abbreviated to TQC).

This definition reveals that quality activities should be as follows:

1 Activities targeted at the consumer in realising the product performance, reliability, safety, usage, economy, servicing and the like that consumers demand.

2 Activities for rationally and economically realising the above objective through utilisation of statistical and other scientific approaches. Rather than insubstantial spiritual arguments, the activities have to enhance and manage the processes for production of satisfactory results through the employment of specific means and techniques.

3 Activities not only implemented by manufacturing divisions such as production and inspection alone, but in which all the individual divisions ranging from surveying, through planning, developing and production, to sales co-operate with one another and endeavour as an organisation for resolution of quality assurance problems and other problems that the enterprise faces.

4 Activities in which everybody participates including the management staff all the way through operators on the floor and everybody advances by playing his role properly under the leadership of the owners, rather than something a handful of designated specialists alone push forward.'

* Japanese Industrial Standard.

The most striking difference between these two definitions lies in the descriptive notes which follow.

It is obvious that the Japanese approach specifically requires the total involvement of all people at all levels for Quality Control to exist. Not only does the European definition not emphasise these same requirements, it is in fact impossible to do so, because it is prevented by the Western system of management and this system must be changed before the concept of Company-Wide Quality Control can be introduced. This point will be better appreciated after reading the next chapter which compares these systems of management in some detail.

Basically the impression given by the wording of these two definitions is that the Western approach to Quality Control is heavily committed to the establishment of sophisticated systems, plans and procedures and inspection, whereas the Japanese approach relies far more heavily upon the development, training and involvement of its people. This is carried out in practical terms through the co-ordinated activities of Quality Circles or other similar concepts such as task force and project group activities. Collectively, these are referred to as 'small group activities'.

3 Development of a people-based philosophy

In the last chapter it was explained why quality was so important in a competitive world. The chapter can be summarised by saying that it does not matter how much Quality Control you have, if people don't really care; if they just do their job according to instructions, then no amount of Quality Control will make any difference.

Quality therefore depends upon involvement, and this chapter is concerned with the effective achievement of just that. In the Western world, participation and involvement has always proved to be an elusive goal. Hopefully the concepts discussed in this chapter will help break through the barriers that have prevented the achievement of these goals.

Comparative systems of management

Taylorism versus craftsmanship

During the critical stages of Japanese reconstruction after the Second World War, labour alienation was the last luxury the Japanese could afford, and the rapid deterioration in labour relations that they experienced in the late 1940s early 1950s came as a shock. This led to considerable analysis of the root causes, with the result that they concluded that the most important factor was the widespread post-war introduction of the American system of management which the Japanese refer to as 'Taylorism'. It seems a little unfair to Frederick Taylor to associate an entire system of management with his name, particularly since he was only one part of its development, but he did have considerable influence during its formative years.

This system requires that work tasks are broken down into their smallest elements, in other words, deskilled, and all problem solving elevated to some management level specialists (Fig. 3.1). These are often referred to as troubleshooters, or problem solvers.

This system also requires jobs to be defined in such a way that each task becomes a fairly clearly stated sequence of operations or work elements, to be performed by the individual. The sequence may be longer in some jobs than others but the elements are still a sequence. This system has now permeated the whole of society around the world and has become the accepted form of management in both industry and commerce. It is just as true for telephone operators, clerical staff, nurses, airline pilots, as it is for production workers in manufacturing organisations. Once the people have learned the job routines, they simply repeat their tasks on a continuous basis. No one asks them anything, or involves them in anything provided that they perform their operations according to the prescribed schedule. If they experience problems, they are

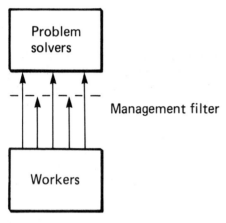

Fig 3.1

usually required to address them to their manager, supervisor, or, in some cases, employee representatives. Unfortunately, problems which are high on their list of priorities are frequently low on their manager's or supervisor's list, with the consequence that rarely is any action taken. This leads the individual to believe that management is not interested in his or her ideas. 'I am just a number on a clock card' or 'cog in the wheel', 'why should I worry?' 'I will just do my job according to instructions, and pick up my salary cheque at the end of the week', are all familiar remarks made at the workplace. In other words, the system encourages the individual to switch off mentally and to perform the task mechanically.

If the work is particularly boring, or dehumanised, such as in many parts of the automotive and other industries, it is not unknown for workers deliberately to sabotage their work to create a distraction in order to retain their sanity.

Why then have we created such a dehumanised work routine? The answer is that this system was good in its time, it served a purpose, and even now is not a wholly ineffective system of management. After all, it is responsible for the standard of living of every member of the advanced nations of the world. The trouble is that the system does, by its very nature, prevent its own evolutionary process. This is best understood by a brief study of the mechanisms which brought the concept originally into being.

The history of 'Taylorism'

So-called 'Taylorism' began to evolve in the United States during the latter part of the last century. Like most developments, there was no one single factor but a conspiracy of several elements which eventually crystallised into a single form.

The most important of these factors included:

1 The work of Eli Whitney—he had discovered the advantages of interchangeability of parts, and found this could be achieved by the development of automatic and semi-automatic machine tools for the manufacture of small arms.

2 The arrival in the United States of vast numbers of immigrants, mostly from Western Europe, who went into the American factories with the object of earning a lot of money quickly and then going out west pioneering. These people were, generally speaking, both unskilled and many of them illiterate.

In order to make use of this unskilled labour it was necessary to take the skill out of the work, and this of course was compatible with the newly developing machine tools inspired by Eli Whitney.

F. W. Taylor believed that management should accept the responsibility for planning and organising work, and that the planning function should be separated from the execution function. His main objective was to treat work and management in a 'scientific' manner and to replace the rather inexact and subjective procedures which had hitherto predominated. His work, combined with that of Frank and Lilian Gilbreath, and others such as Charles Bedeaux revolutionised the concept of work in the United States. It can be seen that even this development was not of cultural origin but was a pragmatic solution to the problems confronting that country at that time.

In any form of organised labour, there are four distinct phases, any one of which may be performed either satisfactorily or otherwise. These are:

Step 1
PLANNING
First of all tasks to be performed and the sequence of events, checks etc., are determined, in relation to the overall objectives of the organisation.

Step 2
DOING
This phase follows the planning phase, where the tasks determined by the planning phase are carried out.

Step 3
CHECKING
During this phase, checks are carried out to ensure that the tasks performed in the doing phase have been carried out in the manner required in Step 1.

Step 4
ACTION
Did the results obtained in Step 3 indicate that the activities carried out in Step 2 meet the requirements of Step 1? If not, then some action is required to improve the plan so that eventually the objectives of the organisation are achieved.

This is just as true for the housewife cooking the Sunday lunch as it is in complex industrial or commercial operations.

This sequence of operations will be repeated continuously throughout the life of an organisation and the effectiveness of each phase will ultimately determine the success of that organisation. Taylorism basically addresses itself to the question of where the responsibility for each of these phases should lie.

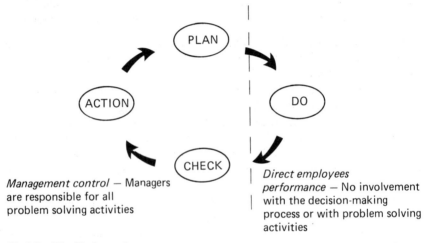

Management control — Managers are responsible for all problem solving activities

Direct employees performance — No involvement with the decision-making process or with problem solving activities

Fig 3.2 The Taylor regime

The Taylor concept requires that management be responsible for the planning, checking and acting and that these phases be separated from the 'doing' phase (Fig. 3.2).

Neither Britain nor Western Europe had any need for the Taylor concept at the time it was developed because they had craft-based labour forces and therefore saw little need to deskill work through the introduction of automatic machinery. Neither was the value of high output production of cheap goods realised.

However, during the years that followed, the Taylor concept was refined and developed. In his book *My Life and Work* published in 1922, Henry Ford publicised the development of flow line production. This development led to even greater demands for sophisticated management specialists such as production engineers, quality engineers, work-study engineers, production

Development of a people-based philosophy

control, Quality Control and the inspection of work by others, thus completing the destruction of the craftsmanship approach and referred to as 'scientific management'.

Scientific management

This is merely the ultimate development of the Taylor System, in which the specialists, together with functional line management, totally control the work process.

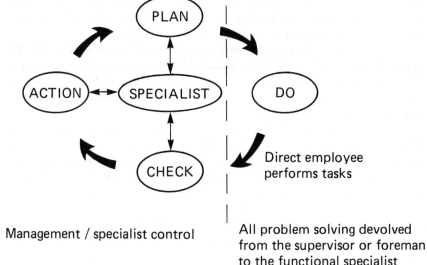

Fig 3.3   Scientific management

Once formed, the 'scientific management' process (Fig. 3.3) becomes self-perpetuating. Management becomes dependent upon the specialist, and the specialist uses this dependence to increase his own influence. There is no pressure from within the loop which will enable the mould to be broken.

This concept of management made its biggest impact on the world at large during the Second World War when the Americans used this system to build their massive armament machine, but it was also used afterwards when they reverted to the manufacture of domestic products and were able to flood world markets with cheap mass-produced products.

This impressed Britain and other European countries, and very soon the world had copied this method of management. American management consultants could earn extremely large fees wherever they went. It was generally assumed that the process represented the nearest thing possible to an ideal model of management. The pioneers of the approach, namely the specialists, and in particular the work-study specialists, then began to introduce the concept not only into office operations but into every form of work activity; hence the term 'Taylorism' which refers to its work-study related origins.

Because the specialists control the system, only those developments which are in the specialists' own best interests are allowed to emerge. Where their professional interest conflicts with the interests of the organisation, the personal interest frequently takes precedence. It can be seen that this method leads to a situation where the individual specialist tends to place his loyalty to his 'profession' before his loyalty to the organisation that employs him. This mechanism effectively stifles any further development and the concept has remained virtually unchanged for the past thirty years. During that time, almost the whole of industry has become so influenced by this approach that most workpeople at all levels have no perception of any alternative.

That is not to say that people have not identified the problems which this approach brings. All the problems associated with treating individuals as mere extensions of their machine or desk have been identified, but the solutions offered have always been cosmetic. No one has ever changed effectively the basic tenets of the system itself.

A good example of this lies in the work of such behavioural scientists as Herzberg, Maslow and McGregor. They each made a contribution to an understanding of the problems relating to personnel needs at work but were unable to provide a vehicle for the satisfaction of such needs because they did not realise that the cause of the problems lay in the principles of the organisational structures themselves.

Japan was the first nation to become aware of the need to break this mould and therefore to avoid these problems. This was because the Japanese had experienced the disadvantages of this approach to management before they had experienced its benefits, and before it had become entrenched in their society. For example, if Japan in the early 1950s is compared with Western Europe and the United States at that time, a vivid contrast can be observed.

The West was going through an unprecedented boom, where most enterprises could sell everything they could make. Economies were booming and most people were relatively well off. Better off, in fact, than at any time in history. It was at that time that Harold Macmillan, the British Prime Minister, coined the slogan 'You never had it so good'.

In Japan, on the other hand, things were different. The economy was weak, the export performance of the Japanese was poor and their GNP was about a third of that of the UK, although admittedly it had recovered to its pre-war levels. They were known as junk merchants to the world, and were noted as cheap imitators of Western products.

An account of the development of this new form of management as it emerged in Japan is given later in Part V entitled 'The History of Quality Circles'. Whereas the West believed its success was due to Taylorism, the

Development of a people-based philosophy 21

Japanese identified the Taylor concept with their failures, and associated it notably with low motivation, low job interest, absenteeism and so forth.

Of course, the West was also confronted with these same problems, but at that time, with the economy in top gear, the disadvantages were easily outweighed by the benefits. Low job satisfaction seemed to be unimportant if

Fig 3.4 The success and failure of Taylorism

the dehumanising aspects of the work method and its social problems were more than offset by high wages and by the workers' access to consumer durables which would otherwise be out of their reach.

Even the quality problems seemed not to matter. Why should a manufacturer worry about quality when he had a full order book and could sell everything he could make? There was even a perverse argument, widely publicised on management training courses, that suggested that there was even a commercial advantage to be gained by deliberately producing poor quality or short-life products. It was argued that this would cause the customer to make frequent replacements, thus increasing the level of demand and the volume of production, while decreasing unit costs. This gave rise to the notion of a 'throw away society'. Unfortunately, this approach only works in an expanding market. As soon as the market begins to shrink, or a major competitor deliberately changes the rules, the process collapses, with possibly disastrous results for those last to react to the change (Fig. 3.4).

This is considered to be one of the most important reasons for Japan's recent success in hitherto safe markets.

The question is, of course, how did Japan manage to change the rules? The answer is that they actually challenged the fundamental basis upon which industrial society is based, and attacked Taylorism. This is something the rest of the world has never done but must do if it has any hope of survival.

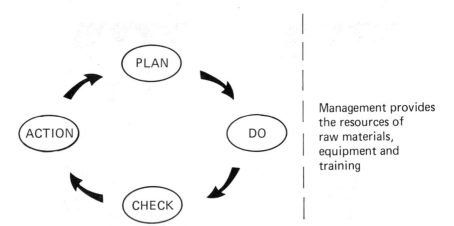

Fig 3.5 The operation of the Craftsmanship system

Craftsmanship system

For many years it appeared that the Craftsmanship system was the only alternative to Taylorism. The Craftsmanship approach is almost the opposite to Taylorism, since by definition a craftsman is responsible for his own quality.

The most fundamental difference between the Craftsmanship approach and Taylorism lies in the question of control. Both systems contain the same basic ingredients of PLAN—DO—CHECK—ACT, but with Craftsmanship, all these phases are controlled either directly by the employee or by the supervisor and the craftsman together.

In the most simple form of the Craftsmanship system, management only provides the means and facilities by which craftsmen perform the entire operation (Fig. 3.5). The system produces high-quality products, but has the disadvantage of high cost, low wages, low output and inadequate forecasting or scheduling possibilities.

Development of a people-based philosophy   23

Inevitably, both systems equally have their advantages and disadvantages (Figs. 3.6 and 3.7) and it has appeared for many years that whilst Taylorism had its problems, these were greatly outweighed by its obvious advantages over the pure Craftsmanship system.

Advantages and disadvantages of Craftsmanship

Advantages	*Disadvantages*
Self-control	High cost of labour
Pride in work	Low output per individual
Self-confidence/self-assurance	Low interchangeability of items
Loyalty to the work	'Unique' product
High level of skill	Scheduling difficulties
Sense of responsibility	Monitoring problems leading to poor control
Motivated and involved	Low wages
Good quality workmanship	
Self improving	
High level of job interest	
'Unique' product	

Fig 3.6

Advantages and disadvantages of Taylorism

Advantages	*Disadvantages*
High productivity at low cost	Control by others
Interchangeability of items	Low worker morale caused by frustration, boredom, low self-confidence of the worker
Low skill workers	Poor quality, absenteeism, lack of job pride, alienation
Lower wage costs/unit	
Accurate forecasting	
Predictable results	Poor company image reflected by workers who interface with customer
Sophisticated highly trained problem solvers	No opportunity for self-development. Supervisory problems
High wages	Loyalty of specialist to specialism rather than to the employer

Fig 3.7

The alternative

To be successful, it is necessary to develop a new system of management that combines all the beneficial ingredients of both systems, but avoids all their disadvantages. A method of management can be developed that is not in conflict with many of the fundamentals of Taylorism, but is more an evolutionary development. There is nothing cultural in such a concept, because everything contained in its approach, has already existed at least in part, in virtually every developed country in the world.

Taylorism has never been challenged in the Western world because it has been assumed that Taylorism and Craftsmanship are mutually exclusive and therefore incompatible. This is in fact a fallacy. It is possible to combine the advantages of both approaches, and almost completely eliminate both groups of disadvantages. This is achieved by bringing the Craftsmanship element back to groups of people rather than individuals (Fig. 3.8), and this is the essence of

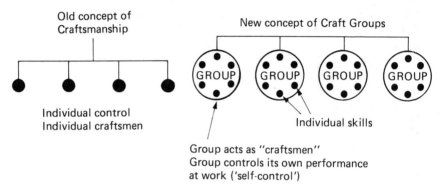

Fig 3.8 Old and new concepts of Craftsmanship

Quality Circles. In other words they introduce self-control. However, whilst we have so far considered the effects of Taylorism on the individual worker, the supervisor's or foreman's role is also a major factor adversely affected by the Taylor style of management.

The role of the supervisor

If the role of the supervisor under the craft regime is compared with the 'Taylor' approach, another major deficiency of Taylorism emerges. Under the craft regime, the supervisor or foreman is usually the leading craftsman in the group. If people are proud of their craft skills, how much more proud are they if they have been recognised as the most highly skilled members of the group. Such was the prestige of the leading hand, supervisor or foreman in the craftsman age that some people might have thought that they were fortunate just to live in the same locality as the leader. The Taylor system destroys that perspective. In fact, in the 1950s and 1960s, at the height of the 'work-study' era, many companies sought to eradicate the supervisor altogether by the widespread use of direct payment-by-results schemes. The advocates of these payment methods frequently identified the reduced need for direct supervision as one of the principal advantages of Taylorism. The emergence of the specialist as a problem solver also serves to accelerate this process. There is therefore a tendency to concentrate less resources on supervisory development,

Development of a people-based philosophy   25

which in turn reduces the influence and respect of the supervisor and increases dependence on the specialist.

In an ideal organisation, there should be a smooth flow of communications from the top to the bottom of the organisation through the line management structure. Corporate policy, objectives, targets and goals should be established at the top level, but the responsibility for achieving those goals should rest with

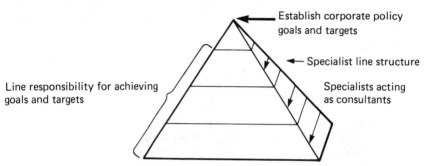

Fig 3.9

line management supervision and with workpeople in the various departments and segments of the organisation.

The specialists should not be a level in that line structure, but separate and parallel to it. Rather than make specialists take responsibility for the achievement of work-related goals, they should, ideally, act as consultants to those that do (Fig. 3.9).

In fact the specialist cannot replace the supervisor, because the specialist has company-wide responsibilities and a separate reporting structure; therefore such dependence creates a breach in the communication path between management and workpeople. It is necessary to heal this breach before Quality Circles are introduced, and for the effective achievement of corporate goals at all levels (Fig. 3.10).

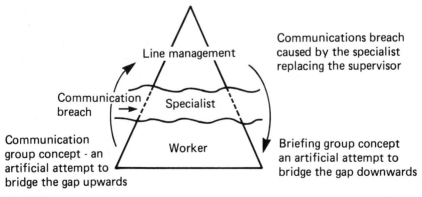

Fig 3.10

It can readily be seen that the supervisor is in fact a key part of the management chain, and the main link between management and direct employees (Fig. 3.11). It is therefore an important feature of self-control by work groups that they concentrate the main drive of their education and training through the supervisory level of management. Many companies would, of course, claim that they do train their supervisors, and this is true in many cases, but even the method of training and subsequent supervisory development is vastly different from the approach necessary for self-control by working groups. The basis of this training will be discussed later.

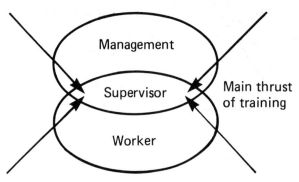

Fig 3.11

Self-control

It is important to realise that the training and education of self-control groups should be regarded as continuous lifetime processes in the same way as management training. Good managers never cease to learn new techniques, and keep abreast of the latest ideas. This is equally true of self-control groups.

Self-control is a revolutionary idea for those organisations that have previously regarded task training as a 'one-off' never to be repeated activity. Whilst in some cases refresher training may be given, this is usually rare but it is essential for training to be regarded as a continuous development process if the potential offered by self-control is to be fully realised. Training in more advanced techniques should be planned to take place as needs demand.

The process of allowing individuals to make presentations of their achievements in work-related problem-solving training exercises is not only a very effective way of gaining confidence, and improving communication, it is found that by allowing supervisors to present their achievements to each other, a very effective means of cross fertilisation of ideas is created as part of a continuous self-improving mechanism.

Not only should supervisors be encouraged to present their achievements at in-house seminars, they should also be given the opportunity to make their presentations at public functions. These functions may be attended by other supervisors and foremen from across industry who attend these functions both as recognition for their own achievements, and to learn from the achievements of others. In Japan this had become a nationwide movement by 1960 and was supported by a magazine *Gemba to QC* (later renamed *FQC/QC for the Foreman*). This periodical was designed both for foremen and for people in the workshop.

Whilst this development has proved to be enormously successful, and that supervisors developed to take managerial responsibility is an impressive advantage, the problems associated with low morale at the workplace remain if

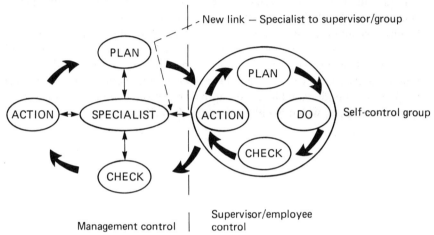

Fig 3.12

the opportunity does not pass down to direct employees. These problems can only be successfully overcome if this concept of the delegation of control can be taken right down to include these individual groups of workpeople.

It will be found that a very effective way of achieving this is to allow the supervisor to train his or her own group of people as part of the supervisor's own personal development (Fig. 3.12). *This specific form of training should not be done by a consultant or outside trainer*, but of course the supervisor must be properly trained to carry out this function.

Presentations

Because the value of making presentations is now realised to be an effective means of continuous development for the supervisor, the same concept may be introduced into the workplace in small group activities. The Craftsmanship concept is based upon trust and respect for the individual. Thus it was necessary to confer this same trust and respect to the groups. That each working group should be responsible for the achievement of its own levels of performance within the framework of corporate goals and targets is an essential feature in the development of self-control.

It will be quickly realised that this can only be achieved by ensuring that each group of workpeople is given the kind of information necessary to exercise this form of self-control, and to do this it is necessary for management to make a clear statement of its objectives, to collect and evaluate data, and to make this data available to everybody: in other words management must treat the groups in the same way as it treats managers at other levels.

Because of the growing awareness of the importance of quality as a means of survival and the need to establish very much higher standards for quality achievement, the bulk of the training given should be based upon Quality Control techniques, for identifying, analysing and solving work-related problems, and the objective should be to create Company-wide Quality Control (CWQC). This concept, which is a philosophy that combines both the system requirements stated earlier, with the people requirements identified in this chapter, is not understood in the Western world; it should not be confused with quality assurance, which is only one part of CWQC.

4 Quality Circles—what they are

The preceding chapters have illustrated how people can effectively become involved in the success of an organisation through the development of self-control in 'small group' type activities. These activities can be organised in several different ways, and can include task force operations, value analysis teams, value engineering, project groups, action centred groups, etc. Each plays a different but important part in participative activities. True 'self-control' can only be introduced through Quality Circle type activities.

The Quality Circle is a specific form of small group activity, and serves a distinctly different purpose from other kinds of group, team or committee activities. The purpose of this chapter is to define precisely what Quality Circles are, and what they represent. It commences with a brief explanation of the stages of development in the life of a Quality Circle.

The principle of 'self-control'

Most Western people confuse Quality Circles with problem-solving groups. Quality Circles in fact represent the form of 'self-control' suggested in Chapter 3. This ultimately goes far beyond simple problem solving, although problem solving is usually the point where they start.

The size of the group that comprises a Quality Circle is important. Too large a group makes it difficult for everyone to participate. If there are more people in the work area than can be accommodated in one Circle, there is no reason why others should not be formed to involve the remaining employees. They are unlikely to conflict with each other. Most Circles have between 6 and 10 people, and the concept works well with groups of this size. Sometimes there are Circles of only 3 to 5 people simply because there are only that number of people in the section.

Circle development

Once a Circle has been formed, all being well, it will pass through three distinct phases of development, to the fourth ultimate stage. Whether or not it ever reaches this final stage is entirely dependent upon the objectives and support of management.

The problem-solving phase

Phase 1—Initial phase During this phase, the Circle will have been trained in simple techniques which will enable its members to identify, analyse and solve some of the more pressing problems in their own work area. These problems will include:

> Wastage of materials
> Housekeeping problems
> Delays, hold-ups, etc.
> Inadequate job instructions
> Quality
> Productivity
> Energy consumption
> Environmental problems
> Handling
> Safety

and, the quality of work life generally.

These will usually be the problems that are uppermost in the minds of most employees.

Phase 2—Monitoring and problem solving After a short time, when several of the simpler problems have been resolved and many others have just 'disappeared' as a result of other improvements in the work environment, the Circle will begin to develop a 'monitoring' mentality. The members will have been trained in simple control techniques, and will use these to maintain the improvements already made.

Phase 3—Innovation—self-improvement and problem solving There is almost a natural progression to the self-improvement phase from phase 2. As the Circle begins to mature, and most of the techniques taught have been well practised and understood, the confidence of the group will have grown considerably. The members will also have gained a wider acceptance by their colleagues in their own and other departments and also by management. In other words, they will be treated with greater respect.

It is about this time that the Circle will progress from 'just solving problems' to the mentality of seeking ways of making improvements. Obviously, this will take longer in some cases than others.

Phase 4—Self-control At the time of writing, it is unlikely that any Circles in Western Europe have reached this stage of development. Whether it is reached at all is as much dependent on managers and others outside the Circle as it is on the Circle members themselves.

Having passed through phases 1, 2 and 3, the Circle will be very mature, and trusted by management. The organisation will have realised much of the potential available from this style of management, and will be both seeking ways of furthering the development of the existing Circles and envisaging new ones.

The latter is only a question of continuing the same form of development with new groups, but the continuous development of existing, mature Circles will be breaking fresh ground in most societies, and is relatively recent among even those companies with 20 years of development. The development of existing Circles involves two factors, internal and external.

Internally, it is necessary for the organisation to ensure that such Circles have access to all the information, training aids and techniques necessary for them to progress. They may indulge in self-study. It will be necessary for management consciously to give them information such as Quality Control data and so forth. They should have access to technical journals relating to their work and attend in-house seminars in order to be kept abreast of the latest developments in their field.

Externally, such Circles should be given the opportunity of communicating with professional educational and specialist institutions, and should make either direct or indirect contact with suppliers when relevant to their activities. They should be permitted to attend conventions where they can meet Circle members from other organisations, and can trade experiences with each other. They should also be allowed to attend conferences and seminars to help them progress in their work.

All this may seem a little advanced at this stage of development, but it does no harm to look ahead to the future. It will be appreciated that if such a stage is reached we will have created a fundamentally different society from that with which we are so familiar today.

Let us now consider again the definition of a Quality Circle: A Quality Circle is a small group of between three and twelve people who do the same or similar work, voluntarily meeting together regularly for about one hour per week in paid time, usually under the leadership of their own supervisor, and trained to identify, analyse and solve some of the problems in their work, presenting solutions to management and, where possible, implementing solutions themselves.

The wording of the definition of Quality Circles is very important to the success of a programme. Organisations which have failed to realise this are usually disappointed with the programme they have developed when it is compared with programmes developed by those who have followed the classic approach.

Taking each aspect of the definition in turn, the basis of each point will be reviewed.

1 'A small group of people who do similar work'

The Circle should comprise a more or less homogeneous group of people, usually from the same work area. They will usually have a similar educational background, speak the same work language, and no one member should be inhibited in any way by the presence of another. Whilst in exceptional circumstances some variation of this important rule may be necessary, generally speaking, such variations should be avoided.

The reason for this restriction will become more apparent in the next section of the book when the mode of operation and the techniques of Circles are reviewed, but basically, it will be found that the more homogeneous the group, the more impressive will be its achievements and the greater its cohesion.

Circles comprising members from different disciplines or with different work experience will find that the more fragmented they are the more difficult it will be for them to select a project which is of interest to all members. Those least directly affected by the potential achievement will show less interest than the other members, and, if some of the work-related jargon is unfamiliar, boredom may be induced, with a resulting loss of morale and possibly the loss of some members.

Another problem may arise if some members have a higher educational background than others. In such cases there is a tendency for the more educated members of the Circle to 'take over' the problem, and solve it on behalf of the group. Whilst in most cases this may not be evident to those outside the Circle, a very important confidence-building aspect of Quality Circles will be lost.

That is not to say that the Circle cannot utilise the services of specialists or others if it so wishes. For example, the members may invite such people into the Circle for a specific project if they feel it will help produce a more soundly thought out solution. In such cases, these guests are really acting as consultants to the Circle, and a supportive management should actively encourage this process.

This arrangement fits in well with the concept of 'self-control' which should be the ultimate aim of corporate management in developing Circles in the first place.

2 'Three to twelve people'

Reference to this feature was given at the beginning of the chapter but some elaboration is necessary. The Circle should be seen as a team and not as a committee. The section members must also see it as 'their section's Circle' and *not* as an elite group in their work area. Although some members of the section may not wish to participate in the weekly meetings, group members should actively encourage them to make suggestions and solicit their ideas on Circle projects.

If the work area contains more enthusiasts than can be included in one Circle, others may be formed progressively once the earlier groups have become established. Those as yet unfamiliar with Quality Circles specifically may fear that such a development can lead to conflict and rivalry between groups, but this is extremely rare. It is far more likely that they will co-operate with each other, even helping to collect data for each other's projects, and occasionally, if need arises, form cross Circle subgroups for the solution of specific problems. Such developments are a sign of maturity in Circle activities and are to be encouraged wherever possible.

In cases where there are only one, two or three people in the work area, it may not be possible to form them into a Circle, but usually, they will have considerable interaction with other more heavily populated sections. Not only will there be plenty of opportunity for them to become involved in the projects of Circles in these areas, but it may frequently happen that the Circle will repay the help that they give by working on some projects of their choice. Again this is a sign of maturity and cannot be expected in the early stages of development.

3 'Voluntarily meeting together'

The meaning of the word 'voluntarily' is hard to define, but basically, in the context of Quality Circles, it means that no one has to join a Circle. People are free to join and free to leave. If someone joins a Circle and subsequently chooses to leave it, there should be no pressure, inquests or recriminations. Obviously, if someone drops out of a Circle it should be regarded as a danger signal that all might not be well in the group, and the Circle leaver should be discreetly asked the reason for leaving. If there is a problem, and it can be overcome, then that individual may, if he chooses to do so, return to the group if the opportunity exists.

The fact that people join a Circle because they want to, rather than because they have to, means that they are prepared to work. You can lead a horse to water, but you cannot make it drink.

The reality of this was very quickly learned by the Japanese when they first began Circles in 1962. Those companies which recognised the value of voluntariness soon developed strikingly more effective programmes than those in which membership was compulsory.

Whilst the number of volunteers may be quite small in the early stages, when people may possibly be suspicious of management motives, the number should begin to increase dramatically as soon as the achievements of the earlier Circles become known and confidence is gained.

If a pilot scheme of say five Circles is successful, then in a matter of days, weeks or months, depending upon the circumstances, people should be saying 'why can't we have a Circle in our section?' or 'why are all the Circles on the day shift? Why can't we have a Circle on nights?' and so forth.

When managers from other departments realise that the areas with Circles are improving their performance, they will soon begin to request an equal opportunity.

The fact that membership is voluntary does not mean that the organisation has to wait until people knock on the door and request a Circle to be formed.

Many people, possibly most, in the early stages have been invited to join but not compelled.

They should be free to drop out at any time if they wish, even in the middle of training. In a sense, they are actually only volunteering to attend the next meeting, although dropping out is fortunately relatively rare.

4 'Meeting regularly for about an hour per week'

Whilst some variation in timing exists, it is generally agreed that when circumstances permit, the regular weekly meeting is preferred to once fortnightly or to irregular times on a weekly basis.

A regular meeting time is habit-forming, and the day of the meeting will soon be associated in the minds of the members as 'Circle Day' and in such cases, members are much less likely to forget to attend. This sometimes happens in other cases.

Two diametrically opposite attitudes are frequently taken to the idea of Circles meeting for an hour per week. Some people cannot imagine that much can be achieved in such a short time; others are more concerned that they might be losing ten hours per week production from a group of ten people. In the latter case, the facts show otherwise, for two important reasons.

1   Circles will usually agree to hold their meetings at a time which causes least interference with work schedules. For example, in process work, they may hold their meetings during a maintenance period, job changeover, or after completion of the weekly work schedule. When this is impossible, they may agree to hold the meeting at the beginning or end of the shift, or during the lunch break. Of course, in these cases agreement as to payment will have to be reached.

2   The activities of Circles are such that a company would be extremely unlikely to detect any loss of production or output from any section as a result of Circle activities. In fact, one of the most striking benefits of Quality Circles is an increase in productivity which will more than compensate for the lost time. This is because Circle members are usually extremely conscious of the factors that interrupt their work, and these problems are likely to become early targets for a Quality Circle.

In the case of those concerned about the short length of Circle meetings, it must be realised that Circles do not work in the same way as committees. Normally Circles do not keep minutes, or spend half the meeting time discussing minutes of the last meeting; they just get down to work straight away. The techniques used by the Circles and described in the next section are extremely effective when used in this type of small group activity, and both members and others are usually amazed how much they achieve in only one hour per week.

5 'In paid time'

We say in 'paid time' rather than normal working hours because there are some cases, such as those described above, when it becomes difficult or impossible to hold the meeting during scheduled work periods.

This may be particularly relevant in shift work operations, when Circles may sometimes span shifts. If the Circle comprises members from each of three or more shifts, it may be possible to hold the meeting during an overlap between two shifts, but the members from other shifts will either miss the meeting, or have to attend outside shift time. The pay arrangements for this will have to be worked out between all concerned, not, of course, overlooking the views or the arrangements of non-Circle members. Contrary to popular belief, Circle members in Japan are also paid for their time when these situations arise.

6 'Under the leadership of their own supervisor'

Some people ask why the supervisor should be the Circle leader. They may say 'why cannot the leader be selected or elected from the members of the group?' Whilst there may be circumstances where this arrangement may be desirable or necessary, they are very few and far between. Even when this is the best alternative, it is rarely ever better than using the appointed supervisor.

Some managers who are unfamiliar with the working of Quality Circles sometimes fear that they will lose control and that the Quality Circle is a way of by-passing them. Supervisors might certainly fear this if they did not have the opportunity of being Circle leaders. Additionally, they would fear that their workpeople might use the Circle as a means of highlighting the supervisor's shortcomings and therefore regard the Circle as a threat.

This would be a tragedy, because nothing could be further from the truth. Management's motives in setting up Quality Circles are to make better use of the existing structure, not to create alternatives. Circles are concerned with work-related problems and not with grievances, wages, salaries or conditions of employment. If these items are contentious then the group must take them up through the appropriate channels in the usual way. Circles are not part of the bargaining, negotiating or grievance machinery, neither do they impinge upon the activities of those who are responsible for these aspects of a company's affairs.

Because the Circle is purely concerned with work-related problems, and because the supervisor is the appointed leader of the group, it follows that direct supervisors should at least have the first option to be the Circle leader.

However, once the group has been formed, the members, and others in the work area will quickly realise that it doesn't matter who the leader is because Circle decision-making is a totally democratic process. When the Circle members are in the meeting room together, everyone has one vote, and no one's opinion is any more or less important than anyone else's.

The smart Circle leader will soon learn that it is not easy to be both the leader and to think up ideas at the same time, and so may, after a short time, offer to rotate the leadership of each meeting around the group. Not only will this enable the official Circle leader to contribute his or her own ideas, but it is also a very effective part of the people-building process, and gives confidence to the members of the group. A leader who develops in this way will usually gain considerable respect from the members as a result.

From the leader's and the organisational point of view, this development may lead to further advantages. If the work area is large, and there are others wishing to form a Circle, the leader may allow the original Circle to become self-propelled while he forms a new Circle in the section. When this Circle has developed, the supervisor may then keep an eye on both groups.

Should there be any reason why the supervisor cannot be, or does not want to be, the Circle leader, then assuming the desire is there amongst the members of the work group, an alternative must be found.

First of all, the supervisor must be given confidence that the Circle, if formed, will not constitute a threat to his or her authority, and the group should be made very much aware of this. The group must be encouraged to discuss its work with the supervisor and where possible solicit his or her ideas. When it comes to the management presentation, the supervisor should always be invited to attend.

In situations where the supervisor neither wishes to participate in the Circle, nor is prepared to allow a Circle to be formed in the work area, it is up to management to make a decision whether one of its appointees should be allowed to continue in a position which obstructs both the wishes of management and workpeople alike, and the action taken in such circumstances is beyond the scope of this book. It is, however, encouraging to note that such situations are extremely rare.

7 'To identify, analyse and solve problems in their work'

The key point about this part of the definition is the fact that the Circles identify their own problems in their own work area. That is not to say that other people may not make suggestions. Indeed, the essence of Quality Circles ultimately should be that the Circles really become managers at their own level.

People can only manage if they are fed with information, and the more information which is fed to the Quality Circle from management, management specialists, people in other departments and so on, the more effective the group will be. 'Self-control' is the foundation of Circle activities.

When people arrive for their very first Circle meeting, they may have been attracted by the possibility of using the Circle as a means of highlighting the faults of others. For example, they may complain about the quality of the products they receive from the previous section; poor quality materials, tools and equipment; inadequate service from specialist departments, and so on. However, when they join the group they realise that this is not at all the purpose of the Circle. They are told that 'whilst we can complain about those other people, we cannot do anything about them'. In almost all cases, there are plenty of problems in their own work area, which can be under their control, and where they can apply their own knowledge and experience to get results.

It is this aspect of Quality Circle activities which gives the members the greatest satisfaction. Because they are not meeting to criticise the work of others, they find that they can make real progress with their projects. When asked what they like most about Quality Circles, one of the most frequent answers comes back: 'we find we can get things done'. 'These problems have been around for years, and now we are making progress.'

8 'Presenting solutions to management'

This is the focal point or highlight of all Circle activities around the World: the presentation to management. Sometimes after weeks of collecting data, trying out new ideas, having discussions with all kinds of people, when the members of the Circle have installed their proposal, or are convinced of the value of their improvement, it is necessary to present their ideas to their manager.

The group is usually proud of its achievement and the teamwork involved. It will probably have worked very hard, may have spent lunchtimes, evenings or even week-ends working on its ideas if its members have been enthusiastic enough, and frequently they are. Consequently, the presentations of their ideas to management are the culmination of all this activity.

It would be unfortunate if they were unable to convince their manager of the benefits of their ideas, simply because they were badly presented or because the members were forced to present their ideas in the form of a report which might not be read. Therefore, training newly formed Circles in presentation techniques is extremely important. They may use two or even three meetings to plan and prepare their presentation.

It would be unfortunate, if an unthinking manager, given the enthusiasm and hard work of a Circle, was 'too busy to listen'. It would probably mean the end of the Circle. Therefore, management has an obligation to allow the group to make a formal presentation of its proposal, and to make constructive comments afterwards.

It is important that all members of the Circle participate in the presentation as members of a team. Whilst there is no obligation on management to accept the ideas of a Circle, they must be given serious consideration. If management decides to turn down a proposal, it really owes it to the Circle to give a good explanation for its rejection. Fortunately, Circle projects are usually so carefully thought through that outright rejection by management is quite rare.

9 'Implementing the solutions themselves'

Because Circles are usually concerned with problems in their own work rather than with those over the fence in the next department, they can often implement the solutions themselves. This is particularly true of housekeeping problems, reduction in waste material, energy saving and so forth. They also frequently find better ways of doing their own jobs. For example, a Circle in the credit control department of a division of a fairly large company formed a Quality Circle. For their first project the members decided to analyse one of their work routines that they found to be particularly tedious. The result was that they reduced the work content by 16 hours per month. In the process of this work they highlighted another problem which, when solved, saved a further 17 hours a month, making a total monthly saving of 33 hours. For their third project, they decided to brainstorm all the possible ways they could make use of the time saved. Someone suggested that they might follow up the invoices with a telephone call. The effect of this idea was to reduce the average credit period by nearly two weeks, thereby making available to that company a considerable sum of money.

Summary of Part I

Chapters 2, 3 and 4

1 Success in business depends upon being at least as good as the competitor in all facets of the organisation's activities, upon generating confidence and creating a good image.

2 To achieve this, it is necessary to establish corporate objectives for the whole organisation, in every function and at every level.

3 It is necessary to design a system for the organisation and deal with Quality Control, budgetary control and all activities.

4 Systems do not motivate people, and if people do not really care, no amount of system will make any difference. People need to be involved.

5 To involve people successfully it is necessary to abandon 'Taylorism'. In other words, it is necessary to introduce the concept of 'self-control' to reintroduce Craftsmanship to groups of people.

6 People need leadership. Therefore, it is necessary to identify and train group leaders or supervisors. This training should be a continuous development process. Each supervisor should be trained in such a way that he has the desire to make each employee the manager at his own level.

7 Quality Circles are a special type of small group activity which form a vehicle for people development and lead to complete self-control within the constraints of corporate policy.

8 Management gets results through people—to be competitive it is necessary to galvanise the resources of the entire workforce.

PART II How Quality Circles work

Preface

The principle 'keep it simple' is the key to successful Quality Circle activities. The techniques are simple, the mode of operation is simple, and initially at least, the problems selected are usually simple.

In this second part of the book, each technique used by Quality Circles is briefly examined and then put into context. Finally, a chapter of case studies is included to depict the ways in which Circles have applied the techniques in a wide range of industries.

5 The basic tools

The most common activity of a Quality Circle is problem solving. Sometimes problems can be solved through discussion and consensus but more generally they are solved by using problem-solving techniques. These are techniques to identify problems, to collect and analyse data, examine causes, suggest solutions, evaluate the solutions, and to implement them. There is also a discipline. All too often people involved in problem solving jump to conclusions and make decisions based on opinions, not facts. Even when facts are used, the results may not match the prediction because the data were inadequate. Many people who have had years of training and experience in problem solving frequently make these types of error, and so great care must be taken to ensure that anyone involved in these activities has been made keenly aware of the pitfalls, and the limitations of both the techniques and his own knowledge.

One of the main fears of managers, who are as yet unacquainted with the mode of operation of Quality Circles, is the fear that Circles made up of groups of people who have experienced very little education, and who are performing unskilled and semi-skilled tasks, may not be able to achieve very creditable results. This is because they do not realise the power of the simple techniques that Circles use to solve problems at their own level.

These basic techniques, usually seven in all, were not invented for Circles specifically; they gravitated into Circles during the formative years in Japan through a process of trial and error. They are referred to as the seven basic tools, because they have proved to be particularly effective when used in this type of small group activity. They are only the basic tools—a sort of 'get-you-started' kit. Later on when the Circles mature, their members will want to use the techniques in more and more sophisticated ways and will add further skills to their list when they are found to be relevant to their work.

The techniques include:

    Brainstorming
    Data collection
    Data analysis
    Pareto analysis
    Cause and effect analysis
    Histograms
    Control techniques

If presentation techniques are included, the list becomes the eight basic elements of Quality Circles. In this chapter each technique will be reviewed in turn.

Brainstorming

The idea of brainstorming is to use the collective thinking power of a group of people to come up with the ideas they would not think of by themselves. It is particularly effective when used in Quality Circle activities.

Brainstorming is the basis of much of the work carried out by Quality Circles, and is used in one form or another at two, sometimes three, stages in a Circle's project. It is used

(1) To identify problems;
(2) To analyse causes; and occasionally
(3) To highlight possible solutions.

Some problems, once evaluated have only certain obvious solutions, and brainstorming would not be used in those cases, but in others there may be an almost unlimited number of possible alternatives and brainstorming is particularly effective.

Why brainstorming?

Over the years there has been considerable controversy about the value of brainstorming. Some academics have provided evidence to show that individuals can produce equally creative ideas on their own without brainstorming. However, this is usually because the brainstorming sessions they refer to are generally conducted differently from those used by Quality Circles.

This approach evolved during the early years of Quality Circle activities, and as with the other basic techniques it is very simple. For example, Circles are not usually taught about creative and lateral thinking as it appears predominantly in most brainstorming training programmes.

Not only is brainstorming itself useful in Quality Circle activities, but the associated discipline helps create cohesion amongst the members and helps considerably to avoid the conflicts that are so common in other group activities such as committee meetings. In fact the way the technique is practised is so effective that it is quite unnecessary to train Circle leaders and members formally in the handling of group dynamic problems because they hardly ever arise.

Circles use brainstorming first of all to identify problems. They do this on a large sheet of paper, usually on a flip chart so that everyone can see what is being written.

The members take turns in which each one is allowed to volunteer one idea per turn to highlight the problems in his or her work area. No idea is censured

46 Quality Circles Handbook

during the brainstorming session and all ideas are written down. No idea should be thought of as stupid or ridiculous, and no discussion is allowed at this stage. In this way, the Circle will usually highlight a large number of problems. Sometimes as many as 200 to 300 ideas have been recorded in such sessions.

These ideas will be wide-ranging and cover almost all aspects of the Circle's work. To this list may be added the suggestions of others. Their manager, the specialists and others in their section may all contribute their ideas to those of the Circle members. When the Circle members feel the list is adequate or complete, and is representative of the problems they are confronted with, they will then commence their evaluation.

Their goal is to highlight just one problem out of the many they have identified which will form the basis of their project. Figure 5.1 shows the results

Insufficient tools	Lack of bench space
Parts incompatible	Wrong working height of benches
Sub-standard materials	Feedback of fault information
Shortages	Personality conflicts
Wrong materials issued	Lack of inspection stages
Wrong tools	No list of alternative parts
Lack of training	Flexibility of labour
Methods	No indication of priorities
Presentation of methods	Bad tasting coffee
Out of date drawings	Service operator availability
Ambiguous work instructions	Standard of supervision
Bad reporting of defects	Insufficient cleaning
Insufficient labour	No job satisfaction
Incorrect change form issued	Safety shoes
Poor quality drawings	Morale
Communication with outside suppliers	Weight of components
	Insufficient data
Poor work station layout	Lack of identification of parts
Badly worn jigs	Poor storage facilities
Too much waiting time	Too many indents used
Acceptable quality standard?	Poor deburring of something? parts
Poor design of tooling	No forward visibility of work
Performance levels unknown	Lack of humour
General untidiness of work station	Air conditioning
Too much walking about for parts	Unused items in work area
No system of tooling recall	Uncomfortable seats
No first aid in area	Job discussion
Poor lighting	Lack of management communication
Insufficient assembly aids	No recreation facilities
Insufficient tooling information	Incorrect standard times
Work instructions	

Fig 5.1

The basic tools 47

of such a brainstorming session in the subassembly of parts. The Circle took just one hour to produce this list. Some may believe this number of problems to be exceptional, but in fact it is quite typical.

One quality manager, when looking at such a list commented 'although I recognise every problem on that list, I have never seen them written on one sheet of paper before and I did not realise that there were so many!' And that was for one single work area!

Because the Circles only tackle one problem at a time, it may seem time-wasting to carry out such an exhaustive classification of problems, but this process is really quite important. It is only through it that the Circle can be sure that the problems identified by each member of the group are given equal consideration. Once the ideas have been listed they are then evaluated.

Basically, they fall into three general categories.

(1) Non Circle controllable
(2) Partially Circle controllable
(3) Totally Circle controllable

Whilst it may not always be possible to separate the second and third categories, it is necessary first of all to remove those which the Circle believes are totally outside its control.

It does this by systematically going down the list one by one, and asking the question 'Can we do anything about this problem?' If the answer is 'no', that item is scratched from the list. For example, the Circle which conducted the brainstorming opposite decided that some of the problems outside their control were:

Insufficient labour
Poor quality drawings
Too much waiting time
Lack of bench space
Wrong working height of benches
Poor coffee
Standard of supervision
Job satisfaction
Safety shoes
Morale
Weight of components, etc.

The members decided that these were matters that they could complain about but could not do anything about. Because they had the rest of the week in which they could voice their opinions about these problems, they felt that they were outside the scope of the Circle.

Of the remaining problems, a new Quality Circle would normally sort them in order of easiness to solve, taking the easiest first. Sometimes there may be a problem which frustrates the group so much that it decides to tackle it regardless of its complexity, and there is nothing wrong with that. It would be as well, however, to warn it not to tackle anything which it feels will be too complex or time-consuming in the early stages, since failure can lead to a loss of confidence at this sensitive stage and the Circle may even disintegrate under such circumstances. A quick success however small is very important to a newly formed Circle. Not only do the members acquire a sense of achievement, but others outside the group will notice that the Circle is getting things done.

Once the Circle has completed its brainstorming and perhaps solved one or two simple problems, it will want to pick a problem which, if it can solve it, will make some impact.

The members of the group will say 'let's pick the problem which costs the most', or 'let's see if we can reduce customer complaints', reduce losses, handling time, or many other items. In other words, the group has now progressed to selecting a theme. If it has decided on a theme, such as 'delays', it will have to identify the problems that cause delays. This will take it back to the brainstorming sheets, from which it will identify all the problems that cause delays, and these will then be listed separately. Naturally the members of the group will want to tackle the problem which causes the longest delays and it may not be obvious which one that is. They will need to collect data.

Data Collection (Check Sheets)

Whilst data collection itself may be easy there are many pitfalls:

> Where to collect data
> When to collect
> How much to collect
> Who is to collect
> What data?

and so on.

One only has to look at the results of opinion polls and compare them with general election results to know that data collection even when carried out by experts sometimes goes wrong.

Obviously, one cannot spend the time and effort giving Circles 'in depth' training in sophisticated data collection and analysis techniques, and so once again, the message is 'keep it simple'. In doing so, one must make sure that Circle members are made aware of the limitations of the techniques they are using and if they need to be more certain about the accuracy of their data, they should enlist the services of a trained statistics specialist to work with them.

The most frequently used data gathering technique used by Circles is the check sheet. Here the items about which the data is to be collected are listed on the left-hand side of the sheet. The time period for data collection is determined and listed in columns across the sheet as shown in Fig. 5.2. The tally check method is normally used as the data is obtained.

CHECK SHEET OF DAMAGED PARTS							
DESCRIPTION							
PART A							
PART B							
PART C							
PART D							
PART E							
PART F							
OTHERS							

Name of Group _____

Date _____

Part Nos ..../ Description ....

Fig 5.2

Before Circles progress to the collection of data, they should be made aware of the dangers of reaching misleading results. Practical training using aids such as bead boxes, dice and rods should be used to acquaint the members thoroughly with the risks of errors due to

(1) Bias
(2) Wrong sample size for accuracy required
(3) Non-repeatability of results
(4) Inaccurate measurements.

Members should also be made aware of the importance of agreeing standards when subjective measurements are being made for such features as 'feel', 'taste', 'colour', 'shade', 'surface roughness', etc.

There can be no doubt whatsoever that the effectiveness of a Quality Circle will be very dependent upon the quality of the training given in these important aspects of its work. Indeed, the foundations laid in the members' basic understanding of simple data will become the basis of all subsequent development of their skills. This training should never be skimped or by-passed, however compelling the reasons may seem at the time.

Pareto analysis

Having collected the data relating to the problems highlighted and listed it on the check sheet, the final column shows the frequency of each occurrence. If the costs of these events are known, then it would be a simple matter to present the results on a cost base, which obviously has more meaning and makes a greater impact on management. However, whilst this data may be meaningful to the Circle members, it will mean very little to others outside the group who have not been involved. A list of numbers is usually extremely unimpressive and it is necessary to present them in a more graphic form if they are to be used to communicate ideas to others. This is where the Pareto form of column graph becomes useful.

Pareto was an American Italian scholar who discovered that about 80% of the wealth was in the hands of about 20% of the population. About the same time another academic named Lorenz found that this relationship seemed to hold good in a wide variety of situations, for example, an analysis of the value of items held in a store is likely to reveal that about 80% of the value is contained in about 20% of the items. The same is frequently true of quality failure costs, such as scrap, rework, customer complaints, etc. machine or equipment breakdown time, delays, telephone usage, etc.

When this relationship exists, a column graph with each column representing a separate feature will usually result in one or two bars being considerably longer than the others, as shown in Fig. 5.3.

However, the Pareto diagram is not drawn in this haphazard manner. Usually the longest column is placed on the left-hand side of the diagram, and each bar moving to the right is the next largest to the one on its left. The final column, regardless of its length, contains the miscellaneous items which were not itemised individually. The Pareto diagram, therefore, when properly constructed, usually looks like the one in Fig. 5.4.

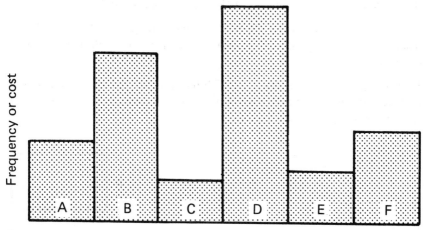
Fig 5.3

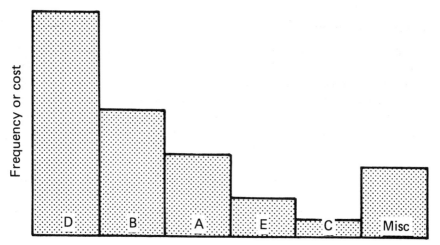
Fig 5.4

This figure shows far more dramatically than a list of numbers that the biggest problem or the most frequently occurring event is item D. There are several advantages in using this approach.

1 The Circle members themselves will be more impressed by the length of the first one or two bars.

2   It is a useful way of communicating the results of the data collection to non-Circle members, particularly those who may have assisted in the collection of the data.

3   It makes a big impact in a management presentation, and shows the thoroughness with which the Circle has carried out its work.

4   Once the data has been illustrated in this way, the Circle can really see whether it has made improvements as it can compare similar data which may be obtained after implementing its ideas.

5   It is a goal-setting mechanism which tends to concentrate the attention of members and non-members alike on the few important problems, rather than spread across the many trivial ones.

Fig 5.5

Cause and effect analysis

When the principal problem has been selected by Pareto analysis, the next stage is to classify the most probable causes. To do this the Circle will construct a cause classification diagram. This diagram is constructed by using the brainstorming process described earlier, but this time, instead of simply listing the ideas, it is helpful if similar or related ideas can be grouped together. The cause classification diagram enables this to be achieved.

The problem or effect is written in a box on the right-hand side of a large sheet of paper, fixed to the wall or on a flip chart where it can be seen by everyone as before in brainstorming. An arrow is then drawn pointing towards the box as shown in Fig. 5.5. The Circle must then decide the most appropriate headings under which the probable causes can be listed. In most cases there are four, and these are:

1   Manpower—the people doing the work
2   Machines—equipment or tooling used to do the work
3   Methods—specifications or job instructions
4   Materials supplied or required to do the work

Occasionally others such as vendor, supplier, environment, office, etc., may be more applicable, or included in addition to those mentioned above.

These headings form the ends of further arrows pointing towards the main arrow already drawn on the sheet of paper (Fig. 5.6).

Once the diagram has been prepared the Circle is ready to commence the brainstorming process of identifying what it thinks are likely to be the most probable causes.

Someone is selected to act as leader, and to write the ideas on the diagram as they are suggested. Because it is frequently possible to write the ideas under more than one heading, for example 'Incorrect setting' could be either a

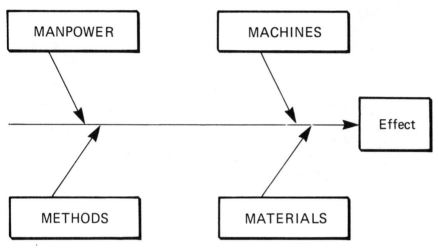

Fig 5.6

manpower problem, or a method problem, depending on whether it is the method which is wrong or whether the person doing the job is using the wrong method; it is therefore necessary for the member to guide the brainstorming leader by prefixing his or her idea with 'under Method incorrect setting' or 'under Machines', and then stating the idea.

Figure 5.7 shows such a cause classification diagram after completion.

As a general rule, it will usually take a Quality Circle one meeting to complete a diagram similar to the one shown above, and frequently this will take place during the same meeting in which the Pareto chart was roughly drawn and the problem selected. Normally though, a Circle will deliberately make the completion of the cause and effect diagram span two meetings. This is for two important reasons:

1 Not all the best or most relevant ideas are thought of in the first brainstorming session, and the problem is only selected at that meeting. Members need time to mull over their ideas, think about the problem on their own, and make observations during their work. At the second session many new and important ideas may come to the surface.

2 It gives non-Circle members an opportunity to voice their opinions and to have their ideas included with the others which have been mentioned. Again, it

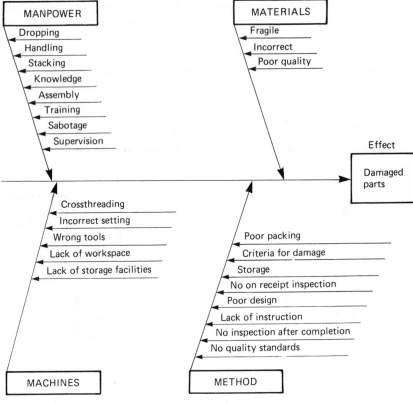

Fig 5.7

is vitally important that other people in the section should see the Circle as 'their section's Circle'.

Sometimes, and it depends to some extent upon the relationships between members of staff, whether this can be done, a Circle will post its diagrams in the work area so that others can add their ideas at any time. Obviously a Circle would not do this if it were likely that graffiti would appear.

As with the basic brainstorming, now that the diagram is complete, it is necessary to evaluate the suggestions.

This evaluation is carried out in much the same way as in the case of the initial brainstorming, except that this time the Circle is attempting to identify the most likely major causes from amongst the many potential causes that have been listed.

The Circle leader will take each idea in turn and ask the Circle members whether they think the particular idea in question is likely to be a major cause of the problem. If the answer is no, then a mark is made against the item to signify that it has been evaluated, and the leader then moves on to the next idea, and so on. If the Circle, by consensus, believes that the idea may be a major cause, then the leader will circle that idea, and again move on to the next. This process continues until all the ideas have been evaluated. At this stage, it is likely that there will be a small number of ideas, usually between one and about four, that have been circled.

The next step is to try to rank these ideas in order of priority, and again, the typical approach is to take a vote. Following this stage the cause classification diagram will probably look like Fig. 5.8.

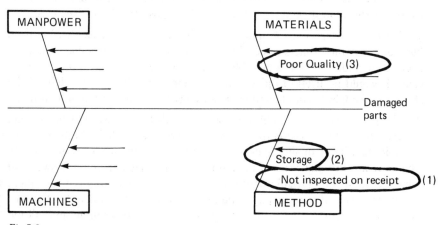

Fig 5.8

In this case, the members of the Circle believe that 'not inspected on receipt' is the prime cause of their problem. They only think it is at this stage. They do not know with certainty, and so now it will be necessary for them to verify their opinion. The subjective assessment just described is really intended to save time and to home in quickly on the most plausible possible causes.

How can the evaluation come about? Well obviously it depends upon the nature of the cause. In the case described above, because the Circle members now know the number of occurrences of the problem from their data collection, they can find the proportion of parts that were damaged on receipt.

It is likely that they will arrange for some form of goods inwards check to be carried out in order to validate their opinion. If they are proved right, they will proceed to develop some kind of incoming material control, possibly recommend some form of co-operation with the supplier and, if the Circle has been well trained, evaluate the costs and benefits of their improvement prior to making a management presentation.

But what if their data collection proves them wrong and shows that incoming parts are not faulty? Then they will go back to the cause classification diagram, and the second most likely cause will be evaluated and verified in the same way.

Of course, different causes may require different methods of verification, and these may include histograms, drawings showing defect locations, polar diagrams, further Pareto diagrams, etc., and the Circle should be trained in these techniques during the preliminary stages of its work. If it does not receive adequate training, its activities will be severely restricted and its achievements relatively unimpressive.

Cause analysis and process analysis

Some problems require a deeper analysis than that which is afforded by the cause classification diagram. In this case, three possible alternatives exist.

1 *Conduct a further cause classification* but this time on the cause that has been highlighted as the prime suspect. For example, on the previous diagram, 'poor packing' was identified as a possible cause. If it were thought to be the prime cause it would be useful to place this problem in the box on the right of the sheet and the Circle could conduct a cause classification session on that topic.

2 *Carry out cause analysis.* This only varies slightly from cause classification but involves the leader in asking questions of the group as a whole. In the previous example, had 'poor quality materials' been selected, the leader would ask 'In what way are the materials of poor quality?' Any member could answer and someone might say 'variable hardness'. The leader would then say 'are there any other causes of poor quality?' and perhaps a suggestion might be that they were 'out of alignment'. This line of questioning would continue until all the ideas had been exhausted, and he would then return to the first idea and ask, 'why is there variable hardness?' and so on. This process is an extremely penetrating method for getting down to the finest detail, and many problems are solved in this way.

3 *Process analysis.* So far, we have discussed problems that occur at only one stage or point in an operation, but sometimes they may occur over several stages. In this case, the Circle may decide to use a further variant of the cause and effect analysis by preparing a 'process analysis' diagram. To do this, again, the name of the problem is written in a box, but this time, the names of the operations are written in sequence in adjacent boxes across the sheet as shown in Fig. 5.9.

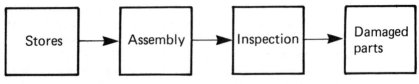

Fig 5.9

At this stage, the Circle conducts a brainstorming session on each box in turn. The leader will ask 'in what way can Stores cause damaged parts?' As before, the ideas are recorded on the diagram. When those relating to Stores are exhausted, the leader will turn to Assembly and finally to Inspection. At this point the diagram will probably look like Fig. 5.10.

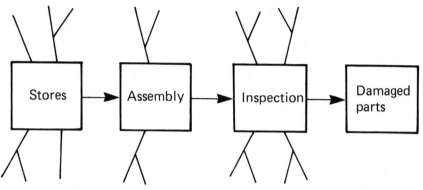

Fig 5.10

Such a diagram is an extremely useful way of lighting common elements. Factors such as lack of job instructions, contamination, or lack of training may be evident at each stage, indicating that there may be serious widespread problems.

Presentation

When the Circle members have completed their analysis and verified their solutions, they will have carried out an extremely thorough piece of work. They will feel proud of themselves. They will have enjoyed working together as a team, and will be looking forward to presenting their ideas to their manager, and sometimes to others who may be relevant to the specific problem they have tackled.

This presentation should be the highlight of their activities. All through their project they will have been mindful of this, and so the presentation will be the climax. It is therefore extremely important that management does not in any way underestimate the importance of this occasion.

Management presentations fulfil the following goals.

1 Give recognition of the Circle's achievements.

2 Allow management to judge for itself the value of Quality Circles.

3 Enable others, possibly less committed, to see how Circles work, in order to gain wider acceptance.

There are many good reasons why Circles may make their presentations on other occasions and in other circumstances, and these will be discussed in a later chapter. In view of the importance attached to management presentations, it is vitally important that Circles are given adequate training to make them and that they receive help to enable them to make them in a professional way.

It must be emphasised again that management is under no obligation to accept a Circle proposal if it does not wish to do so. It is the responsibility of the Circle members to 'sell their idea in such a way that it appears attractive to management'. They should be trained to speak the manager's language, in other words to present their ideas in the context of measures which are uppermost in the minds of most managers, namely:

    Cost improvements
    Quality improvements
    Scheduling or inventory improvements, etc.

Rejection by management of Circle proposals is fortunately extremely rare. This is mainly because there are usually few secrets in Circle activities, and if it becomes obvious that a Circle is heading towards a totally unacceptable conclusion, there are usually many opportunities to warn it of this. If the members still insist on pursuing the idea, that is up to them, but the Circle will be encouraged to offer alternative ideas to give management a choice when it comes to the presentation.

Following the presentation, and hopefully the acceptance of the proposal, the Circle will begin thinking about its next project. At this stage the members may wish to brainstorm all over again, or in many cases, take the next problem on the list. It can be seen therefore that the brainstorming sheet is a work sheet. They will only conduct a further brainstorming when they begin to feel that the list needs topping up, or that many new problems have surfaced, or when they have noted problems relating to them on other Quality Circles' brainstorming lists. They may also add items retrieved from Quality Control defects analysis, customer complaints or suggestions from non-Circle members.

Occasionally, the company may decide to initiate a quality awareness campaign, and may invite Circles to participate in some activity, such as a poster competition, or the design of a novel product. Once Quality Circles have become established, there is an endless variety of activities in which they can participate. The most important thing to remember is that the one hour per week is 'the Circles' hour'. Self-control is the ultimate goal.

6 Quality Circle data gathering and analysis

Learning the Techniques

For Quality Circles to be effective, it is necessary for them to acquire a basic understanding of data: how data can be collected, analysed and controlled.

Two of the basic techniques for handling data, check sheets and Pareto analysis were briefly reviewed in the previous chapter. In this chapter we shall look at data collection and analysis as it applies to Quality Circle work in order to show the depth of training that should be given to new Circle members.

Types of data

Basically there are three kinds of data:

1 Variable, i.e. speed, temperature, time, volume, weight, length, voltage, resistance current, pressure, etc.

2 Countable—or attributable—i.e. number of errors, right/wrong, is/is not, black/white, broken/not broken, etc.

3 Subjective—to the senses, i.e. taste, feel, sound, appearance, etc. This can also be treated as countable in many cases.

It is necessary for Quality Circles to be able to deal with each of these categories, all of which are likely to occur at various times and stages in Circle activities.

100 per cent inspection versus sampling!

The question of how much data to collect is always difficult to answer. Of course, a statistician will have no difficulty because he will know how to use formulae or sampling tables to give him his answer. Generally speaking, Quality Circles do not have this level of knowledge and for the majority of Circle activities, a fairly rough and ready result is all that is required. Nevertheless, the Circle will need to have some guidance on this point.

Assuming a perfect inspector and perfect measurements, 100% inspection will provide the answers we need. However, this is not always possible or practical. For example, 100% inspection of one day's production of washers when output is in the order of tens of thousands per day could not be justified financially, unless of course it could be done automatically. Therefore, sampling of some kind would be necessary. In any case, inspectors are rarely perfect and sampling is frequently more accurate if it is carried out properly.

In the case of a continuous process, it will be necessary to agree on a representative period over which the observations will be made. In this situation there are two basic risks present in sampling:

1 We think something has changed when in fact it has not.

2 We think it has not changed when in fact it has.

Whilst these risks will always be present to some extent, they are in fact directly related to the size of the sample. The bigger the sample, the smaller the risk. The Circle must decide roughly how much risk it is prepared to take, or the degree of certainty it wishes to have to be reasonably confident that it is correct.

It is not necessary to bombard a newly formed Circle with deep statistical theory in order to be able to do this. Most people, in their everyday experience of life, added to skilful teaching and guidance, are capable of developing an awareness of the limitations of the data they are collecting. There are several alternative ways this can be achieved, depending upon the kind of data to be collected.

Example

With countable data, boxes of various coloured beads can be used for a simple demonstration. If one colour of bead is classified as a defect, and all the remainder are classified as good items, the following demonstration can be carried out.

Equipment

1 Box containing approximately 1000 beads or other similar items carefully mixed with a fixed percentage nominally defective

2 Chart papers ruled off into columns or rows with the rows marked 0, 1, 2 progressively.

Method

The trainees working as a group take a fixed-size sample from the box (100 items), the number of defective items in the sample is then recorded on the chart paper using the tally check method. This procedure is repeated approximately 50 times and the result recorded each time.

If the number defective is then changed slightly and the demonstration repeated, three separate sets of results may appear as shown in Fig. 6.1.

Quality Circle data gathering and analysis 61

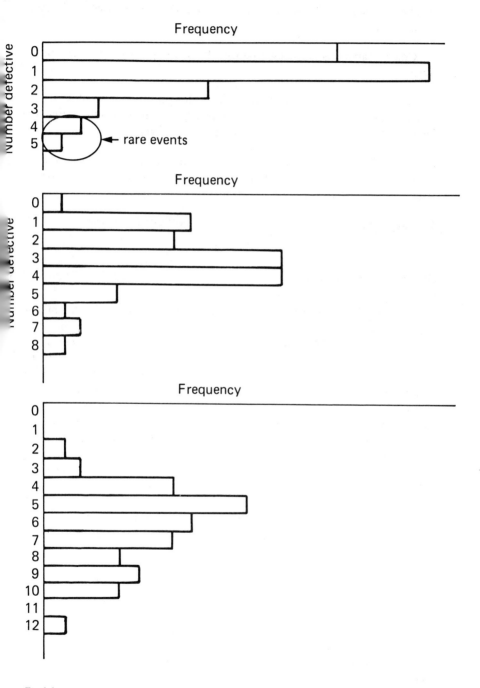

Fig 6.1

The frequency distribution diagram produced can be used to illustrate several points.

1 Chance variations normally produce a unique shape when recorded in this way.

2 By conducting the demonstration using different proportions of beads, the pattern will change, and this will demonstrate to Circle members that this method of recording data can be useful to detect changes.

3 It will show the members that they must not jump to conclusions when changes appear to have occurred in a process. It may only be a chance variation in the data similar to that observed in the demonstration.

4 They can also use the information they have collected as a basis for control.

Use of data for control

By observing the results shown on the diagram it will be noted that the bulk of the results centre about the mean value. This is to be expected, and more important to the Circle will be the less frequent events which occur at the extremes, shown circled in the diagram. These are relatively rare events. Of course they do occur occasionally, as observed. Once this fact has been established by the data, the Circle now knows that these are rare events and it will watch out for them. If on one occasion seven defects occur, the members will say, 'well, that is a rare event, and it has to occur once in a while!' but what if it occurs again fairly soon afterwards? Then the Circle will be suspicious because it will have been taught that two similar rare events occurring consecutively are extremely unlikely. It will know that it is far more likely that something has changed, and it will take action accordingly.

The same process can be used by a Circle to compare two different methods or processes. It can be seen that a Circle can make considerable use of this type of data without needing sophisticated training in statistical techniques. That doesn't mean to say that such training should not be given. The main reason why our society is less numerate than it might be is possibly because we usually try to teach too much too quickly. The greatest power of statistical techniques lies in their most elementary form. Considerable use can be made of basic statistics without any knowledge of the mathematics of probability theory, or even the standard deviation, but both of these will be very much more meaningful when the student can appreciate the value to him in learning these concepts. If a Circle is taught the basic ideas already outlined and begins to use them in its activities, it will not be long before the members will want to learn more.

Variable data

This type of data can be handled in much the same way as countable data, as, for example, if we want to record temperature variation at various intervals in a process. It is first of all necessary to determine the maximum range over which the variations are expected, and their value, i.e. suppose we expect the extreme variation to be 30°, with a minimum of say 20°. We know then that we are very unlikely to record a value less than 20° or greater than 50°. These can be written on the vertical axis of the chart (Fig. 6.2) as shown.

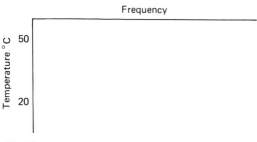

Fig 6.2

The Circle will then have to decide the intervals of measure within which the various readings will be grouped. If we assume also that the Circle believes 5° intervals are likely to be satisfactory, the chart will then look like Fig. 6.3.

```
              Frequency
         ┌─────────────────
      50 │ X X
      45 │ X X
      40 │
      35 │ X
      30 │
      25 │
```
Temperature °C

Fig 6.3

All recordings above 20 and up to 25 will be recorded in the 20 row and so on. If the members were right in their estimate, the completed chart will probably look like Fig. 6.4. It can readily be seen that this diagram is similar in many respects to that produced for countable data, and in many cases diagrams of this kind can be treated in similar fashion.

For example: if two apparently identical processes are compared side by side, the diagram (Fig. 6.5) may show that they are different. Here it can be seen that

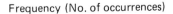

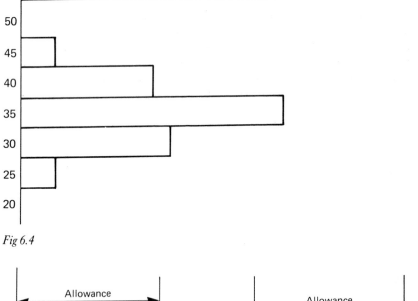

Fig 6.4

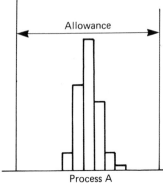
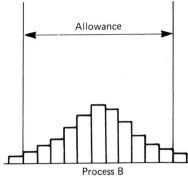

Fig 6.5

process B is well able to keep within its allowance, whereas process A is in trouble at both extremes.

The techniques shown above are both extremely simple to use. Circles of cleaning staff, labourers, unskilled and semi-skilled workpeople have all been trained by DHA to use these techniques in a very short space of time without difficulty. More important, they are actually using them in their everyday work. They also like using them. The reason why a great majority of people shy away from mathematical concepts is not because they are not interested. It is usually because they lack confidence in themselves, and do not believe they can learn. Once they find that they can understand what they have been taught, and that the ideas are useful in their work, they become more interested and develop a desire to learn more. These techniques should be regarded as the basic building blocks upon which more sophisticated concepts can be built later.

Drawings showing defect locations

This remarkably simple technique is a great favourite amongst Quality Circle members. It is used by Circles when they want to establish whether or not any pattern exists concerning the problem they are studying.

Let us take the example of a group of workers in a garment factory. Their task is to perform several different operations, such as sewing together the

Fig 6.6

various component parts of the garment, stitching hems, and so forth. They may wish to discover whether more defects occur in one part of the garment than another.

To do this they will make a drawing of the product and post it in a convenient place in their work area accessible to Circle members. Each time a defect is noted, a Circle member makes a mark on the drawing at the appropriate location. After some time the drawing may look like the one in Fig. 6.6. It will be noted that the majority of defects are grouped in two distinct areas, and there must be some reason for this. The Circle will then concentrate its attention on these aspects. It can be seen that this technique has a similar effect to Pareto analysis and again helps to focus on the few important problems rather than spread across the many less important ones.

This technique is quite versatile. Circles use it not only to improve products but also in the design of forms and the location of errors. The design of a work area might be an example. For instance, in one place in the Potteries, a Circle made a drawing of its work area in an attempt to see where most breakages occurred. After four weeks, a distinct pattern emerged and enabled the Circle to design a better layout. This greatly reduced the number of breakages.

Other groups projects that have benefited from the technique have included:

> Printed circuit board manufacture and assembly
> Injection moulding faults
> Form design, etc.

Check lists

Many of the activities of Quality Circles result in much more clearly defined work routines. Frequently there are several alternative ways of doing the same job and the Circle will seek to establish which is best. When this has been achieved the Circle will often design a check list to ensure that its proposals are properly implemented and maintained. Check lists include such items as:

- Training routine for new employees in the work area.
- Ensuring that all elements of a task have been completed, i.e. similar to the countdown of a rocket.
- Essentials for the production of procedures manuals.

Graphs and charts

Circles are taught that whilst words may be used to communicate their ideas, pictures, charts or graphs are usually far more effective. It has been said that a picture is worth a thousand words. Apart from the value of charts and graphs, Circles enjoy using this approach to presenting their ideas and so training is given in these techniques. Basically there are six types of charts and graphs:

>Line graphs
>Scatter diagram graphs
>Column or bar charts
>Pie graphs
>Pictographs
>Organisational graphs

An additional advantage to be gained from the use of such techniques is that it enables the Circles to present their ideas in the way that is familiar to most managers. They give a good impression, and are far more likely to be listened to.

The techniques in perspective

To conclude this section of Part II let us look at the way in which these techniques would normally be applied.

1 A new Circle, or one which has exhausted its previous list, or one which feels that new and important problems have arisen in its area will conduct a brainstorming session.

2 When the list is complete the Circle will segregate the ideas into

>Not Circle controllable
>Partially Circle controllable
>Totally Circle controllable

3   Several smaller problems easily dealt with will be given priority.

4   The Circle will vote on a theme. Possible themes include

Waste materials
Lost time
Safety
Energy
Customer complaints
Materials handling
Housekeeping, etc.

5   Having selected a theme, the Circle will list the problems relating to it, that were highlighted during brainstorming.

6   Next the members will produce a check sheet in order to determine the relative importance of each item.

7   From the check sheet they will produce a Pareto diagram. This will highlight the few important ones and separate them from the many trivial.

8   The problem thus selected will be analysed using cause classification.

9   The cause classifications will be evaluated by using the job knowledge of the members to identify what they believe to be the most likely key causes.

10   The first potential key cause will be evaluated to determine whether or not it is the true cause.

11   This evaluation may involve the use of further cause classification relating to the cause now highlighted.

12   Alternatively it may call for cause analysis, process analysis, histograms, drawings showing defect locations, check sheets and Pareto analysis depending upon the circumstances.

13   When the true cause has been established the Circle must seek a solution. This may involve either brainstorming or experimentation or both.

14   Alternative solutions may be evaluated in order to establish the best solution, or to offer management a choice.

15   Following the establishment of the 'best' solution, the Circle will prepare a management presentation.

16   The management presentation will involve all of the members of the Circle and sometimes two or three meetings will be required to prepare their materials and the method of presentation.

17   The management presentation will be made to the manager of the section together with others who may be affected by the suggestions.

68 Quality Circles Handbook

18   When relevant, management will make a decision whether to accept, partially accept, or reject a Circle proposal.

19   In the event of partial acceptance or rejection, it is important that management give the Circle clear reasons for its decision, which, if carried

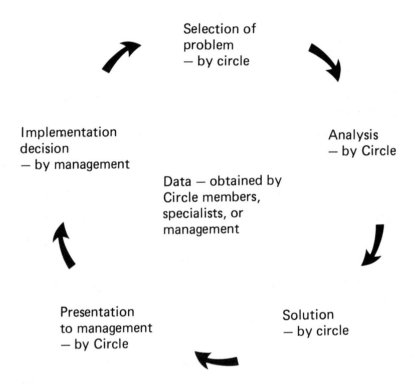

Fig 6.7   The problem-solving process

tactfully, will normally be accepted, albeit reluctantly, by the Circle. Rejection can usually be avoided when it is expected by presenting management with a choice of two or more alternative solutions. These should, of course, be evaluated prior to the presentation.

Figure 6.7 shows the Quality Circle problem-solving process, and Fig. 6.8 shows the sequence of problem solving.

Fig 6.8 The Circle problem-solving sequence

7 Case studies of Quality Circles

The author would like to make a special point of thanking the directors and managers of the companies who have offered case study material, their Quality Circles, and facilitators for their co-operation in submitting the following case studies for inclusion in this book. This co-operation is typical of the open spirit which is so much a characteristic in Quality Circle activities, and the stimulation to become so involved in the concept has been greatly enhanced by the enthusiasm of these and other wonderful people.

The case studies included here give a perspective of the variety of projects, different organisations, and methods of recording Circle projects. They have been presented in alphabetical order of companies, but there is no special relevance to this. Only minor editing has been carried out to increase clarity.

The Wedgwood project has been reprinted in exactly the form received because it is a good example of how Quality Circle projects may be recorded. At the time of writing this book, Wedgwood Circles had completed several hundred projects which are all collated conveniently in A4 ring binders.

Case Study 1: A.G. Ceramics Ltd, Stoke-on-Trent

FAULTFINDERS QC (CERAMIC FLOOR TILE SELECTORS AND PACKERS)
JOB DESCRIPTION
To visually inspect floor tiles for shade variations and quality prior to packing into boxes.

A brainstorming session was held in order to list all the problems in the Circle's working area. This resulted in a total of 60 problems being identified. The next step was to categorise these into their relevant areas such as:

(i) Circle problem
(ii) Circle problem with outside help
(iii) Outside Circle control and Circle influence.

A short list of 'Circle problems' was then listed and the merits of each problem discussed in detail. Voting took place to select a problem to tackle which resulted in 'Fireflash Tiles' being selected.

A Fireflash tile can best be described as a dark narrow spray effect applied to one edge of the tile only. This is done to produce an antique effect and also to minimise the inherent shade variations of ceramic floor tiles.

Although identified as a Circle problem the application of the spray takes place in another department whilst the tile is in clay form, prior to firing. The Circle felt, however, that it was a major problem when selecting the tiles and that the finished quality of the product could also be improved.

The main problems of the selectors are:

(i) Variations in spray density
(ii) Width of spray
(iii) Overspraying
(iv) No spray at all.

All this often meant as many as five 'shades' of tiles to be packed at the same time—not an easy task when tiles are moving along a conveyor belt at the rate of 40 tiles per minute.

The Circle then constructed a data gathering check sheet (Fig. 7.1) which would record the quantities of the various flashes applied over a three-week period.

With the approval of local management and the full support of non-Circle members the data gathering exercise was undertaken. The results were then collated and a master check-sheet drawn up. To give a clearer picture, the figures were transferred to a Pareto chart. This showed that 61% of the flashing was acceptable, being either light or dark and of a consistent narrow width. Of the remainder, 13% had no flash, 12% were questionable, 10% double flashed, 1.8% dark wide and 1.2% light wide.

It was decided to investigate thoroughly the incidence of non-flashing and, to further confirm the figure of 15%, a check was made of non-flashed tiles over a four-day period on one machine. This time the result was 23% non-flashed. The circle was then satisfied that this was indeed the primary problem.

The problem was then put to the cause and effect technique although the words 'bad flashing' were substituted for non-flash in an attempt to incorporate all spraying problems (Fig. 7.2).

The most important factors were listed in order of priority as:

1. Use of correct liquid
2. Visual inspection of liquid levels
3. Spray nozzle cleaning
4. Air pressure settings

Photographs were taken of the existing spray system to be used in the final presentation.

A brainstorming session was then conducted on the most probable cause of no flashing which was that there was no flash liquid in the header bucket above the spray unit. The present system uses galvanised buckets which are positioned at such a height that the liquid level cannot be seen. The Circle proposed the use of semi-transparent buckets to replace the galvanised type and made this their main recommendation (see Fig. 7.3).

As an alternative to semi-transparent buckets the Circle investigated the use of a level probe that would give either an audible or visual warning whenever the liquid had fallen below a predetermined level. The cost of this was estimated at £100 per spraying unit and the circle felt that the simple transparent buckets would be the best solution.

The Circle also observed that the outlet control valves fitted below the buckets were often set in different positions with no directive as to which was the correct position. The Circle therefore recommended the

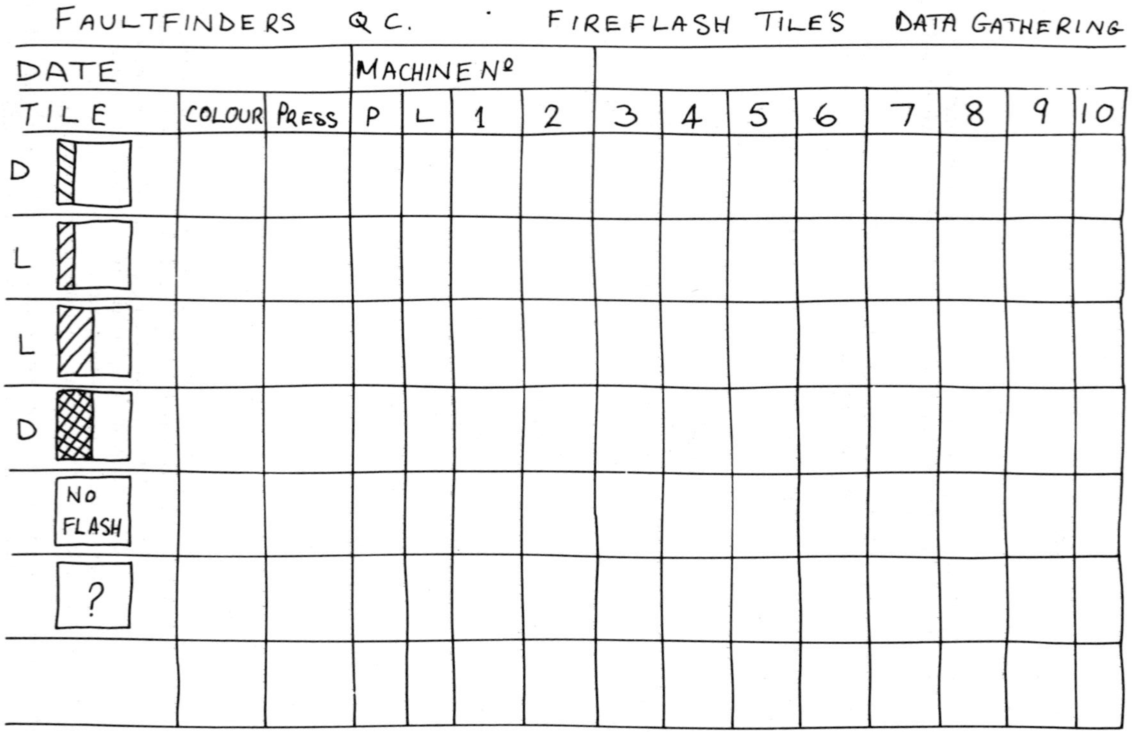

FAULTFINDERS Q.C. · FIREFLASH TILE'S DATA GATHERING

DATE				MACHINE Nº									
TILE	COLOUR	PRESS	P	L	1	2	3	4	5	6	7	8	9	10
▨ D														
▨ L														
▨ L														
▩ D														
NO FLASH														
?														

Fig 7.1

Case studies of Quality Circles 73

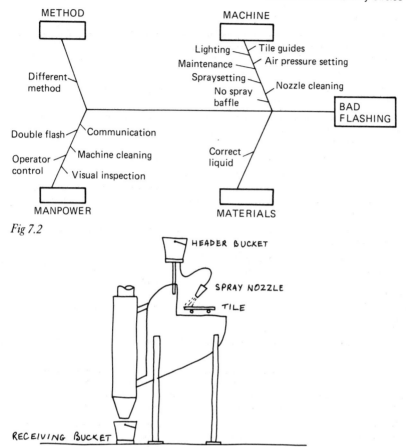

Fig 7.2

Fig 7.3

fitting of a simple sheet metal indicator to the valves so that all settings could be set to the same position on all spray units.

The Circle then investigated the nozzle cleaning aspect of the problem but first conducted a simple cause and effect exercise into the reason why nozzles were blocking in the first place, and looked at the spraying system in detail.

Fig 7.4

Two major causes were very apparent:

   (i) Particles of clay dust were being carried over during spraying and eventually depositing in the receiving bucket.

   (ii) Airborne dust at ground level was also contaminating the liquid in the receiving bucket.

The contents of the bucket were being transferred into the header bucket and topped up with fresh liquid.

The result was that dust contamination became progressively more dense in the liquid with the passing of time, increasing the possibility of blockage in the nozzle.

The Circle's recommendations from these findings were:

   (i) To install fine wire mesh filters onto the receiving bucket.

   (ii) All contents of the receiving buckets should be put into a large settling tank to allow the removal of deposits before returning the liquid back into the system.

The Circle then listed the benefits to be gained if their recommendations were followed. These were:

   (i)   Reduced number of shades to select.
   (ii) Longer runs of consistent shades.
   (iii) Reduced monitoring of shaded tiles in warehouse prior to despatch.
   (iv) Reduced floor area required in the warehouse for various shades of tile.
   (v)   Increased accuracy of selection.
   (vi) Reduced number of pallets per selecting machine to stack and remove.

The presentation was then made to the steering committee members and local management. It was met with great enthusiasm. Members were congratulated on the professional way they had tackled the problem, presented their findings and put forward their recommendations.

A follow-up meeting held a few days later with management to discuss the implementation of the recommendations produced some rather startling results. The presentation had obviously prompted management to think seriously about the problem and they realised that much more could be done to eliminate bad flashing.

They proposed to the Circle that whilst their recommendations would be implemented, they would also be investigating other likely causes of the problem. These were:

   (i)   The replacement of metal with plastic atomiser needles in the spray heads which had a tendency to corrode and block.
   (ii) To introduce a stain into the spray liquid which would then remain visible on the tile and be seen more easily by operatives.
   (iii) To increase the cleaning frequency of all spray units on a fixed cycle.

Further meetings were held periodically with management reporting to the Circle on progress made with their recommendations.

The final result was a tremendous communications exercise between management and Circle and an awareness that all shared the same benefits of a Circle's project.

Bad flashing has now almost completely disappeared and the standard of quality has risen from an average 86% best to 92.5%. The number of shades for selection has reduced from 5 to 3.

Case Study 2: Ciba-Geigy Ltd, Plastics Division, Cambridge, England

'OCTET' QUALITY CIRCLE
Bonded Structures No. 1 Factory

The main function of the factory is to produce various types of adhesives for use in the aerospace industry. The adhesives are made in 'film' form to ensure ease of handling and consistency. The 'Octet' Circle is concerned with the mixing of the adhesive (resin) before it is converted into the 'film'.

The resins are mixed in special mixers and according to the resin are either mixed hot or cold. After every mix the mixers have to be thoroughly cleaned to prevent contamination. The only way to clean the sticky residue from the mixer is by using a strong solvent: to make the cleaning easier the solvent is usually heated.

Once the mixer had been cleaned the warm solvent was, in the past, poured into a large open top tray. This was then carried about 40 yards outside the factory to a waste solvent area. The waste solvent was then poured into a large drum by means of a funnel.

One of the many problems identified by the Circle at its brainstorming session was waste solvent disposal. All of the Circle members had at one time or another had the job of carrying the waste solvent — all of them knew there was a better way of doing it. The decision to investigate and solve the problem was unanimous.

The next stage was to brainstorm the Circle's requirements and alternative methods of carrying the waste. Several methods were chosen for further investigation. The Safety Department was consulted about the possible hazards of the proposed methods; several of the suggestions were thought to be unsafe and were discarded at this stage.

The Engineering Department was consulted about possible alterations to the layout of the mixing room. It was found during these discussions that the mixers were going to be raised off the ground for ease of working.

As a result of the various discussions the Circle agreed that a mobile container would be the best option for moving the waste solvent. The Circle members then submitted various designs for discussion at their meeting. From these submissions a design for a mobile container was agreed which would cover all of the Circle's requirements. The design was drawn by a Circle member and given to an apprentice in the Engineering Department as an exercise.

The container is mounted on wheels so is fully mobile (no more carrying!); it has a built-in pump and is fully sealed so there is little risk of spillage.

The Circle members are justifiably proud of their mobile solvent container which in practice has proved to be quicker, more convenient and safer than the old method. The Circle have named their creation 'K9'.

76 Quality Circles Handbook

Case Study 3: Corning Medical, Corning Ltd, Sudbury, England

''THE ENGINEERS'' QUALITY CIRCLE PRESENTATION

OCTOBER 1983

PROJECT: REJECT AND REWORK REDUCTION

PRESENTATION PROGRAMME

(1) INTRODUCTION (5) SOLUTIONS
(2) SLIDES AND PHOTOGRAPHS (6) TOOLING
(3) REJECTS (7) COSTING AND SUMMARY
(4) REWORK (8) QUESTIONS AND ANSWERS

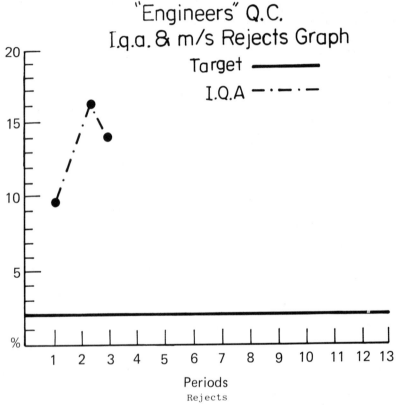

After considering all the machine shop associated problems that were listed during brainstorming sessions, the Circle decided by method of voting to choose the subject of 'Rejects' as its first problem to work wi⌐
I.Q.A. reject rates were 12.6% for the first two periods of 1983.
It was felt by all that this fact alone was very damaging to the machine shop's professional reputation, and that any reduction would be of great benefit to the Company.

"ENGINEERS" Q. C. Reject check sheet

date	mon	tue	wed	thu	fri	sat
incorr. mat.						
out of tol.						
h ll tol.						
threads i/o						
finish						
mat. alloc.						
others						

Rejects check sheets

Check sheets were designed for the purpose of collecting data in order that listed information could be examined.

A time period of four weeks was determined for this exercise and all shop floor personnel were invited to participate in the process.

The sheets contained the main criteria thought to be responsible for rejects.

Q.C. Magic dust

Data gathering for rejects resulted in virtually blank check sheets.

It would appear at first sight, that the Circle had cured the problem of machine shop rejects without actually doing anything.

In reality, it was agreed that a concerted effort (either conscious or subconscious) by everyone had contributed to the near elimination of rejects.

It can more easily be explained by the appearance of the magic dust effect using its influence within the machine shop.

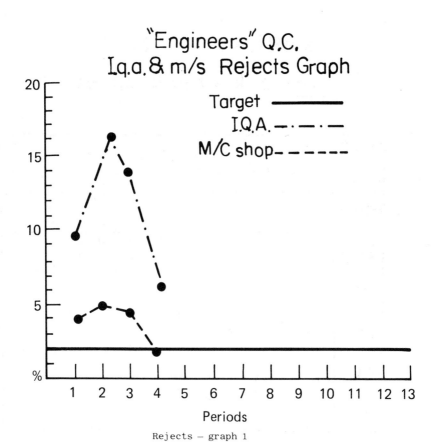

Rejects – graph 1

I.Q.A. reject rates were seen to have fallen to 5.95% in period four. This was regarded as further evidence that the Quality Circle's conclusions were correct.

It was decided that reject rates should still be monitored carefully by the Circle in order that any sudden rise could be dealt with accordingly.

Agreement was then reached to substitute the problem of 'Rejects' with 'Rework'.

"Engineers" Q. C. Rework check sheet

date	Brass	Ali	Branz	stain. steel	plastics	mild steel	mills	C/lathe	Drills	cap 5·1	cap 5·2	Auto.	others
mon	I											I	
tue			I						I				
wed					I	I							
thu													
fri					II			I		I			
sat													

Rework check sheet

Check sheets were once again designed and distributed on the shop floor.

Participation by all machining personnel was critical for this stage of data gathering, as each individual was responsible for reporting his or her own rework.

The time period for data gathering was scheduled for two periods. This somewhat lengthy time spell, guaranteed as broad a reflection of rework as possible.

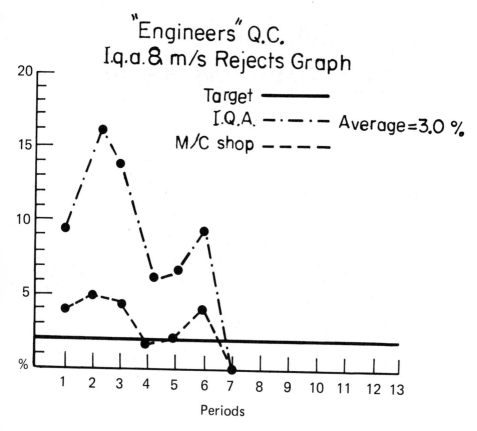

Rejects — graph 2

Bearing in mind that rework could lead to rejects, the Circle decided at this stage to monitor rejects and rework in more detail.

With the enthusiastic co-operation of I.Q.A., period reports on rejects and rework were forwarded to the Circle and analysed with future prevention in mind.

In order to give a more accurate picture of machine shop reject rates, a second monitoring line was added to the graph. The purpose of this was to reflect rejects as a percentage of the total number of jobs leaving the machine shop, as opposed to the I.Q.A. method of reflecting them as a percentage of the number of batches checked.

I.Q.A. reject rate for end of period six: 9.3%
Machine shop reject rate for end of period six: 3.72%

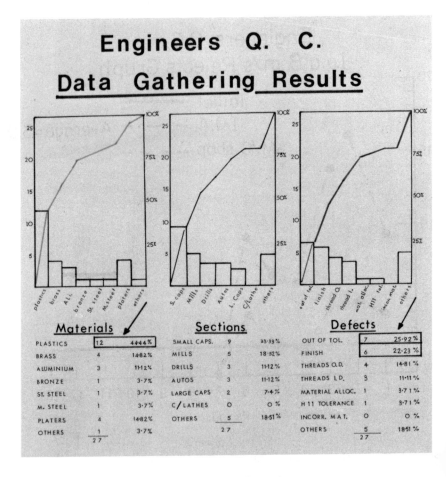

Pareto charts and results

Using the results from rework data gathering, Pareto charts were drawn in order to prioritise the problems and to present to the Circle a visual analysis.

Conclusions drawn were that the main areas for concern were PLASTICS, FINISH and TOLERANCE.

Machine section results were not included for further analysis but used as supportive evidence that the conclusions were right.

Each column containing others, represents mostly plating and subcontract work. Both considered to be outside the Circle's sphere of activity and control.

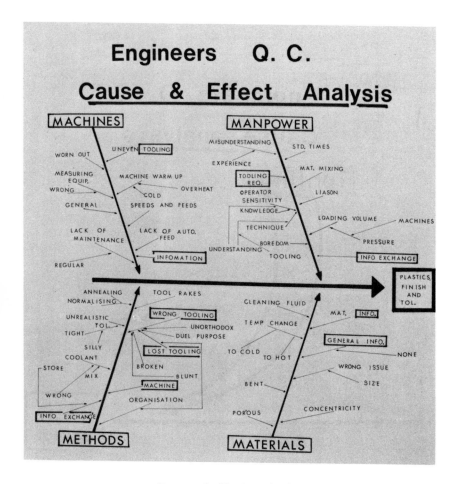

Cause and effect analysis

The technique of cause and effect analysis was used to further investigate the prime areas for concern as a result of the data gathering findings.

It was concluded that the following were the main causes on the effects of PLASTICS, FINISH and TOLERANCE:

1. TOOLING
2. INFORMATION EXCHANGE
3. MACHINES

The problem of machines was discounted from further analysis as they were deemed beyond the Circle's relative control. Nonetheless, the machining of close tolerances on outdated machinery remains a problem to be resolved.

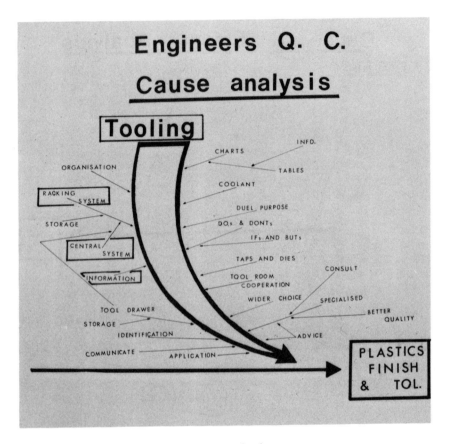

Cause analysis

Tooling was regarded by all the Circle members to be a subject deserving of further detailed analysis. Therefore, cause analysis was practised in order to complement this desire.

This provided the Circle with the following conclusive factors that were felt to have contributed most towards the problems of tooling.

1. Need for racking and job box system.
2. Need for central stores for plastics tooling.
3. Greater information.

Engineers Q. C. Information card

PART NO. 940 01 001			TITLE. PLUNGER	MATL. DELRIN
OPERATIONS	SPEEDS	FEEDS	TOOLING	REMARKS
CAP.LATHE 51				JOB BOX
TURNING TOOL	1250	280	12°FR 10°TR 15°SR HSS	USE LARGE MULTI TOOL HOLDER
BORING TOOL	850	360	12°FR 10°TR 15°SR HSS	BORE OFF SIZE
DRILLS	1250	160	SLOW SPIRAL	WASH TO A CLEAN FINISH
COOLANT	—	—	SIM COOL	
MILL 001				USE VERTICAL MILL
FLAT	750	N.F	END MILL ½ INCH	MILL FIXTURE RACK 2
SLOT	750	N.F	F.C.3 CUTTER	MULTI ST FIXTURE FORM FOR C.NC RACK 2
DRILL 006				FOBCO (4) DRILL
DRILL	1020		SLOW SPIRAL 2.5	USE JIG RACK 1
TAP	MED.		SPIRAL FLUTE (PARADUR N.L.M.)	

Systems and information card

After leaving all the findings to incubate for two weeks, further discussion within the Circle led to what was thought to be a final solution towards the reduction of rejects and rework.

The Circle seeks management permission to install an information card system on the shop floor, to run parallel with job issue cards.

Also to install and equip an efficient job box system and central stores for plastics tooling.

Milling N.A. Block
Ref. Block

EXAMPLE OF MULTI-STATION MILLING FIXTURE DEVELOPED TO MACHINE UP TO 22 902 N.A. BLOCKS AT A TIME AND 12 902 REF. BLOCKS AT A TIME.

A time reduction of 30.5% for N.A. Blocks and 34.0% for Ref. Blocks was achieved as a result of these developments.

Case studies of Quality Circles 87

Turning – Ref. Blocks
Turning – K. Blocks

As a spin off from the development of multi-station milling fixtures, fast loading and quick release turning fixtures were designed.

The increased reliability and repeatability of the tolerances on the blocks made this possible, and resulted in a reduction of the standard times.

Picture of N.A. Block

Whilst developing new methods of tooling for plastics, the Circle has experienced one or two temporary failures.

One of these failures concerned the experimentation of triple boring and drilling tools for machining 902 N.A. Blocks on a multi-station fixture.

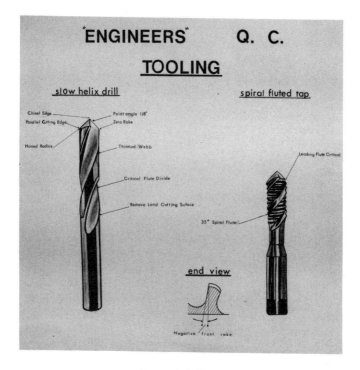

Tap and drills

The majority of components made from plastics have at some time or other to be drilled and tapped. Problems with these operations are usually considerable.

For this reason, long and involved experiments were conducted as regards to tool angles, speeds and feeds, negative rakes, critical flute divides etc.

Correspondence with tooling specialists as far afield as West Germany resulted in vague and generally minimal information.

Drawing upon the talents and experience that exists within our own machine shop, the Circle has developed certain geometrical requirements connected with tooling designs.

These developments are now being used in the machine shop with a high degree of success.

Quality Circles Handbook

CIRCLE EXPENDITURE

902 REF. BLOCK FIXTURES

    2" × 2" × 18" GROUND STOCK £30.00
    50 − 5.0 mm DOWEL PINS £3.30
    LABOUR − 9 HRS × £5.14 £46.26

902 N.A. BLOCK FIXTURES

    3" × 0.5" × 18" GROUND STOCK £15.00
    75 − 5.0 mm DOWEL PINS £4.95
    LABOUR − 7 HRS × £5.14 £35.98

TURNING FIXTURES

    2 TURNING FIXTURES FROM SCRAP
    MATERIAL AND MADE IN CIRCLE
    MEMBER'S OWN TIME
    COST TO COMPANY ZERO

STATIONERY £20.00

PRESENTATION SLIDES AND PHOTOGRAPHS £12.25

MEETINGS

    154 HRS × £5.14 £791.56

PROPOSED SOLUTIONS

    ZERO

TOTAL COSTS = £959.30

DIRECT SAVINGS − 1984

ALL COSTING AT LABOUR RATE £5.14

902 N.A. BLOCK: MILLING

    TIME SAVED TO MACHINE ONE BLOCK = 0.46 HRS
    ESTIMATED NO. OF UNITS FOR 1984 = 1560
SAVING: 0.46 HRS × L.R. £5.14 × 1560 = £3688.46

902 REF. BLOCK: MILLING

    TIME SAVED TO MACHINE ONE BLOCK = 0.32 HRS
    ESTIMATED NO. OF UNITS FOR 1984 = 780
SAVING: 0.32 HRS × L.R. £5.14 × 780 = £1282.94

902 K BLOCK: TURNING

    TIME SAVED TO TURN ONE K BLOCK = 0.04 HRS
    ESTIMATED NO. OF UNITS FOR 1984 = 780
SAVING: 0.04 HRS × L.R. £5.14 × 780 = £160.36

902 REF. BLOCK: TURNING

    TIME SAVED TO TURN ONE REF. BLOCK = 0.05 HRS
    ESTIMATED NO. OF UNITS FOR 1984 = 780
SAVING: 0.05 HRS × L.R. £5.14 × 780 = £200.45

480 ROTOR HOUSING: PROTOTYPE TAPS

    ESTIMATED NO. OF ROTOR HOUSINGS 1984 = 520
    NO. OF NORMAL TAPS REQUIRED
    = 104 AT £1.48 EACH = £153.92

NO. OF PROTOTYPE TAPS REQUIRED
= 10 AT £5.25 EACH = £52.50
SAVING: £153.92 − £52.50
= £101.42

TOTAL DIRECT SAVINGS = £5433.63

QUALITY IMPROVEMENT SAVINGS

All calculations are based on:
1. A department hourly rate of £5.14.
2. Broadload figures and estimates provided by Planning.
3. Reject data and year end estimates provided by I.Q.A.
4. An assumption that 80% of rejects involve rework.

ACTUAL DATA FOR 1982

Broadload hours including contract and O.E.M.	43000
Year end rejection rate at 7.1%	3053
Given 80% of rejects involve rework	2442
Rework costs based on £5.14/hour	£12.6K

ESTIMATED DATA FOR 1983

Broadload hours including contract and O.E.M.	40000
Year end reject rate 2.0% (P1 − 10 = 2.08%)	800
Given 80% of rejects involve rework	640
Rework costs based on £5.14/hour	£3.3K

ESTIMATED QUALITY IMPROVEMENT SAVING

1982 Actual costs	£12.6K
1983 Estimated costs	£3.3K
Indirect saving	£9.3K

> Engineers Q. C.
> Rework — Conclusions
>
> 1. a, Tooling
>   b, Information Exchange
>   c, Machines
>
> 2. Tooling
>   a, Job box system
>   b, Central tool store
>   c, Greater info.

Summary slide

FINAL PROJECT SAVINGS

Direct financial savings (tooling etc)	£5433.64
Less Quality Circle expenditure (meetings etc)	£959.30
THEREFORE TOTAL DIRECT SAVING	= £4474.30
Indirect cost saving (Quality Improvement)	£9300.00
TOTAL PROJECT SAVING	= £13774.33

DIRECT BENEFIT/COST RATIO = 5433/959 = 5.7:1

SUMMARY AND ACHIEVEMENTS

1. Reject rates reduced to below Management target of 2% and the potential exists to progress further.

   BENEFITS
   (a) Greatly improved quality.
   (b) Increased pride in work and higher morale on the shop floor.
   (c) Increased motivation within the machine shop.
   (d) Less disruption to plans (due dates, etc.) and smoother work flow.
   (e) Reduction in loss of output and disruption down line.
   (f) Fewer increased labour charges to cover overtime work to recover output. Also less subcontract charges to cover overloads.
   (g) Reduced material costs of scrap.
   (h) Less frustration.

2. Development of various aspects of plastics tooling that assists operators and reduces standard times.

3. Improved working relationships with other departments through Quality Circles.

4. Encouragement of specialists within the Company to share completely their professional knowledge.

5. Increased customer confidence as a result of all the preceding achievements, and hopefully leading to future sales and job security for all Corning personnel.

Whilst the Circle views with much pride its achievements in the reduction of rejects and rework rates, everyone recognises the fact that the real challenge is yet to come.

The machine shop as a whole is totally committed to containing reject rates at as low a figure as possible.

The validity of this achievement can only be tested by time and a commitment on our part, shared with management's continued support towards quality improvement.

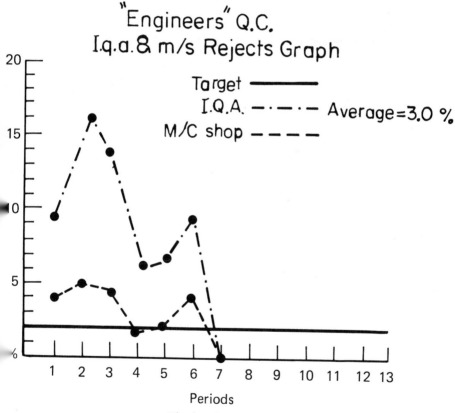

Final rejects graph

This achievement in reducing rejects to zero reflects the contribution made by everyone in the Machine Shop at Bocking.

The members of the Engineers' Quality Circle would like to express their thanks to all those who have assisted and advised them during their training, problem solving and first management presentation, namely:

DENNIS JACKSON
DEREK WRIGHT
SID WHITEHEAD
STILL SKILLS Q.C.
ALL OUR COLLEAGUES IN THE MACHINE SHOP
BARRY BRAYBROOK
ROBERT PORTER
BRENDAN CARR
I.Q.A.
PETER FENN – TOOLING CONSULTANT
GUHRING LIMITED, WEST GERMANY
GUNTHER AND COMPANY LIMITED, WEST GERMANY
JOHN GARRARD – FACILITATOR
MANAGERS AND THE STEERING COMMITTEE

Case Study 4: Honeywell Control Systems Ltd, Bracknell

This report summarises the findings and background pertaining to a problem raised in the I.P.G. Inside Sales Quality Circle.

The final presentation of the findings, and the preparation of this report, were the work of a small 'task force', but all members of the Circle contributed to the gathering and assessment of the information, essential to the preparatory phase.

Corporate Communications and Mailing/Switchboard Departments also provided information, advice and help and the Circle members were grateful to them for their assistance.

REPORT ON CORRESPONDENCE AND
PROBLEM TELEPHONE CALLS

1.0 INTRODUCTION

At the formation of the I.P.G. Inside Sales Quality Circle in early 1982 a list of items for attention was drawn up, two of which were 'incorrect routing of telephone calls' and 'incorrect routing of correspondence, telexes, etc'.

When the time came to deal with these problems it was decided that, as many of the related factors were the same or similar for both problems, they should be combined as:

'Incorrect routing of telephone calls and correspondence'.

Several 'brainstorming' sessions involving all members of the Circle, and checks with the switchboard and mail room, culminated in the production of a 'possible causes' list and subsequently one of 'possible solutions'.

A presentation summarising our findings and their background was made on Friday 11 February 1983 and this report is the written, expanded version of that presentation.

This report is in eight sections:

1) Introduction
2) Recommendations

3⎫
4⎭ Explanatory notes on recommendations
5) Benefits
6) Background on telephone calls
7) Background on correspondence

2.0 RECOMMENDATIONS

2.1 IMPROVE <u>OUR</u> INFORMATION TRANSFER TO POTENTIAL AND ACTUAL CUSTOMER BY MEANS OF:

2.1.1 Revised letter heading
2.1.2 Sticker for attaching to outgoing letters, compliment slips, specification sheets, etc.
2.1.3 Acknowledgement card
2.1.4 Revised visiting cards with 'inside contact' information
2.1.5 Contact information to be added to specification sheets, brochures, etc.
2.1.6 Contact information to be incorporated in advertisements

2.2 APPOINT CORPORATE CO-ORDINATOR(S) TO WHOM DIFFICULT TELEPHONE CALLS AND LETTERS ARE REFERRED, SUPPORTED BY:

2.2.1 Product/customer/divisional lists
2.2.2 Specific switchboard operator/mail-sorter training
2.2.3 Divisional/departmental co-ordinator

3.0 SUGGESTIONS FOR REDUCING THE OCCURRENCE OF THE PROBLEM

In checking the reasons for misdirection of telephone calls and correspondence, etc., it became clear that outgoing information in the form of letters, advertisements, catalogues, etc., was sometimes unclear and often actually misleading.

Examples, with suggestions for improved information, are given in the following pages under the headings:

3.1 Letterheads
3.2 Sticker for outgoing letters, etc.
3.3 Acknowledgement card
3.4 Visiting cards
3.5 Specification sheets/brochures
3.6 Advertisements

4.0 EXPLANATORY NOTES ON DUTIES OF CO-ORDINATOR(S)

4.1 One of the many advantages of the official appointment and recognition of corporate and/or divisional/departmental co-ordinators is that definite responsibility rests with named persons. They can be trained as necessary, and have access to equipment and information required to 'solve the problem'. This avoids the 'hit or miss' nature of the present situation.

A full-time co-ordinator's responsibility could extend to follow-up activities, to ensure that the correct allocation of a letter, 'phone call, telex, etc., has resulted in customer's requirements being met.

4.2 Up-to-date and complete product lists should, and in some areas may, already exist, and can be used for many purposes other than that proposed in this report, e.g. training of new employees, supplementing quotations, providing information for new and potential customers, encouraging inter-divisional business (we certainly place orders with outside suppliers on occasion for equipment which could be obtained from another division).

Quality Circles Handbook

3.1 Letterheads

Honeywell

Your Ref:

Our Ref:

Your Contact is:
Extension:

Honeywell Control Systems
Charles Square
Bracknell
Berkshire.
RG12 1EB
Telephone: Bracknell 24555
Telex: 847064
Cables: Honeywell, Brac

This is our standard "Letterhead".

Note that the address at the bottom which perhaps comes more prominently to the eye is the registered office at Brentford.

No pre-printed information is given to encourage the insertion of "Your Reference", "Our Reference", "Please reply to ...", "Divisional/Departmental Name" etc. information.

Refer to enclosed circles for suggested improvements.

Yours faithfully,

A. N. Other
Account Executive
(Process Control Division)

Delete from here & move to top of page.

HONEYWELL CONTROL SYSTEMS LIMITED, CHARLES SQUARE, BRACKNELL, BERKSHIRE, RG12 1EB
TELEPHONE: BRACKNELL 24555 (STD CODE: 0344) TELEX: 847064 CABLES: HONEYWELL, BRACKNELL

A SUBSIDIARY OF HONEYWELL INC.
REGISTERED OFFICE, HONEYWELL HOUSE, GREAT WEST ROAD, BRENTFORD, MIDDLESEX: REGISTERED No.217803 (ENG

(IN MUCH SMALLER LETTERS)

Case studies of Quality Circles 97

3.2 Sticker for outgoing letters, etc.

One common solution to the omission of Honeywell Contact Information on outgoing documents, at relatively low cost, is the "sticker". A two section, preferably coloured, "sticker" is suggested, possibly reading as follows:

PLEASE ATTACH TO YOUR REPLY	FOR THE URGENT ATTENTION OF: A.N. OTHER, P.C.D.

This sticker could be used on letters, specification sheets, compliment slips etc.,

An alternative, larger "sticker" could combine contact details and reply addressee information:

YOUR CONTACT IS: A.N. OTHER, P.C.D. EXT:- XXX	(PLEASE ATTACH THIS TO YOUR REPLY) FOR THE URGENT ATTENTION OF: A.N. OTHER, P.C.D.

3.3 Acknowledgement card

Suggested possible basis of design for Acknowledgement Card.

```
                    ACKNOWLEDGEMENT
                              DATE ........................
  WE ACKNOWLEDGE WITH THANKS RECEIPT OF YOUR ...............
  ................ DATED ....................................
  YOUR REF .................................................
  OUR QUOTATION/ACKNOWLEDGEMENT/LITERATURE WILL
  FOLLOW WITHIN ............................................
  YOUR CONTACT IS ..........................................
  PHONE NO ................... EXT .........................
  IN CORRESPONDENCE PLEASE QUOTE:
                    YOURS FAITHFULLY,
```

Such a card was in fact used some years ago by several departments within the Company. It would be useful as a simple and speedy acknowledgement of any customer contact by 'phone, telex or letter.

3.4 Visiting cards

S PICKWICK

Senior Sales Engineer
Industrial Products Group

Honeywell Control Systems Ltd.,
Honeywell House,
Charles Square,
Bracknell,
Berkshire RG12 1EB
Tel   0344 24555
Telex   847064

Honeywell

Inside Sales Back-up
— see overleaf

```
FRONT OF CARD - "INDUSTRIAL PRODUCTS GROUP"
COULD MORE APPROPRIATELY BE REPLACED
BY "PROCESS CONTROL DIVISION".
```

INSIDE SALES SUPPORT

J. Wardle	—	Inside Sales Supervisor
B. Snodgrass	—	Senior Inside Sales Engineer
R. Wozenham	—	Senior Inside Sales Engineer
J. Marley	—	Senior Inside Sales Engineer

```
BACK OF S. PICKWICK'S CARD GIVES NAMES
OF INSIDE SUPPORT PERSONNEL - USEFUL FOR
TELEPHONE CONTACT AS S. PICKWICK USUALLY
"OUTSIDE" BUT APPARENTLY NOT APPROVED
BY HONEYWELL.  TRANSFER INFORMATION (EDITED)
TO FRONT OF CARD.
```

3.4 (*contd*)

MARK TAPLEY

Senior Sales Engineer
Test Instruments Division

Honeywell

Honeywell Control Systems Ltd.,
Honeywell House,
Charles Square,
Bracknell,
Berks. RG12 1EB
Tel   0344 24555
Telex 847064

FRONT OF CARD - BACK IS BLANK.
"TEST INSTRUMENTS DIVISION" IS A GOOD LOCATING DESCRIPTION (AS COMPARED WITH "INDUSTRIAL PRODUCTS GROUP" - SEE COMMENT ON S. PICKWICK CARD). <u>FRONT</u> OF CARD SHOULD ALSO PROVIDE INSIDE CONTACT DETAILS, AS SUGGESTED ABOVE.

The product lists should be programmed into existing and/or new mini-computers, thus providing the twin benefits of simple updating and speedy access. The 'hard-copy' lists could then be obtained from the computers via printers.

A 'Guide to Products and Services' is already under development in Corporate Communications, and it may well be that it will meet some or all of the requirements stated above.

4.3 The present training of switchboard operators should be supplemented by more specific instruction regarding methods for clarifying caller's requirements. A list of questions, perhaps in the form of a simplified logic diagram, would be useful. The continuing use of the words 'Industrial' and 'Commercial' when questioning callers should be discouraged, as they tend to confuse rather than clarify.

<u>5.0 BENEFITS DERIVED FROM RECOMMENDATIONS</u>

5.1 Improved customer relations and company image.
5.2 Less lost or delayed mail (and possibly fewer 'lost orders').
5.3 More efficient switchboard and mail room operation.
5.4 Less non-productive time spent by inside sales|contract engineers et al.
5.5 Improved inter- and intra-divisional communications and product knowledge. (This was also a major issue identified in the recent 'Attitude Survey').

3.5 Specification sheets/brochures

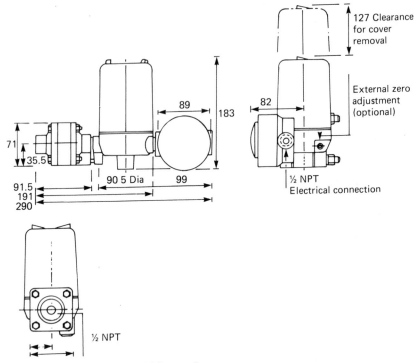

Dimensions (mm) of Mid range PP/I transmitter

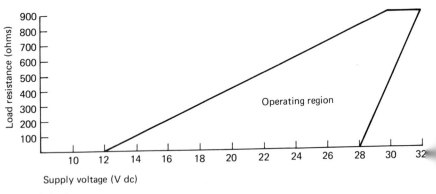

Usable load range

This is typical of the back page of many of our Specification Sheets, and gives no basis for contact to obtain further information, quotation etc. If overprinting is impractical or too expensive, the ''sticker'' suggested in Section 3.2 would be appropriate.

Case studies of Quality Circles 101

3.6 Advertisements

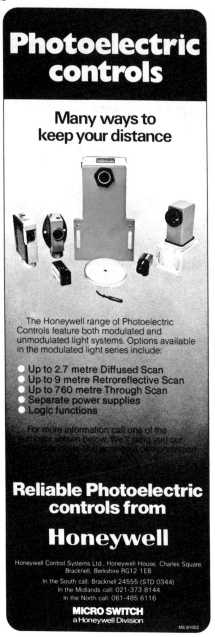

This Honeywell Microswitch advertisement does provide the information necessary to correctly locate any resulting enquiries, although it could be argued that the ''Microswitch'' reference should be incorporated in the reply address.

102 Quality Circles Handbook

3.6 (*contd*)

ADVANCED DESK-TOP COMPUTER GRAPHICS CAMERA SYSTEM

The Honeywell Model 3000 is the very latest in microprocessor-controlled bench-top colour graphic camera systems, providing the ability to produce brilliant colour or sharp black and white photographs from information presented on a computer VDU.

Hard copies can be gained on paper or film transparency in sizes from 10" × 8" to 35mm slide format.

The Honeywell Model 3000 is an advanced and compact computer peripheral with its own built-in "self-test" procedure and offers many benefits to industry, geophysics, medicine and business management.

Please send further details without obligation to

Name *GR WILSON* Position *Collect*

Company Name and Address *GWENT COLLEGE*
ALLT-YR-YN, NEWPORT, GWENT 0333 - 51525

Postage will be paid by licensee

Do not affix Postage Stamps if posted in Gt Britain, Channel Islands, N Ireland or the Isle of Man

BUSINESS REPLY SERVICE
Licence No. WLV 130

HONEYWELL CONTROL SYSTEMS LIMITED
CHARLES SQUARE
BRACKNELL
BERKS RG12 1EB

This reply paid advertisement card finds Bracknell - but then who? Not even the Division is identified. It would be better if the actual Department/Section was identified - in this case Test Instruments.

6.0 BACKGROUND ON TELEPHONE CALL PROBLEMS

6.1 Telephone calls are received at an average rate of 1600 per day.

Of these approximately 10% or 160, cannot be placed with certainty, and 1% or 16 cannot be identified at all.

Yearly therefore, taking into account public holidays and weekends, uncertain and unidentified calls total 40 000 and 4000 respectively.

Assuming only 5 minutes is spent on correctly placing each uncertain and unidentified call, the total time wasted amounts to two full-time employees' services per year.

6.2 The negative effects of the above can be summarised as:

6.2.1 Wasted time on the part of the switchboard operators and more often, relatively expensive part-time troubleshooters in the various divisions.

6.2.2 Delays in dealing with customer requirements, resulting in frustration at least and no doubt disillusion and loss of business at the extreme.

6.3 INCORRECT ROUTING OF TELEPHONE CALLS

PROBLEM

Telephone calls are for obvious reasons the hardest of our subjects to document. We stopped short of taping conversations.

However, we have identified some common problems. Misdirected calls seem to happen more often in the afternoon. They are not restricted to industrial but common to all divisions, in fact the more I have investigated the more it seems that we are all at some time during the day talking to other divisions' customers.

The most common cry from customers seems to be 'you are the fifth person I have spoken to in Honeywell, what are you going to do about it?'. I have had a call, this week from a customer in Cardiff asking for dampers, which seemed to be a Commercial application. I took the customer's details and then went on the route he would have taken if he was transferred. Firstly, I rang Commercial Sales in Bracknell, who in turn passed me on to Building Services in Bracknell. As the customer was in Cardiff, I was passed on to Building Services in Birmingham, but when I rang them, they told me Building Services for Cardiff is now dealt with from a new office in Bristol. So after five calls, the customer would have arrived at the correct office.

This example shows just some of the problems a customer can encounter when ringing Honeywell. He was lucky I knew the product he was talking about. Many employees have heard of the newer divisions, but we have very little idea of what they sell in any detail.

From a survey done on the switchboard over a period of a month, we have some idea of their workload and the problems they face.

No. of calls: Average 1600 per day

No. of calls that cannot be placed with certainty: 10% or 160

No. of calls that cannot be identified: 1% or 16

The way problem calls are dealt with at present is to pass them through to certain 'trustee' employees within the various divisions who know a fair amount about their own division. These people are most commonly inside sales engineers, but others are also involved.

EFFECTS

There are three main effects of this problem.

Firstly, and most important, is the image customers get of Honeywell when they decide to ring us. The sheer frustration they can experience can put them off Honeywell for life. Many of the industries we deal with have very good 'grapevines' and word soon gets round about the bad points of dealing with a company. All of this after spending £XXXXX on the communication budget. Our advertising and merchandising can be first rate, but no customer is going to negotiate an obstacle course to get a Versapak!

Secondly, when we look at the problem calls, we can see that over a year, taking into account public holidays and weekends our 10% of uncertain calls and 1% of unidentified calls come to 40 000 and 4000 respectively per annum.

If we look on these calls as time wasted by the people they are put through to, the cost to the company can be quantified.

For a person earning £6000 per annum, who spent five minutes on each call, this would cost £12 000 p.a. or 2 person years.

The figure for salary may be on the conservative side and does not, of course, include the other costs of employing a person, such as pension, national insurance surcharge and training. The time spent on a call is also on the conservative side. My example of the call from the customer in Cardiff took me twenty minutes.

The third effect is on the employees who have to take these calls. After two or three in one day their attitude towards the customer becomes less helpful than even they feel it should be. A comment I have heard is that they know how customers should be dealt with, but they end up hearing themselves making all the classic mistakes of ineffective communication. It is very difficult to sum up in words the effect this has on people, but the frustration is there and is not going away.

SOLUTIONS

Our brainstorming session produced the following list of possible solutions.

1. Product lists (cross-referred to appropriate divisions, depts, etc.)
2. Customer lists (cross-referred to appropriate divisions, depts, etc.)
3. Experienced operators
4. Switchboard troubleshooter
5. Divisional/departmental troubleshooter
6. Corporate troubleshooter
7. Better operator training
8. Ceefax terminals in switchboard room
9. Computer accessed lists
10. Message recorder

7.0 BACKGROUND ON MAIL AND TELEX PROBLEMS

7.1 Statistics quantifying these problems have been obtained from the mail room as follows:

In an average month, the mail room in Bracknell 1 received 13 000 pieces of mail.

Of these, at least 28% or 3200, are simply addressed to the company, without reference to a specific person or department.

Mail room staff route this 'unidentifiable' mail to the 'most likely' department or person. However, in many instances their best guess is incorrect, and several transfers of the document from one department/division to another can result, before the correct destination is found — if indeed it ever is. (Some letters are almost certainly 'lost' en route.)

7.2 The negative effects of the above can be summarised as:

7.2.1 Wasted time on the part of mail room and telex staff and more often, relatively expensive part time troubleshooters in the various divisions.

7.2.2 Delays in dealing with customer requirements, resulting in frustration at least and no doubt disillusion and loss of business at the extreme.

7.3 INCORRECT ROUTING OF MAIL AND TELEXES

MAIL

This problem, though very real, is less 'urgent' than telephone calls which obviously must be resolved 'on the spot' whereas written communications can be temporarily put on one side for identification.

In an average month, the mail room in Bracknell 1 receives approximately 13 000 pieces of mail. Of these, at least 28% (3200) are addressed simply to the Company in general without reference to a specific person or department. A further 90 are 'real problems'. Whilst items addressed to a named person or department are forwarded 'as received', the remainder need to be opened and any enclosures stapled to the covering letter and then sorted by reference to the heading or any recognisable reference. Assuming, that this procedure takes 30 seconds per item, it occupies more than 1½ man-hours per day. An additional hazard is that enclosures can become separated from their parent correspondence. In one specific instance a set of customer specifications were divorced from the remainder of the enquiry for 7 days, having inadvertently been routed with another piece of correspondence from the same customer to another division.

As with telephone calls, mail room staff route unidentifiable mail to the 'most likely' department or person. However, in a large percentage of cases their 'best guess' is incorrect and can result in correspondence circulating through many departments before reaching its correct destination.

The flaws in this method are obvious.

(a) It is dependent on the goodwill, knowledge and availability of the initial recipient.

(b) Delays in handling.

(c) Additional costs to the company in the use of time spent by sales engineers in these extraneous tasks.

DEFINITION OF 'PROBLEM' CORRESPONDENCE

(a) Letters addressed to 'the company', i.e. no divisional, departmental, or name reference.

(b) Letters addressed to individuals with common surnames but without initials. We have SMITH (8), JONES (5) and WILLIAMS (5).

(c) Lack of any Honeywell reference, e.g. quotation or order number, typists reference, etc.

(d) Letters or enquiries for obscure or specialist products. Honeywell's continuing expansion into new fields and product ranges results in enquiries for items with which the majority of staff are unfamiliar.

(e) Letters from customers unfamiliar with the diversity of Honeywell divisions who address mail to 'Head Office'.

TELEXES

The problems encountered with telexes (of which we receive some 2500 in an average month), are in general similar to those listed above, but are less easy to resolve. Incoming telexes are routed via mail room and any ambiguities are initially handled under the 'best guess' routine.

Should this 'guess' prove incorrect, the recipient will either attempt to resolve it or pass it back to the mail room.

In very few cases does a telex give the customer's name. Most have an 'answer-back' code which often bears no relationship to the customer's name: e.g. XYZ Company is SETL G.

Thus it is necessary to send a telex to the customer requesting 'name and address' before any further action can be taken.

NEGATIVE EFFECTS

1. Time wasted by:
    (a) Mail room
    (b) Telex operators
    (c) Recipients of misrouted mail.

2. Poor service to customers due to:
    (a) Delay in replying to enquiries/literature requests.
    (b) Delay in actioning orders with consequent failure to meet deliveries (particularly for items normally ex-stock).
    (c) Delay in providing information on delivery status of existing orders.
    (d) Apparent lack of interest.

The overall effect can be loss of business due to erosion of customer confidence in our organisation.

Examples of 'good' and 'bad' correspondence are shown in the appendix.

POSSIBLE SOLUTIONS

1. Basic 'product knowledge' training of mail room staff.

2. Production of an 'in-house' listing of products and divisions (including addresses as necessary). This could be produced and updated with minimal cost, i.e. in the same way as the internal telephone directory.

3. Appointment of a corporate troubleshooter to whom all such problem correspondence should be passed.

4. Making it easy for customers and prospective customers to address mail correctly by:
    (a) Affixing a sticker to all items of outgoing mail giving name, division and possibly telephone extension of person to contact.
    (b) Incorporating into all sales literature the correct and full title and address of the relevant Honeywell location.
    (c) Reintroduce the 'Acknowledgement of correspondence/enquiry/order' postcard used some years ago with great success. This could be a general-purpose card. See sample.
    (d) Incorporate name of 'inside sales' back-up on all visiting cards and identify with division/department name.

Subsequent discussions resulted in the deletion of solution 10 and the

ACKNOWLEDGEMENT

DATE ....

WE ACKNOWLEDGE WITH THANKS RECEIPT OF YOUR ....

.... DATED ....

YOUR REF ....

OUR QUOTATION/ACKNOWLEDGEMENT/LITERATURE WILL FOLLOW WITHIN ....

YOUR CONTACT IS ....

PHONE NO .... EXT ....

IN CORRESPONDENCE PLEASE QUOTE:

YOURS FAITHFULLY,

---

setting aside at least for the present — of solutions 4, 5, 8 and 9. Our best considered solution was 6 — the CORPORATE TROUBLESHOOTER with back-up from 7 BETTER TRAINING FOR OPERATORS, 1 and 2 PRODUCT and CUSTOMER LISTS and 5 DIVISIONAL/DEPARTMENTAL TROUBLESHOOTER. The lists would be prepared and up-dated by divisions and could eventually be accessed via microcomputer and/or Ceefax terminals.

Taking these one by one:

Better training for operators

This is a fairly easy process of training not in their job but who does what and where in Honeywell.

The corporate troubleshooter

Would be responsible for all customers whose calls cannot be placed. He would be fully conversant with Honeywell, its divisions, products and services. He would be responsible for updating and improving on the product and customer lists. All divisions would have to update him on new products, deletions from ranges and any new services offered.

Maybe in the initial stages he would have to be supported by a divisional troubleshooter whom he would go to, to find products or services in the division. This divisional troubleshooter would be responsible for updating the corporate person as outlined above. This could be performed by current personnel and would not be a new appointment.

I have been in touch with a company in Bracknell who are of a similar size to Honeywell and have the same problems on phones that we have. As of the 5 April, they are employing two people experienced in telemarketing techniques.

These people will have any calls that cannot be placed passed to them. They will have to take a person's name and number, etc. They will know most of their products and services and will get the person concerned to phone the customer. If they do not know what they are being asked for, it will be their job to find out.

The nice point that the other company makes, is that these calls do not stop here. The customer information service people will phone customers back 24 hours after a call and ask if they have been contacted, and if the person who contacted them has been able to help, and if not, why not.

CONCLUSIONS

The Circle would recommend that the company appoints a troubleshooter to deal with customers along the same lines as the other company. This has the advantage of saving engineers' and other employees' time and relieving the frustrations caused by these calls.

The image Honeywell presents to the customer can only be enhanced from the one they get at present. We believe this solution along with our other recommendations is the most cost effective answer for Honeywell as the company expands and our product and service base becomes more and more diverse.

Case Study 5: Rowntree Mackintosh

Rowntree Mackintosh is a leading international company manufacturing a range of confectionery and snack foods. It operates a number of UK factories including one at Fawdon, Newcastle, which produces a range of well-known lines including Lion Bars, Fruit Pastilles, Smarties and Jellytots. Approximately 900 people are employed at the factory, many of them on shift work.

This case study describes the progress, week by week, of one Circle the 'Solvits', in identifying and solving a problem in its workroom. All the members of this particular Circle are female and are employed in a section in which Fruit Pastilles are packed into large tubes.

Week 1

A brainstorming session was carried out to establish problems in their working area. The brainstorming results are shown in Diagram 1.

From this list the Circle short-listed four particular problems according to the priorities indicated and finally decided to concentrate on 'filling giant tubes' as their project.

Week 2

The Circle carried out a cause and effect analysis to identify the possible causes of their selected problem. The cause and effect analysis is shown in Diagram 2.

Week 3

The problem was formally identified as a 'difficulty experienced when pouring a measured quantity of Pastilles through the funnel into a giant tube, and is caused by sweets jamming in the mouth of the tube. In order to make the sweets drop into the tube it is necessary to bang it repeatedly which, over a full work shift, is very tiring'.

The group decided to bring a selection of tubes and funnels to the next meeting to examine the problem under experimental conditions.

```
            WORK PROBLEMS
  Weights of pastilles_____  4
  Items on floor
  Ink on hands
  Radio not played long enough
  Missing equipment
  Heating system
  Faulty equipment
  Lack of hot water in toilets
  Chairs
  (New) towels
  Men
  Overalls
  Waste _____ 3
  Slippery floors
  Canteen cups
  Badly formed cartons_____ 2
  Giant tubes filling _____ 1
```

Diagram 1

Week 4

Tests were carried out on a selection of tubes and funnels and it was found that in addition to the difficulty of putting sweets into tubes, it was also very difficult to get them out. It was decided to talk to a marketing colleague about customer reaction to this.

Tests were carried out with oval-shaped sweets (strawberry, blackcurrant, and lime) which proved that such a shape, unlike the shapes of other flavours, could be packed with no problem. In other words, the shape of the sweet affected the filling. The facilitator agreed to look into this and report back.

At the same meeting the group tried tests with various funnels and funnel positions and it was found that leaving a small gap between the bottom of the funnel and the top of the tube helped results.

Week 5

The facilitator reported back that the exclusive use of oval sweets would increase the manufacturing costs of the sweets prohibitively. The group asked for a wooden jig to be made to hold tubes whilst being filled.

Week 6

The group carried out tests with the wooden jig and found it was difficult to remove the tubes from the jig due to sweets standing proud to the top of the tube, and the use of a jig was abandoned.

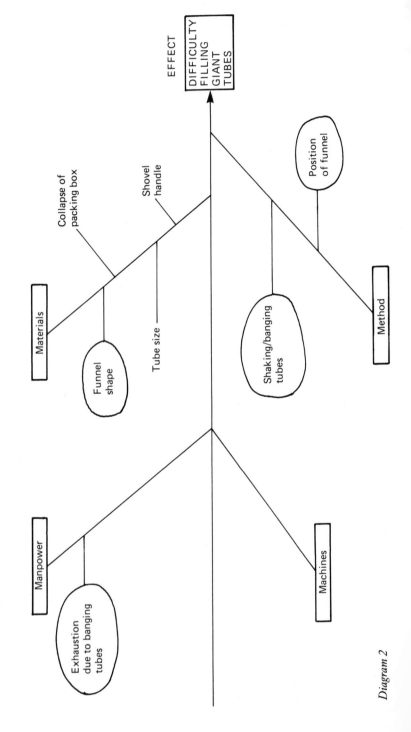

Diagram 2

Week 7

Further trials were carried out using different shaped funnels, made by the sheet metal-working section at the factory. It was found, by trial and error, that a gap of 11 millimetres between the funnel and tube produced the best result. It was also found that cutting the bottom of the funnel at an angle did not help the flow of sweets.

Week 8

More tests were carried out and a further funnel designed as per Diagram 3.

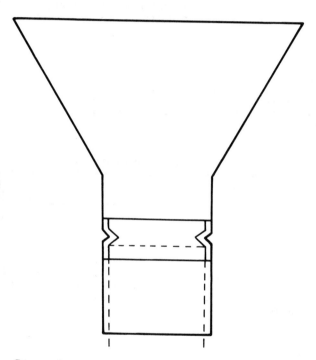

Diagram 3

Week 9

It was finally agreed that the best design incorporated the 11-millimetre gap but that a wider diameter top and stop ring to help 'seat' the tube should be included. The facilitator arranged with the sheet metal-workers for a further test funnel to be made to this design.

Week 10

The new funnel was tested against the old type. In timed trials the new funnel proved:

1. Easier to handle
2. Faster to fill tubes
3. Responsible for less spillage.

Week 11

The results proved a time saving of 24 seconds (average) to fill one dozen tubes. More importantly to members, the new funnel virtually eliminated the need to bounce the tubes to settle sweets. It was agreed that the test results were worth while and that a presentation to management should be prepared.

Week 12

The group asked to see the sheet metal-worker who had co-operated by making the funnels to explain what they had been doing and to thank him for his help. The group prepared a presentation for the departmental manager and production manager and at their suggestion a shop steward was invited to attend.

Week 13

It was decided to include a practical demonstration during the presentation. Each of the Circle members tried the demonstration and one member was chosen. The group practised the presentation and made sure that each member knew exactly what she was doing at all times.

Week 14

The presentation was made to: production manager, departmental manager, personnel manager, forelady and chargehand. The production manager agreed to the necessary expenditure to make a batch of funnels.

Following a discussion about the weight of the funnels it was decided to order some in light-gauge tin and some in plastic.

Results

The new funnels are now used by all members of the department, both the tin and plastic types being equally successful, and it is unanimously agreed that the work of the Circle has made the job easier to perform, and that the new funnel is a significant improvement on the funnel which had been in use for about twenty years.

Case Study 6: Tioxide UK Ltd, Grimsby

'FAULT FINDERS' QUALITY CIRCLE

Tioxide UK Ltd manufactures titanium dioxide pigments at its Grimsby works. The laboratory complex consists of four laboratories covering process control and pigment testing. The purest water used in the laboratories was distilled water from a total of five separate water stills of the traditional laboratory design using electric heating elements.

New process developments, requiring very pure, demineralised, water had just involved a supply being installed some 10 metres away from the laboratory. The obvious proposal to extend the line received the comment 'demineralised water is very expensive, and all you will save will be a little bit of electricity'.

Laboratory Quality Circle 'Fault Finders' decided to check the facts. They knew that the system used excessive amounts of cooling water, had to be regularly cleaned, and required expensive spares. They suspected that the 'bit' of electricity was actually quite large.

A survey of costs and quantities was begun, using QC data-gathering methods. The results showed that a project to replace distilled water by demineralised water had a payback time of only 28.4 days, and that the annual cost of providing pure water for laboratory use would become less than 1% of its existing level.

Cost of Distilled Water

(a) Electricity
 Daily average for five units: 132 kwh per day
 Cost 2.7p per unit   Annual cost £1395   A

(b) Cooling water
 Usage varied with cleanliness of piping
 Average was 1 litre in 46 seconds for each unit
 Annual flow 3428 m^3
 Cost £44.28 per 1000 m^3 Annual cost   £152   B

(c) Maintenance Costs
 Cleaning (1 man per day per month)   £230
 Acid for cleaning   £ 10
 Replacement tubing   £ 10
 Replacement elements   £ 61
 Replacement flasks   £ 56
 Replacement condensers   £ 23.50

                            Total   £390.50   C

Total cost of distilled water
  A + B + C   =   £1937.50 per annum

Cost of Demineralised Water

Annual usage = 61 m^3
Cost per m^3 = £0.171
Cost of demineralised water   =   £10.40 per annum
(Installation cost – Year 1 only – estimate £150)

Cost Benefit – Distilled v Demineralised

Cost of providing distilled water   £1937.50
Cost of providing demineralised   £   10.40

  Annual benefit   £1927.10

Annual benefit = £1927.10

Cost Benefit – Year 1

Annual cost benefit   £1927.10
Installation cost estimate   £ 150.00

                                        £1777.10

Payback

$$\frac{150}{1927.1} \times 365 = 28.4 \text{ days}$$

114   Quality Circles Handbook

Case Study 7: Josiah Wedgwood Ltd, Stoke-on-Trent (Example of a one-page A4 Circle report)

Situation: Giftware of different sizes is put into rigid wrapped boxes prior to dispatch. The operative first places the empty box over a vacuum table (which holds down the bottom half and lifts the top half off, prior to putting in the product. Boxes are from 6 in x 6 in x 1 in to 23 in x 24 in x 23 in.

1. Cause and effect

2. Brainstorm on improved methods

Action	Reaction
Make fitting less tight:	Bottom could fall out when product inside.
Blow compressed air into box with hollow needle:	Unless pressure and volume balanced carefully box exploded! Also lets dust and insects in.
Put holes in bottom to let air in:	
If a vacuum is used holding base down why not have a similar device on top on end of piston.	*Excellent. Could work. Bring pneumatic engineer in.*

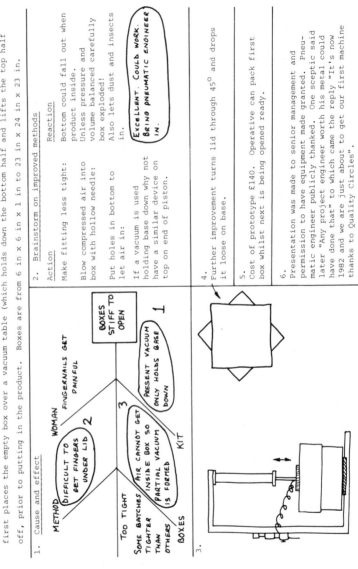

4. Further improvement turns lid through 45° and drops it loose on base.

5. Cost of prototype £140. Operative can pack first box whilst next is being opened ready.

6. Presentation was made to senior management and permission to have equipment made granted. Pneumatic engineer publicly thanked. One sceptic said later "Any project engineer worth his metal could have done that" to which came the reply "It's now 1982 and we are just about to get our first machine thanks to Quality Circles".

Summary of Part II

Chapters 5, 6 and 7

1   Quality Circles are trained to solve problems and to make improvements in their own work.

2   The basic techniques include brainstorming, data gathering and analysis, Pareto Analysis, cause and effect analysis and histograms.

3   Data includes three types of data: variable, countable and subjective. It is important that Quality Circles are trained when, where and how to collect data, and that they know how much data is necessary for the conclusions they seek.

4   Quality Circles select the problems themselves; others may also nominate projects. The problems from which the projects are selected will always be work-related and from within the Circle members' own work area.

5   Quality Circles can be formed in any department where people work together and share common problems. The case studies show Circles from production, packing, sales, engineering and laboratories.

PART III Preparation and introduction

Preface

This Part is intended to assist those responsible for the planning and preparation that is necessary, prior to and during the development of a Quality Circle programme.

The key to success with Quality Circles lies in secure foundations. Every minute spent in preparation before commencement will be repaid a thousand-fold later.

It is hoped that the content of this Part will be of value to all those within an organisation who will be responsible for defining corporate objectives, setting up the steering committee, and defining and implementing its policies.

8 Organisational development

For Circle programmes to be successful it is necessary to prepare a smooth path for their introduction. Failure to do this is almost certain to lead to disappointing results. If Circles are going to alter the culture of an organisation for the better, people must be made aware of and prepared for such changes. Even in the earliest stages a Quality Circles programme will make at least some impact on top management, middle management, supervision, specialists, trade union representatives and non-Circle members at each location of the organisation where Circles are being established.

Conversely, the attitudes of each of these groups will greatly affect the newly formed Circles whose members will be very sensitive to adverse reactions from their seniors and elected representatives.

At the time of writing this book, the number of failed Circle programmes in the UK far exceeds the successes. This is probably true of the whole of the rest of Europe and the USA also. At the same time, the author and his colleagues have trained Circles in over a hundred locations in the UK and have met very few major problems. The reasons for this success are twofold:

1 Very careful preparation of each of the groups mentioned above has been made before commencement of the programme.

2 Every key group in organisations trained by David Hutchins Associates has been fully briefed on the full implications of Quality Circles prior to their introduction.

Friends from companies trained by DHA frequently say that they have been contacted by various organisations who have attempted to introduce Circles without outside help, and have come unstuck.

In many cases the training has been almost non-existent. 'We showed them a video tape', or 'Our Training Officer gave everyone a talk' are extremely frequent replies to questions about their preparations. There are also an incredible number of organisations who seem prepared to entrust the introduction of Quality Circles into their companies to self-appointed experts with the weakest of credentials, simply because they are local or inexpensive. It is quite extraordinary that the owners and directors of sometimes quite large companies are prepared to risk the potential of the most profound change they are ever likely to contemplate in their entire careers to an 'expert' who had probably never even heard of Quality Circles or their philosophy more than a year or two previously at the most and who is unable to supply a list of satisfied clients.

Even the most expert advice available in the world need not be expensive, and a properly introduced programme will pay for itself over and over again. In fact, some companies go so far as to claim that they would not have survived the

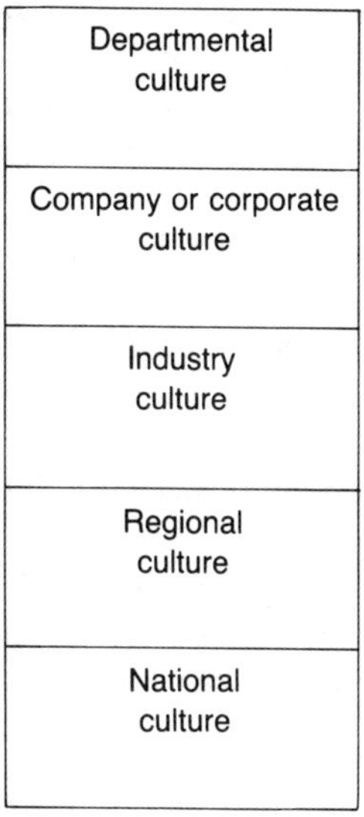

Departmental culture
Company or corporate culture
Industry culture
Regional culture
National culture

Fig 8.1 The five levels of culture

recession if it were not for Quality Circles. The disillusionment that can follow a failed Circle programme may mean that it is better not to start than to start and fail.

The first question to consider once the decision has been made to commence a programme is the question of culture. There are five different levels of culture (Fig. 8.1). The 'culture of the organisation', the 'culture of the industry', the 'local' or 'regional culture' and 'national culture', down to the individual department or section itself, i.e. 'departmental culture'.

People will frequently attempt to use the fact that different cultures exist as an excuse to avoid taking action. 'It will never work here' is a very well-worn comment and is frequently heard when Circles are mentioned.

Let us take national culture first. Of course there are vast cultural differences between Japan and the rest of the world. The Japanese were isolated from the civilised world for over 200 years prior to the Meiji Restoration in 1868; they are one of the few pure races left on earth, and their religion which is a mixture of Buddhism, Confucianism and Shintoism, makes them unique in the world. This uniqueness, together with the traditional Japanese culture, is a constant source of fascination to the rest of the world, and stories about their strange customs and ways make good entertainment in magazines and on television.

All this unfortunately clouds an extremely important issue: namely, the question whether management concepts which evolved in such a unique culture, could possibly have any relevance in another. It is the fact that virtually no one thought this to be possible until nearly twenty years after the original developments began that accounts for the long delay in Quality Circles being taken seriously around the world. The reason that Quality Circles do work in non-Japanese companies is not because the concept is cross-cultural. This is quite untrue. Circles do require a certain culture to exist in the organisation prior to implementation, after which they will themselves create a totally new culture as they become established.

The important point is that the culture we are referring to is not the national culture, but the company culture. Not only Quality Circles, but many other aspects of modern Japanese management can be introduced unmodified into non-Japanese companies, provided that the company culture is made suitable. Admittedly some important aspects of Company-Wide Quality Control cannot be successfully introduced without the supporting national infrastructure, but this is a practical consideration, not a cultural one.

Quality Circles and Company-Wide Quality Control can only be successfully introduced if the organisation is willing to develop a consensus style of management. This style of management is extremely rare, possibly non-existent outside Japan or South East Asia.

Why Circles fail

In the West particularly, most organisations have a more individualistic style of management. In many cases, interdepartmental rivalries are quite strong, and such competition between departments or locations is frequently more important in the minds of some managers than the threats from their real competitors. This type of environment is not conducive to Circle activities, and whilst the existence of the Circles themselves will tend to correct this attitude, it is nevertheless necessary for top level management to make a conscious effort to commence this process prior to the introduction of Circles.

It is the failure to recognise this necessity that has led to the majority of failed Circle programmes. All too frequently the following scenario takes place. Operations Manager 'G' has discovered Quality Circles either by attending a seminar, reading an article, or by contact with a colleague in another organisation. If the concept appeals to him he is faced with three optional strategies.

1 Inform his superior and recommend that the company takes action.

2 Discuss the idea with colleagues at his own level in the hope that they ma

collectively recommend the concept to top management at a forthcoming management meeting.

or 3 Regard the concept as a personal opportunity for advancement and, rather than 'give' the idea to others, decide to go it alone and implement the concept in his own department.

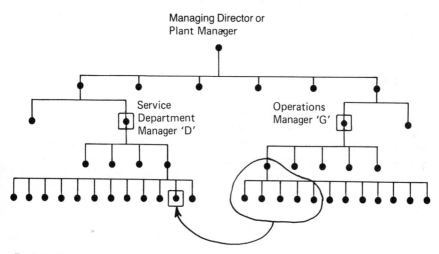

Fig 8.2 Organisation chart for a single location plant

Strategy 3 would be extremely unlikely in a Japanese organisation, but may be quite likely in many others, and in fact happens all too frequently.

Let us assume that the Operations Manager 'G' adopts Strategy 3. He will obtain as much information about Circles as possible but will do it in a very low key way in order to avoid alerting others. He will probably then set up two or three Circles in his section. Before very long one of the Circles will want some help or information from another department. Let us say Department 'D'. Probably one of the Circle members has a friend in that department, or they meet in the canteen at lunch times. The employee from Department 'D' then begins to co-operate with the Circle, and perhaps carries out one or two tasks to help its members (Fig. 8.2).

It will not be long before the manager of Department 'D' discovers what is happening. Given the individualistic style of management mentioned earlier, it is quite likely that Manager 'D' does not like Manager 'G' and will not want his staff to co-operate in any activities outside the regular scheduled arrangements. Co-operation will be quietly discouraged with the consequence that the Circle will not get the support that it needs.

This problem will not just occur in one area; it will happen across the entire organisation. The Circle members will quite rightly perceive that they do not have management support and in all probability will disband the Circle. Even if the Circle does not disband, it will limp along at such a slow pace that its manager, who was hoping for such big things will soon come to believe that Circles are not a magic cure after all. He will probably then disband the Circle and subsequently claim 'we tried it once and it did not work!' He is unlikely to be keen to make a further attempt. Additionally, he will have another reason for not wanting a further attempt. He will think that the first failure was a reflection on his managerial ability. This could of course be partly true, but really, the failure was due to the culture that existed in the company at the time.

Changing the culture

People talk about culture as if it were carved in tablets of stone and could never be changed, and yet cultures are in a constant state of change. Whilst cultural change at national or regional level may be a slow process, the rate of change in culture in an organisation can sometimes be quite dramatic. It changes every time a new managing director takes over, particularly if he has a powerful personality. Sir Michael Edwardes made a dramatic impact on British Leyland as did Ian McGregor on British Steel. That is not saying that these changes were either good or bad, only that they took place.

Fortunately, the changes necessary to create an environment that will support Quality Circles are also possible. Of course they will not happen overnight. Whilst people may change dramatically at a superficial level, some older people will have spent an entire lifetime in their previous environment and it will take time for them to become accustomed to a different approach.

The changes necessary to support a Circle Programme are both at corporate level and in the way people are managed. It is necessary for corporate management to move towards consensus management: in other words, to develop throughout management a sense of corporate consciousness; to develop a sense of fraternity throughout the organisation so that managers, specialists and supervisors are mutually supportive rather than antagonistic; to develop a sense of mutual corporate pride, and entrepreneurial drive to promote the success of the operation rather than just that of their own departments.

People management change

Of equal importance to the problem of interdepartmental rivalry between managers is the problem of management perceiving Circles in their own work area to be a threat to themselves. Some managers may be afraid that the Circle may expose their own weaknesses.

In considering some of the case studies presented in Chapter 7, it would be easy for a cynic to say 'That was a simple problem! You did not need a Circle to do that! Why did you not solve the problem yourself?' Such remarks, if not pre-empted by the preparation of staff at all levels, could be extremely damaging if the manager saw them as a criticism of his competence. Even if they are not stated, given the type of environment they are working in, some managers may 'feel' that others are thinking such statements. This being the case, the manager, who is presumably concerned with his own status in the eyes of others, is unlikely to be over-enthusiastic about a concept that will expose him in this way.

A further equally damaging potential situation arises after a Circle has completed a successful brainstorming session. Again a question is prompted: 'How come you have all those problems in your work area? I didn't think you had any problems!' Fortunately, these seemingly intractable problems can be avoided by careful preparation.

Management gets results through people!

Prior to the implementation of Circles it is necessary for top management to convince middle management that Circles are not seen by it as some form of inquisition. Top management must give confidence to both middle management and to direct supervision that it recognises that of course there are problems in its work area; there are problems in everybody's area, there are problems right across the whole organisation. 'We know that, we accept it, and believe that Quality Circles can help get them solved'. If Circles are successful in a given work area, then that work area manager should be congratulated, because it is obvious that he or she supports the Circles' activities.

To show management how it affects the performance of its staff, it is necessary to compare different styles of management and their effect on people. Managing people involves three factors:

Attitudes
Motivation
Work environment

It is important for managers to realise that they control neither the attitudes of their people nor their motivation. The only factor controlled by management is the environment in which its people work. Not noise, smell and dust, etc., but the environment created by those managers' style.

Management is capable of creating two diametrically opposed managerial styles. Whilst both extremes undoubtedly exist, most managers may be identified as being somewhere between the two. Some may vary from one extreme to the other in different situations. The late Douglas McGregor once summed up these differences when he postulated the theory 'X' and theory 'Y' management concept. The theory 'X' manager is authoritarian and the theory 'Y' manager participative.

The theory 'X' manager says 'work people are lazy, slothful, indolent and inherently work-shy. Therefore I need to use threats, fear, and carrot and stick methods to achieve my performance goals'.

The theory 'Y' manager on the other hand says 'work itself is as natural as breathing and sleeping. Man has an innate desire to work, to justify his existence, as part of his social relationship with others in the community, to satisfy his creative desires and to achieve job satisfaction. Therefore it is necessary for me to make the work of my people rewarding and interesting in such a way that it will give them what they want, which means in turn, that they will respond by giving me what I want'.

Quality Circles should be seen by management not just as a problem-solving process, but as a way of creating a theory 'Y' type of environment. If management can accept this principle, then the true nature of Quality Circles is revealed. Managers need to accept the following points:

- The one hour per week is the Circle's hour.
- It is budgeted out on the basis that it allows the members to indulge in those projects that they think are important and not necessarily those uppermost in the minds of the manager.
- Circle meetings should be enjoyable.
- Circles should be given an opportunity to display their creativity, which can be in the form of:
  Presentations
  Presentation aids such as view graphs, slides, models, etc.
- They should have the opportunity to meet their Circles and exchange ideas.
- They should be encouraged to develop a spirit of self-control.
- All these points should be seen as the Quality Circle members' attraction to the concept.

Management's reward comes from the following:

- Work itself becomes more interesting through greater involvement. Many other problems will 'just disappear' through less carelessness on the part of work people.
- General productivity will increase through higher morale.
- Lower absenteeism because of greater job interest.
- Fewer grievances.
- Greater team spirit.

Quality Circles therefore should really be seen as pure theory 'Y' management.

Top management must convey to middle management that it believes in this approach, and that managers are expected to manage that way because it is the company's policy for them to do so. It is the responsibility of middle management to convey the same attitude to their supervisors, and once this has been achieved, the culture will have been changed totally and irrevocably. However, it is sometimes necessary to use a little theory 'X' to get some theory 'Y'.

In one extremely successful company which was trained by DHA, the plant director had a private discussion on the concept prior to a formal presentation to fifty of his senior managers. When introduced to them at the start of the presentation, he said 'This guy's going to tell you all about participation, and I want you to listen to him, because afterwards we are going to do it!'

9 The role of top management

The visible and real support of plant or corporation top management is essential to the success of Quality Circles. Circles are only part of a corporate policy which goes far beyond the Circles themselves. Top management's role in Quality Circles has seven vital aspects:

1. Establishment of corporate policy and corporate plan
2. Setting corporate goals and objectives
3. Management commitment
4. Allocation of resources
5. Monitoring
6. Auditing
7. Support

This chapter is intended to give guidance to top management on how this role is fulfilled, if the goals of this book are to be realised.

1 Establishment of corporate policy and corporate plan

Before any organisation can make the final decision to go ahead with Quality Circles, top management must first of all be certain that it actually wants to proceed, and that it intends to do so without reservation. This may sound obvious, but it is surprising how many top management teams think that they only have to give the OK for Circles to take place, and then take no further interest. Such programmes always end in failure.

Different managers may have a different perspective of what Quality Circles really are, and a clear understanding of them is essential. There may also be differences about:

> when to start
> where to start
> how many Circles to start with
> what we actually intend to achieve through the programme and *why* we wish to start

The answers to these questions will, in effect, establish the corporate policy of the organisation. This should be the collective decision of the board of directors.

The most likely reason for starting a Quality Circle programme is to help make the company or organisation better at what it is doing: more successful, more profitable, in accordance with the requirements of the owners, whether the organisation is state-owned or private. It must be believed that Circles will help achieve these objectives and the consensus support of all directors must be received before the process of informing others in the organisation is commenced.

Part I of this book explained that Circles are not an entity in themselves but are a part of Company-Wide Quality Control (CWQC) which embraces every facet of the organisation. A definition of CWQC was given in Chapter 2. Many organisations ignore this because it seems too complicated, but lose almost all the true value as a result.

A company policy statement may look something like the one in Fig. 9.1.

It is the policy of the XYZ Company so to develop the resources of our people, systems and technology as to make our organisation leaders in the field, in all aspects of the business, notably profitability, to enhance our corporate image, increase customer satisfaction and make our company a better place to work in.

We recognise that the success of our organisation is dependent upon its employees. It is the policy of this organisation to galvanise the resources of all of our people to work towards the ultimate goals of the enterprise. This will be achieved through the development of a sense of:
    corporate identity,
    corporate pride,
    corporate loyalty
and by encouraging people to feel that their company is better for their being there, and for the recognition of their achievements.

Every employee should be given every possible opportunity to continue his or her own personal development, for the benefit of the organisation as a whole.

This policy will be put into operation through the rigorous application and development of company wide quality control, and the encouragement of Quality Circle activities at all levels in the organisation.

        Signed..............................Chairman
                                or President

Fig 9.1 Company policy statement

2 Setting corporate goals and objectives

The policy statement is really a statement of intent. It is necessary to be more specific in relation to each function and department, and so goals and objectives for each must be determined. Ideally, as we proceed downwards through the organisation each level of management should be more specific about these targets and goals. Top management is responsible for establishing the overall policy, but it is the responsibility of senior management to interpret that policy in relation to its own department or division. Each subsequent level downwards should conduct the same operation all the way through to the direct employee.

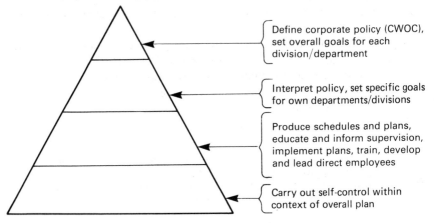

Fig 9.2 The development of responsibility

When this has been completed, the resulting goals and target proposals should be resubmitted upwards and re-evaluated at each level. Finally, the aggregate of these detailed appraisals will become the corporate goals for the coming year.

The responsibility for achieving these goals and targets should ideally rest within the line management structure rather than be assigned to the specialist support functions. These functions should be developed to fulfil a consultancy relationship with line management which should retain ultimate responsibility (*see* Fig. 9.2).

3 Management commitment

This is a favourite term amongst management consultants, but its meaning is rarely ever explained. Of course, every programme requires management commitment, and in terms of Quality Circles, it refers to the visible interest in and awareness of the activities of all levels of staff and management relating to Company-Wide Quality Control. Undoubtedly, the most successful programmes are those where the managing director and other directors take an active long-term interest. They attend meetings, raise questions about Circles at management meetings, ask to sit in at Circle presentations.

In one large company the chairman told the facilitator 'If a lack of resources ever impedes the continued development of Quality Circles, you only have to ask'. This was a real shot in the arm for that Circle's programme, which happens now to be one of the best in the UK.

In another company of international proportions the managing director of the entire operation attended the first Circle presentation in the organisation, at one of its many locations. Afterwards he wrote a personal letter to all the Circle members individually, congratulating them on a job well done, and inviting them to make a video tape of their project. Imagine the effect that this had on the small group of young ladies who were carrying out printed circuit board assembly work.

Management commitment at the highest level can have a great influence on managers at lower levels, particularly if some of them are reluctant to support the programme. In such cases, the evident enthusiasm of the line manager's report or that of higher management can be very persuasive. As has been stated at the end of the last chapter, sometimes a little theory 'X' is required to achieve theory 'Y'.

4 Allocation of resources

Resource considerations for Quality Circles can be listed under four headings:

(a) Cost
(b) Manpower
(c) Facilities
(d) Materials and equipment

(a) Costs

Contrary to many people's impression, the introduction of Quality Circle programmes should not be expensive, but neither is it free. A good consultant should train a company to build its own programme rather than come in and run it for them. All being well, his total fee is likely to be more than recovered during the first few months of operation, but this cannot of course be guaranteed. This is because Circles do not necessarily start to work immediately on cost reduction problems. Over the course of a year, many projects will have saved money, and it is usual for the programme to show a benefit to cost ratio of approximately 3 to 1 or better in the first year, and this will improve constantly in subsequent years.

In addition to deciding the resources to be budgeted for the initiation of a Circle programme, there will also be maintenance and development costs, and a policy decision will be needed to determine how any savings made by the Circles will be used. This latter aspect is covered more fully in Chapter 16. The most important costs to be considered are:

Consultancy fees
Time lost during training
Facilitator's salary (*See* Chapter 15)
Steering committee meeting time (*See* Chapter 14)
Cost of new equipment
Cost of training aids
Cost of Circle meeting time
Budget for Circle projects
Allowance for motivational activities (*See* Chapter 16)

(b) Manpower

The only additional manpower requirement for the introduction of a Circle programme should be the appointment of the facilitator. The implications of choosing full or part time facilitators will be fully discussed in Chapter 15. In a larger company, further facilitators may be required. As a general rule, one facilitator can adequately support about fifteen Circles once the programme is under way. In some cases the facilitator may be supported by a member of the training department, but this is unlikely to strain existing resources.

(c) Facilities

Meeting rooms for the Circles, free from distractions, are the most important consideration. Initially, this aspect is unlikely to cause problems when there are only three to five Circles, but later on extra facilities may be required.

In the Wedgwood factory in Staffordshire the programme grew so quickly that at the end of the first year there were approximately 70 Circles, which used up all the meeting room facilities. Such was the commitment of management that it built a special Quality Circle centre with a number of new meeting rooms, to enable the continued expansion of the programme.

Quality Circles need some *storage facilities* such as cabinets, lockers, cupboards, etc. to keep their worksheets and materials. Sometimes, when they are collecting samples of some feature they are studying, they may even need a small room to keep their materials, where they are unlikely to be disturbed by others.

(d) Materials and equipment

Circles need very little in the way of basic equipment and many companies will already have most items, which include:

Flip charts—very popular in Circle activities
Kodak or similar carousel slide projector
Tape recorder/player with synchro pulse to connect to projector
Overhead projector

5 Monitoring

Monitoring a Circle programme at regular intervals gives lower levels of management the clearest possible indication of the importance attached to Circles by their superiors.

A Circle programme can be monitored by the following parameters:

- Cost/benefit ratios
- Quality improvements
- Productivity improvements
- Absenteeism
- Grievances
- Morale—attitude surveys
- Sick leave
- Accidents/safety
- Energy saving
- Waste reduction
- Inventory control
- Schedule improvements
- Housekeeping
- Timekeeping

and possibly others relating to specific industries.

It must be understood that whilst the overall cost benefit ratio is an important consideration in assessing whether Quality Circle activities are generally of value to the organisation, individual Circles must not be compared with each other on that basis.

At Circle member level, the most crucial consideration is the level of morale both in the Circle and in the section generally. If an individual Circle appears to be making large financial savings, this should be regarded as a bonus and attributed to the Circle programme as a whole. Without the existence of the other Circles, these savings would not be achieved.

The report which monitors the programme will usually be prepared by the facilitator, and endorsed by the steering committee prior to submission to top management. This is likely to be an annual activity, but in some cases may be six-monthly.

6 Auditing

A regular audit by top management is unfortunately all too rare. In Japan, an audit by the company president of every activity within the scope of Company-Wide Quality Control is an essential ingredient in the success of the concept. Not only does it give satisfaction to top management that its policies are being carried out and are working, but it also demonstrates to staff at all levels that top management is not only interested in, but thoroughly understands what is going on. Top management may also instruct the finance department to make an independent audit of cost achievement claims so that all measures of Circle activities are impartially monitored. This will reduce the likelihood of one of the biggest problems in Circle activities—the Circles race!

This is particularly a problem in large multi-site operations. Plant 'A' may justly claim, say, 30 Circles. At Plant 'B', in order to give a good impression, a claim of 40 Circles may be made when in fact it has fewer. This could also apply to claims of savings. One plant makes one claim, which the second plant feels compelled to upstage. Eventually, this rivalry may develop to such an extent that the entire programme becomes a fabrication. The independent audit will reduce the likelihood of such problems.

7 Support

Suspending meetings

Occasionally, production pressures and other problems may cause some managers to be sensitive about the time being spent on Circle activities. There may be occasions when there is a desire to suspend such activities. It is on occasions such as this where the support of top management will be crucial. Suspension of meetings should only be advised in the most extreme circumstances. Usually a Circle will volunteer to meet in its own time, if it will overcome some crisis in the department.

Management musical chairs

Direct top management support is also vital in multi-site operations. If management at group level is not aware of Circle activities at each location, or does not take an active interest, an otherwise excellent programme can be disastrously affected if the general manager of the location is changed, and the new appointee is less committed to the concept.

In order to make an impression on the balance sheet, he may decide to curtail Circle activities, particularly if he is unaware of the level of support for the programme at group headquarters. This problem has unfortunately already occurred at a company which was developing a small but otherwise excellent programme.

10 The role of middle management

The attitude of middle or line management towards Quality Circles is quite critical. The vitality of individual Circles will frequently be a direct reflection on the relationship between the manager and the Quality Circles in his or her section or department. In Chapter 8 considerable attention was given to the perspective that middle managers may have of Quality Circles in the initial stages, and the effect of this important group must never be underestimated.

Initially, because Circles are normally only started in a small way with three to five Circles, it is unlikely that every manager will be affected. When managers have been briefed on Quality Circles, different attitudes will become evident. Some managers will say: 'it's all been tried before' or 'I don't think it will last'; 'It is OK in other companies but it won't work here', and so on. In reality they are expressing a fear that they themselves may not be able to make it work, or that they will feel that they may be exposed in some way. Fortunately, such feelings rarely, if ever, present a major problem. Usually, if the initial briefings are carried out successfully, there will be a number of other managers who see things differently. These managers are likely to respond by making such comments as 'I think it's a great idea, pity we didn't think of it twenty years ago', etc.

It is highly recommended that the initial Circles are formed in departments led by such managers. 'Start where the grass is greenest' is a good maxim. Supportive departmental managers are essential to the success of a Circle programme.

Once the early Circles have been established, all being well, there should be notable achievements which will not go unnoticed by other managers. Eventually, some of the initially more negative managers will request Circles to be started in their work areas. Of course, there may be some who will never wish to start. Such hardened attitudes will require management decisions beyond the scope of this book.

Middle management support

Enthusiastic middle managers will want to know how they can best help the Circles in their areas. In the early days of Quality Circles in the UK it was thought that the manager should keep well away from the Circles' activities until they requested an opportunity to make a presentation. Experience, however, has shown this to be wrong. Provided that the manager does not actually 'interfere' in the Circles' activities, or attempt to steer them forcibly in one direction or another, a healthy interest can be of great benefit. Circles like to think that their manager is interested in their work.

The manager must always be aware that the ultimate object of Quality Circles is to develop a 'self-control' working environment and must always remember the following golden rules, some of which were initially mentioned in the previous chapter.

- The Circle selects its own problems.

- The one hour per week is the 'Circle Hour', and the way the hour is used is at members' discretion. Management must not appear too concerned about the time a Circle spends on a project.

- Management's 'pay-off' comes in the other 38 or 39 hours of the week. Any advantages which accrue directly from Circle projects should be regarded by management as a bonus.

- Circle meetings should only be postponed in the most exceptional circumstances, and preferably only after discussion with a higher level of management or with the steering committee.

- Individual members including the leader of the Circle should not be prevented from attending a meeting, except in the most exceptional circumstances. If this is absolutely essential, it may be preferable to rearrange the meeting time in order to give all members an opportunity to attend.

- The time for Circle meetings should be mutually agreed between the manager and the Circle and should occur at the least inconvenient time in relation to the work of the department.

- Wherever possible, it is preferable for Circle meetings to take place at the same time and same day in the week. The day then becomes identified as 'Circle Day' and people are more likely to plan other activities to avoid this time. People are also less likely to forget to attend. This sometimes happens in other cases.

There is nothing wrong in the manager 'looking in' occasionally during a Circle meeting. It shows a healthy interest and the Circle will usually be pleased to see him. Sometimes the manager may have some information relating to the subject matter being discussed by the group, and his giving this information to the Circle directly is probably one of the strongest indications of support that can be given.

Sometimes the manager may wish the Circle to look at a problem that affects the department and is of great concern to him or her. Provided that the reasons for this are explained to the group, and that its members are not pressurised to do so, the Circle will usually be flattered by such a request and will generally respond positively. If it happens too frequently the Circle may feel that the manager is attempting to 'take over' the Circle.

Relationship with other Circles

A manager's main concern will most probably be with the Circles in his own department. Sometimes, perhaps frequently, they will need help, advice or information from specialists or people in other departments. Co-operation between managers in cross functions will greatly help in this situation, and therefore managers who are keen to promote Circle activities would do well to foster good relationships with their colleagues. Conversely, Circles in other areas may require help and information from that particular manager's department, and his attitude towards such requests will greatly affect the support given by others to his own group's activities.

Management Circles

Some companies are beginning to realise that Circle activities need not extend only to direct employees. The concept works equally well at both management and supervisory levels. Such groups are generally referred to as task forces and can work in conjunction with Quality Circles. Circles of specialist troubleshooters may be referred to as project groups.

Whilst Circles of managers are still relatively rare, there are now many Circles of supervisors.

Management Circles have several advantages.

- By working in the same way as a Circle, managers can more fully appreciate the type of relationship which develops amongst the members.
- Communications across functions are improved, and lead to greater co-operation.
- Managers are more likely to develop a 'corporate spirit' rather than a 'departmental spirit'.
- Development of a consensus style of management is encouraged by these activities.
- It is a very effective way of solving management problems.
- Management becomes familiar with the language and techniques of Quality Circles, i.e. brainstorming, Pareto analysis, cause and effect etc., and is more sympathetic to their work.

- Management will not feel threatened by its people appearing, at least to itself, more impressive than managers themselves.

Management's role in people development

In Chapter 8 it was stated that management gets results through people. People are the most important asset of an organisation. However dull and boring a person's job may be, and however alienated people may feel, they have a certain loyalty to their work and to their organisation. When they meet their friends socially outside work they often boast about the company's products or its reputation and they want to be involved.

A good manager should recognise this and build on it. Quality Circle activities are an opportunity for them to do so, and the following guidelines are intended to help managers who wish to get the most from their people. The most important considerations for middle management may be put under the four headings:

Responsibility
Recognition
Education and training
Job rotation

Responsibility

If the principle of *self-control* is valid it really means that people need responsibility and will generally accept it. Giving a person responsibility, however small it may be, is recognition of that person's talents and ability. It engenders trust and loyalty.

Taylorism (*see* Chapter 3) denies people the opportunity to take responsibility. By breaking jobs down into their smallest elements and elevating problem solving to a management specialist, responsibility is removed from individuals and they become mere extensions of their machines or desks. It creates a massive contrast between their lives in and out of work.

Outside work they have a great deal of responsibility. They may be husbands or wives, they may have families. From their income they have to manage their own economy, pay the rent or mortgage, save up for holidays and Christmas, obtain passports, repay hire-purchase debts, and raise their children. Most people are perfectly capable of doing this. They maintain the same standards as the rest of their community, and are trusted and respected by their friends. They may have hobbies and pastimes, where they have developed considerable skill or acquired considerable knowledge. They may even be regarded as experts. They may be members of some local committee, where their ideas are listened to and acted upon, but the tragedy is that most of them will be required to hang their brains on the gate when they walk into work in the morning and pick them up again when they leave at night. No one asks them anything, no one involves them in anything, and it is no wonder that they switch off mentally. When this happens, their performance is purely mechanical. In some cases, the enormous boredom may be so great that they make distractions to break down the monotony. In the extreme, this may even result in the deliberate sabotage of the company's products.

Although this problem is normally identified with manufacture, it does not just relate to production workers doing repetitive tasks, it relates to all forms of work where the individual is confined to a detailed job specification. The sequence may be longer in some jobs than others but it is still, nevertheless, a sequence. Once the sequence has been repeated several times it can contain little interest regardless of its length.

The theory 'Y' manager described in the previous chapter will continually be aware of the dangers of this, and should always be seeking means by which the problems of boredom, fatigue, carelessness due to low job interest, and sullen attitudes, can be overcome. Many can be significantly reduced through Circle activities provided that the ultimate goal is self-control.

By deliberately feeding Circles with management information such as quality control data sheets, output targets, variance analysis, data and so forth, not only does this indicate trust and respect from the manager, it also enables the Circle to appreciate management's dilemma, and is far more likely to lead the Circle towards projects concerned with improving the performance of the section.

Recognition

This is one of the most important forms of motivation. A golfer would derive little satisfaction from his first 'hole in one' if there was no one there to witness the event. This is no less true of people at work. People want to be listened to. They like their manager to show an interest in their ideas. It is particularly true of Quality Circles. Good theory 'Y' managers will not only take a keen interest in the projects of their Circles, they will always be prepared to make the time available to attend their Circle presentations. They should see these events as being amongst the most important highlights of the Circle process.

The Circles will be proud of their achievements, and will want to tell their story. Their own manager, to them at least, will be the most important person in the audience.

Education and training

It should be the responsibility of each manager to identify the training needs of his or her department in order to ensure that the staff are adequately prepared to perform their tasks in a satisfactory manner. This aspect becomes even more important if the principle of self-control explained in Chapter 3 is to be realised.

Departmental training programmes should be designed to:
- Increase task-related skills
- Improve abilities to identify, analyse and solve problems
- Increase confidence to accept responsibility
- Build teams
- Develop leadership
- Create a sense of corporate identity/loyalty
- Encourage self-improvement and self-development

Some people may not immediately realise the importance of each of the items listed in situations where people are doing highly repetitive low-skill operations, such as packaging items into cartons, etc. In fact these aspects of training are even more important in such situations. The people concerned are probably no less intelligent than others involved in very much more demanding activities, and something needs to be done to occupy their minds. It was the realisation of this fact which was one of the critical factors which inspired the Japanese to develop Quality Circle type activities in the first place.

Job rotation

Flexibility at the workplace is a great advantage to management and this may be developed through Quality Circle activities. During crises, or when a key individual is absent, it is obviously an advantage to be able to switch people around. Of course, in areas where demarcation problems exist, such flexibility is not always possible, but much can be achieved in many situations.

Flexibility is not just an opportunity for management. It should be seen as an advantage for everyone. Whilst undoubtedly there are some people who are content to perform a single operation repeatedly, this is not true of most. People like variety, and a change of activity creates renewed interest. People also like to feel that they have acquired a broader range of skills. They feel more useful. Some organisations recognise this and even award certificates for attainment which are displayed in the work area.

Job rotation gives opportunities for Quality Circles, particularly where the repetitive nature of work creates problems of carelessness, fatigue, boredom, etc., and at the same time gives greater emphasis to the idea of self-control.

For example, in a Japanese factory, a shop full of employees was involved in the assembly of portable radio cassette tape players. The shop was working on the conveyor-belt principle, with six rows of operatives in lines which ran the length of the floor. The majority of the operatives were involved in the hand insertion of components into printed circuit boards which were the size of an A4 sheet of paper.

During our tour of the work area, some members of the author's study group became concerned that the operatives appeared so intent on their operations that not one of them even appeared to be aware of our presence, and they were working at a very high rate. This was somewhat unnerving to those accustomed

The role of middle management   141

to repetitive work in the UK. There, not only would the pace have been slower, but the operators would have taken at least a passing interest in the visitors.

After the tour the study group tackled a senior manager about this observation. At first the manager could not understand why the group should be surprised at this apparent level of job interest. Then he said, 'They did not look up because they were interested in their work'. The group asked how they could possibly be interested in such repetitive tasks, and he replied 'Ah, well that is because they belong to Quality Circles. In their Circles' activities they will discuss problems relating to monotony, boredom, fatigue, human unreliability, mistakes, etc., and will seek to reduce them. Although you saw them performing specific operations during the walk round, they would not perform the same task throughout the day. Most probably, one individual would be doing hand insertion of components for approximately one hour, then switch to visual inspection for one hour, then a different assembly operation, then another, making four separate tasks altogether. They would then repeat the same tasks in the second half of the shift. This arrangement of tasks would not be determined by either the manager or the supervisor but by the operatives themselves, in order to attain the best results possible. In other words, they were setting their own goals!! This is the ultimate in self-control'.

This form of self-control would of course be impossible if departmental management had not first accepted the responsibility for training the operatives in these diverse skills.

Improvement in ability, to identify, analyse and solve problems

A Quality Circle is only as good as the techniques it has been trained to use. The basic techniques which will enable a work group to get started in Circle activities were outlined in Part II of this book. However, these should be seen as foundation techniques and not as the ultimate development. If Quality Circles are working properly, they should be part of a continuous development process. Additional techniques can be learned in two ways:

1   Formal training through courses arranged by the Company.
2   Self-development through reading, evening classes or correspondence courses.

Formal training needs must be identified by departmental managers, budgeted for, and included as part of the overall company training programme.

Self-development of Circles is an ongoing process, which will happen to some extent regardless of supervisory or managerial input. However, there are several ways in which this can be both accelerated and encouraged. Managers can make books, periodicals, technical journals available to the group and make facilities available so that Circles can make contact with Circles in other organisations, for mutual exchanges of ideas. Managers can sanction any or all of the following.

- Allow them to correspond with institutions and learned societies.
- Encourage attendance at relevant seminars when the work schedule permits.
- Participation in conventions for Circle leaders and members.
- Mutual visits to other organisations supportive to Circle activities.
- In-company seminars.

All these activities will tend to increase the scope of Circles, heighten their enthusiasm, and encourage others to participate in such activities.

Increase confidence to accept responsibility

The more that responsibility can be delegated to others, provided that recognition is given for their achievements, the greater will be their respect and loyalty. Responsibility equates to trust and respect, and it is rare that a normal person would ever violate trust. The more scope that a manager affords to his or her Quality Circles, the greater will be their satisfaction, and their respect for the manager.

Of course the devolution of responsibility must be a gradual process, and measured against the confidence of the individuals concerned. Too much devolution too soon can have the adverse effect if the group lacks confidence. Part of the manager's task, then, in Quality Circles development is always to seek ways of increasing the group's self-confidence. The best way this can be done is by thanking the members and congratulating them on their achievements.

Team building

By their nature, Quality Circles are a team-building process. Where the department includes people who are not members of the Circle, this may present a problem. During the training of Circles, Circle members must be very carefully schooled to regard themselves as 'their section's Circle' and not an elite group in the work area.

This problem is made worse when the manager attempts to use undue influence on the Circle to 'tackle his problems'. The Circle will then more than likely be accused by the non-Circle members of being 'management's favourites'. However, if the manager understands fully the true nature of Circles, not only is this unlikely to happen, but he or she can help develop a team spirit throughout the department.

The Circle should be encouraged to solicit ideas from non-Circle members, ask for their ideas about possible projects, and involve them in data collection.

Some departmental managers encourage Circles to make their presentations to the rest of the department prior to their presentation to management. On such occasions the non-members may make constructive suggestions on how the presentation may be improved. It may even encourage them to form another Circle, if the existing group has ten or twelve members. There is nothing wrong with having more than one Circle in the same department. They will not conflict with each other. Normally, they will be mutually self-supportive and greatly enhance the co-operative spirit of the section.

Leadership development

During the many years of Taylorised management, the role of the supervisor or management-appointed group leader was in many cases seriously eroded. Quality Circle activities can provide an opportunity not only to re-establish the leader's role, but also to develop leadership and identify future leaders.

A good supervisor acting as Circle leader will quite often rotate the leadership of the group meetings. Not only does this allow the official leaders to think up their own ideas, but it also makes the group more self-reliant. Such a leader may eventually allow the group to run itself whilst a new group is formed elsewhere in the section. The leader will then oversee both groups.

Managers must be keenly aware of the importance of leadership development amongst supervisors and should take every opportunity to encourage their supervisors to take up places on corporate training schemes if full self-control is ever to be achieved.

Creation of corporate identity/corporate loyalty

Loyalty to one's family, group, community, or organisation is a natural human characteristic which is latent in most people almost regardless of the way they are treated. Of course, if someone is treated badly or feels unloved, such loyalty is likely to be vigorously suppressed. The importance of loyalty, or the means of achieving it are often overlooked in organisations, which is surprising because the visible expressions of loyalty by staff are probably the most impressive features of a successful department or organisation.

This is especially important at the point of interface between the supplier and the customer. At company level, the entire status of an organisation in the market place can be influenced in many cases more by the visible signs of loyalty of company employees than by the quality of the product or service itself. Loyalty breeds confidence. Loyalty usually equates with pride, and the desire to do a good job.

Of course, one individual manager cannot by himself change the corporate image of the entire operation, but neither can any other on his own. Top management can obtain the loyalty of its senior managers, and the senior managers can obtain the loyalty of their subordinates, and so on down the line. At department level, therefore, it is the responsibility of the manager to obtain the loyalty of his own staff within the context of the organisation as a whole.

Managers may think this aspect to be less important when their section or department does not interface with the user, but this is wrong thinking. Management should instil in the minds of its people the concept of 'next downstream operations are the customers. We, in turn, are the customers of upstream operations.' Those departments that are able to generate this sense of pride and loyalty will find that it becomes infectious in both directions. Not only will the section be more appreciated by the following departments, it will also find that many of the problems it is confronted with among its own suppliers will simply disappear.

Eventually, the organisation will become the sum total of the collective effort of all of its employees. Theory 'Y' management is the only way to achieve that loyalty.

Self-improvement and self-development

Members of staff collectively and individually should be given every encouragement to continue their own development. To read books, attend evening classes, even in non-vocational activities. All these possibilities tend to give confidence, and low self-confidence is one of the biggest problems hampering organisational performance today.

A manager should encourage this form of development and take an interest in his people's attainments.

11 The supervisor as Circle leader

Recognition of the importance of the supervisor's role in management in Japan preceded the development of Quality Circles by at least ten years. During that period, the Japanese developed an extremely sophisticated approach to supervisory development which has no equivalent anywhere in the world.

By the time Quality Circles emerged, Japanese supervisors were highly trained and were better trained managers than many people two or three levels higher in non-Japanese societies. Consequently, Quality Circles were almost a natural extension of this development. Obviously, it would be unrealistic to expect non-Japanese organisations to spend ten years reproducing this same development before commencing Circle activities. Fortunately that is not necessary.

It has been found that Circles can be formed successfully even in cases where the supervisor or group leader has received no formal management training whatsoever prior to the decision to commence Circle activities. This is provided that training and development is conducted in parallel to Circle activities. These must never be overlooked. If supervisory development does not take place, it is fairly certain that the Circle programme will suffer, if not fail completely, and some form of supervisory development will always prove to be an extremely worthwhile investment provided it is done properly.

In this chapter we shall look at the role of the supervisor in a post-Taylor environment, the selection of supervisors as Circle leaders, supervisory development and training, and problems relating to Circle leadership.

The supervisor in the post-Taylor environment

It has been explained in previous chapters that Quality Circles are a form of self-control which combines the advantages of Taylorism with the advantages of the Craftsmanship concept, to form a new style of management (see Fig. 3.9) based on the individual work groups with the supervisor as group leader.

The success or otherwise of this approach is highly dependent upon both the supervisor and the line manager. Both may be required to adopt a different style of management from previously, and their selection and training is a crucial consideration. As Circle leader, the supervisor has two different relationships to consider:

(a) The everyday relationship with people in the department which may contain both Circle and non-Circle members.

(b) The relationship with the Quality Circle members during Circle meetings.

The critical factors under item (a) that are relevant to a successful Circle programme are:

1 Ensuring equal treatment for everyone in the department regardless of their attitudes towards Circle activities and Circle members.

Circle members must not be seen as an elite. Some people in a department may be extremely sensitive about this, and the supervisor must ensure that any such accusations are groundless if they arise.

2 The style of management or supervision that is conducive to the development of a sense of loyalty and co-operation.

This requires the adoption of a style of management that can range from consultative at one extreme to participative at the other.

A supervisor who adopted other styles—autocratic or paternalistic, for instance—would be unlikely to create an environment conducive to the spirit of Quality Circles. He would also need to show contrasting styles inside and outside Circle meetings that would be impossible to maintain.

The style of leadership demanded inside the Circle at Circle meetings is critical.

It is vital for the Circle leader to remember at all times that when the door is shut and the Circle members are in the room together, everybody has one vote, and no one individual opinion is any more or less important than any other. During Circle meetings therefore it is necessary for the supervisor to adopt a consensus style of leadership. The main objectives of the Circle leader are twofold.

1 To act as a source of knowledge, and to be an adviser, trainer and developer of the group.

2 To ensure the participation of all Circle members.

In the early stages of Circle activities the Circle leader, together with the facilitator, will be concerned mainly with the training and development of the group. However, as the weeks go by, and the Circle begins to mature, the training element will gradually reduce. Simultaneously, the Circle leader's confidence will have grown, and a healthy relationship with the group will have been developed.

The Circle leader will realise at this stage that it might be worthwhile to allow the leadership of individual meetings to rotate amongst the members. Not only will this continue the people-building aspect of the members; it will also give them increased confidence in the leader and in the open nature of Circle activities. Beyond that, it will enable the leader to contribute his or her own ideas to the meeting. This is not easy when acting as leader and member simultaneously.

After a short time the leader may judge that the Circle has become self-sufficient and is no longer totally dependent upon the leader's presence. In a large work area, this may provide an opportunity for the leader to start another Circle and subsequently appoint deputy leaders. The supervisor may then simply keep an eye on each group and 'sit in' on meetings when necessary. It must be said that this form of development is not essential, only desirable, and it should happen naturally, not by force. In a high proportion of Quality Circles, the supervisor will remain Circle leader permanently.

It may be seen that Quality Circles are by themselves an excellent form of supervisory development. In one company trained by David Hutchins Associates, the plant manager commented: 'the most significant development since we formed the first Circles a year ago is that our supervisors are now talking like managers. Even if the Circle programme had achieved nothing else, in my opinion, this fact justifies the entire cost'.

Selection of supervisors as Circle leaders

Because the introduction of Circles is not usually preceded by years of specialised supervisory development, the selection of the initial Circle leaders is critical.

Normally, it would be unwise to consider the creation of more than five or six initial Circles at a given location. There are several reasons for this, the most important being:

1 First impressions are extremely important, and because the organisation is unlikely to have any previous first-hand experience with Circles, it is necessary to be able to give the new Circles all the support they need.

2 A large-scale development is likely to frighten those who are as yet uncommitted, into a defensive position. People feel less threatened by a pilot programme, which can easily be terminated if necessary.

3 There will be a wide range of management styles, relationships and attitudes within the organisation, some of which may be adverse to the Circle concept. These cannot be changed overnight. Only a small proportion of managers and supervisors have attitudes conducive to Circles in the early stages.

Item 3 above demands that before Circles are contemplated it is necessary to review the styles, relationships and attitudes of managers and supervisors throughout the entire location.

The answer to the question 'where should we start?', is, as stated earlier, 'where the grass is greenest!'. In other words, start in those departments where the supportive supervisors and leaders already exist.

Again it is impossible to emphasise too strongly the importance of supportive management in the section or department where Circles are to be organised. Having located the most supportive managements, the potential Circle leaders may be selected. This requires much the same approach as that used to find the supportive managers, and the first Circle leaders should be those who already have a good relationship with their people. They should have a natural tendency towards theory 'Y' management, and easily adopt a consultative or participative style with their people. They should also be selected from amongst the more self-assured and confident people.

Whilst they will have been invited to become potential Circle leaders, it must be emphasised that the voluntary nature of Circle activities applies as much at this level as it does at member level. If they do not want to lead a Circle, they should not be forced to.

If they do not want to lead a Circle, and both management and direct employees want to form a Circle, then management is faced with two options:

1 Ask the supervisor if it is acceptable to them for a Circle to be formed with the group electing their own leader.

or alternatively

2 If the answer to (1) is negative, management will be faced with the choice of either abandoning the idea of a Circle in the area initially, or of moving the supervisor to another area.

If (1) is accepted, it is imperative that the supervisor is kept in touch with the activities of the group, and that he or she should always be given the opportunity to attend Circle presentations. He or she should never be by-passed.

The above advice will enable most organisations to make a start. Some will find the general attitudes of managers, supervisors and workpeople more favourable initially than others, but it is highly unlikely that the positive factors will be totally absent and a pilot scheme will almost always be possible. This pilot scheme should be seen as being rather like a new-born baby. It will need nursing, and caring for until it is strong enough to stand on its own feet.

If the first leaders are carefully selected, the first Quality Circles are likely to be successful. Success breeds success, and all being well others will be impressed with the results, and will soon want Quality Circles in their own area. The rate at which this demand will increase cannot be forecast and varies from one company to another. At one extreme, a company may commence five Circles and only progress to seven or eight a year later. At the other extreme, some companies, such as Wedgwood, have created a phenomenal 180 Circles in just over two years. Paradoxically, whilst the success of the early Circles may greatly influence other supervisors to start Circles, the converse may also happen amongst a minority.

Some supervisors, perhaps those who have the least self-confidence, will be reluctant to start Circles because they are worried that they may not equal the achievements of the earlier groups. Such supervisors may need additional training designed to increase their self-confidence before they are given the opportunity to lead a Circle.

Supervisory development and training

Whilst some supervisors will display the necessary characteristics to be considered for Circle leadership, they will still require initial training in the basic techniques and group dynamics of Circles before they ask for volunteers amongst their workpeople.

It has been observed that some consultants who claim to be experts in Quality Circles attempt to train the leader and the Circle at the same time. There are several serious defects in this approach.

1 The client is permanently dependent upon the consultant because no one in the company will have acquired the basic training skills.

2 The environment will remain 'Taylorised' because the key aspect of self-control through the development of the leader will not emerge.

3 The leader is suppressed into the group and will not develop leadership skills.

4 The leader has greater credibility with the group than the outsider who does not share work-related jargon.

Circle leaders should be trained to train their own Circles as part of their own development. Of course, there are few Circle leaders who would be able to do this entirely unaided, but the initial Circle leader training should be designed to achieve this with the help of the facilitator.

After leader training which normally takes three or four days, the leader and the facilitator together should train the Circle. The facilitator's role in this training is supportive. At the first meeting of the group, in most cases, the facilitator will probably do most of the work. However, if an informal atmosphere is created, even the most nervous new Circle leader will break in to explain some of the points. As the leader's confidence grows, he or she will take over more and more of the training. The facilitator will gradually recede into the background when it is judged that the leader has effectively assumed control. The rate at which this withdrawal of the facilitator takes place will vary from one Circle to another. In some instances it will happen quite quickly. The leader may already have experience as an instructor, or have been a football or netball coach, and will therefore quickly take over. Others without such experience may require more initial support.

Ideally, supervisory development should precede the development of Circles in the same way that it did in Japan. Because this is not essential, it does not mean that it can be overlooked entirely. Whilst a Circle leader training programme for supervisors will be sufficient to commence Quality Circle activities, it must be regarded as only basic training. Supervisor/leader training should be a continuous development process which may carry on indefinitely within the company's corporate plan.

The training should be designed to be 'people building' and not simply be concerned with the acquisition of knowledge for its own sake. For example, Etsuro Tani of the Nippon Steel Corporation writes in a paper: 'Indispensable for the promotion to the foreman (kocho) rank is to finish the formal special course and the assistant foreman study course, and the foreman cannot be promoted to the general foreman (sagyocho) unless he completes the latter special course and the general foreman education course. In this way education is inseparably related to promotion.'

Formal courses of importance to supervisory development are summarised in the following:

(a) Introductory Course, full day course ... 10 days.

General introductory lessons about company life are given to all operators newly employed. Inculcated into their mind are the importance of the iron and steel industry, the outline of Nippon Steel Corporation and the pride and consciousness newcomers shall have as Nippon steel men. This is similar to induction training courses conducted by some Western companies, but has considerable depth.

(b) Foreman's Special Course, 3 hours, twice per week for 40 weeks totalling 240 hours.

Employees of middle standing with over three years experience are to be trained in this course on Quality Control with daily standard work operations as the basis for the training. The aim is to give practical and special knowledge essential for jobs assigned to foremen and equivalent in problem solving and leadership.

(c) Assistant Foreman Study Course, full day course of 6 weeks duration.

This course is aimed at building up the capabilities of assistant foremen practically to carry out leadership in the capacity of foreman and at teaching the basic techniques to accept leadership in the workshop.

(d) Latter Special Course, full day course of 5 months duration.

Trainees are foremen and their equivalent who are expected to become general foremen, to teach them the technical knowledge they will require to perform the general foreman's duties.

(e) General Foreman Education Course, full day course of 2 months duration.

The trainees are candidates for the general foreman rank, to build up their abilities for management control work and the actions essential for good management'.

In addition to these courses, supervisors and foremen are encouraged to study in correspondence courses, described as self-improvement programmes, and are given the opportunity to attend seminars, give papers, take journals and operate Quality Circle activities as a part of their normal work activity.

This intensive process of training in management skills does not just apply to Nippon Steel; it is common to the whole of Japanese industry. If other countries really want to achieve the same level of progress in their industries as is currently happening in Japan, it is necessary for them to develop a similar level of intensity of training. The courses should not be designed by colleges which cannot be responsive to individual needs but by the companies themselves as part of their own development programme, and based on their own specific requirements identified in the corporate plan. At the beginning of each year, the education and training programme for each division or section should be determined from the overall policy and goals of the enterprise. Preferably, this should be worked out by a special committee comprising the heads of each division or section.

The techniques selected to be introduced through the training should be those which will enhance the skills already acquired, so that the individuals may do their work more effectively rather than for purely academic purposes. Basically the objectives should be to

(a) Create the sense of corporate identity/corporate loyalty and corporate pride
(b) Give a greater awareness of corporate goals
(c) Improve decision-making ability
(d) Improve problem-solving skills
(e) Improve leadership skills
(f) Improve communication and presentation skills
(g) Develop training skills
(h) Increase self-confidence
(i) Improve relationships with managers and with workpeople

Problems of Circle leadership

A Quality Circle is comprised of a group of individuals, each with his or her own personal characteristics. There are many texts which cover the behavioural aspects of small group activities: the threats, fears and conflicts that emerge; the differences between the behaviour of assertive, altruistic, and analytical types; and the ways of dealing with aggressive, or shy characters, etc. It would appear from the complexities which result that the leadership of Quality Circles would present horrendous difficulties to the supervisor who does not have an honours degree in group dynamics.

It therefore comes as a surprise to most people that 'in depth' training in these skills is rarely given in Circle leader training courses, and is found to be unnecessary. This is due in the main to three important factors.

1   The voluntary nature of Circle activities means that people can drop out if they wish. Although this rarely happens in properly trained Circles, the fact that they are able to do so seems to put pressure on the individuals to come to terms with each other's point of view.

2   The techniques themselves tend to reduce the likelihood of conflict. The basic rules of brainstorming are really good rules for any kind of meeting. For instance, the rule that requires all ideas to be written down, and not evaluated immediately almost completely eliminates the risk of conflict.

When the idea is later challenged by a group member it becomes an attack on the idea and not the originator. In other forms of meeting such as committees the attack is made immediately the suggestion is made with the intention of preventing it from reaching the Minute Book. In other words, it becomes an attack on the originator, not the idea.

3   A third important factor is the rule that everyone takes turn in offering suggestions and is allowed only one idea per turn. This ensures that even the most shy member of the group has a say equal to that of the most assertive type.

This does not mean to say that the leader will not have problems, only that they are less likely, and that the problems which will be encountered are unlikely to be disastrous provided that the rules are followed. The problems that frequently occur are as follows:

- A strong-willed member of the Circle attempts to force the Circle to tackle a problem of his or her choice—frequently an industrial relations problem.
- The group is made up of people with disparate skills and finds it difficult to choose a problem which all members want to tackle.
- The Circle tackles a problem which proves difficult to solve.
- A non-Circle member is trying to demoralise individual Circle members.
- The departmental manager proves to be less supportive than was expected.
- One or two members are less interested than others in the group and forget to attend meetings, or perhaps hold private conversations at the meeting.
- Fluctuating work demand makes it difficult to fix the timing of Circle meetings.
- The Circle thinks management has been slow in implementing a previous suggestion and are becoming demoralised.

- The Circle believes that it has run out of problems. Usually, it means it is not brainstorming according to the rules.

All these problems are likely to occur at some time or other. They are rarely more than a nuisance, and most companies overcome them without seeking outside help.

The first two or three on the list are perhaps the worst. The strong-willed member, if not prepared to accept the democratic or consensus approach, could bring about the collapse of the group and sometimes does, if the problem cannot be handled. More often though, the group will either bring such members into line, or it will effectively squeeze the individual out of the group. In the last resort, the leader and the facilitator will have to deal personally with the problem.

The second problem sometimes arises in small offices where it is only possible to form a Circle of staff from different sections. If their skills are too diverse, and it is desirable to attempt to form a Circle, it might be a good idea to suggest different types of project so that everyone can participate. For example, they may choose to design posters for a company Quality campaign or organise functions for the other Quality Circles.

The third problem is frequently avoided by allowing Circles to bring in specialists if they wish. It must always be remembered, however, that it is the Circles' problem, and that the specialist is acting as a consultant or adviser because they requested it. There is always the risk that the specialist will take over the problem and this must be vigorously discouraged. If the specialist happens to discover something important relating to the project he must present it through the Circle and not independently.

12 Trade unions and Quality Circles

This chapter is intended to assist trade union officials, representatives and members to formulate their opinions about Quality Circles and their effect on trade union interests. It is expected that the topic will attract much discussion amongst union activitists as the concept of Quality Circles begins to gather momentum.

Any change in work relationships constitutes both a potential threat and potential opportunities for trade unions, and it is hoped that this chapter will help those concerned to gain a clear understanding of these important aspects of Quality Circle operations.

It is also intended that this chapter should assist those managers responsible for planning the introduction of Circles in the initial preparation stage. Hopefully the content will enable them to obtain a clear perspective of the matters that are likely to be of greatest interest to trade union representatives, and stimulate the necessary co-operation that is so important to the success of any programme.

Background

At the time of writing this book no British trade union had published a policy either in favour of, or against Quality Circles, although several leading trade unionists have made varying comments and the British Trades Union Congress published a guidelines document in April 1981. This will be reviewed later in the chapter.

In general, David Hutchins Associates' experience in dealing with trade unions at company level has so far revealed that no one union is either more or less supportive than any other. That is not to say that there have not been problems, or that individuals at all levels have not expressed opinions based upon the knowledge they had at the time. Union attitudes towards Quality Circles at plant level have varied from both extremes, total hostility to total acceptance and co-operation. However, these differences invariably relate either to the personalities of individuals or to the environment within the company and its industrial relations record, and not usually to the union itself.

In some cases the union representatives on site have been supportive but the local full-time official hostile. On other occasions the reverse has been true

Whenever there has been a hostile local official, it has frequently been due to the fact that he or she has already had a bad experience of Quality Circles elsewhere in the territory, but this was because the companies concerned had made a bad job of implementing the concept.

Currently, this is the greatest hazard in Quality Circles. There are so many consultants, all offering their own variant of the concept, that it is easy for a misinformed client to introduce a programme that violates the basic rules. In other cases, in order to cut costs, some companies have attempted to introduce Circles without proper advice, with similar unfavourable consequences.

The biggest fear of those of us experienced in helping to establish Quality Circles is that such ill-conceived programmes may bring the entire concept into disrepute and give a wrong impression before sound Quality Circles are properly established. It would be a major tragedy if any trade union were to declare a national policy of hostility to Quality Circles based on feedback from such badly introduced programmes.

To illustrate the importance of this point, two examples will be given of situations that occurred within the experience of DHA. In the interests of confidentiality it will not be possible to name the organisations concerned.

Example 1

A company trained by DHA had a successful Circle programme which had been in existence for about nine months.

Suddenly, one day and without warning, all of the members of the biggest union in the factory received a letter from their full-time district official saying 'on no account should any member have anything to do with Quality Circle activities'. It was later discovered that the same letter had been sent to every member in the district.

The employees who were members of Circles were extremely shocked and upset by this and could not understand why it had happened. They made representations to the branch and found that the problem had originated in another company in the same locality and in the same industry. Apparently, the other company had commenced a Quality Circle programme without assistance. Obviously it did not understand the concept properly, and initiated one Circle in each of its three factories with instructions to look into anomalies in the piece-work system. Apart from the fact that true Quality Circles should be free to choose their own problem, it is a hard-and-fast rule that Circles should not be allowed to tackle problems relating to wages and conditions of work. This is because there are other channels for dealing with such matters. Circles should be concerned with problems related directly to work.

It happened that the shop convener in one of these factories was the wife of the local official, and apparently it took just thirty minutes for her to contact him, with the result that he wrote the above letter.

Fortunately, DHA had been kept informed of these events and were able to contact the company in question. They were offered a presentation on Quality

Circles and this was given after normal working hours in the canteen. The following day the district official sent a further letter to the members saying that he had no objection to their being involved in Circle activities provided that they kept within certain guidelines. These guidelines had been spelled out at the presentation the night before.

Example 2

In another company, the author had just finished a half-day presentation to the twenty-two senior shop stewards representing the ten unions with members at that location. As the people were about to leave, the most senior steward, representing the largest union on site said 'my full-time official has told me to have nothing whatsoever to do with Quality Circles'. He then promptly left the room together with his colleagues. Things indeed looked black.

The manager who had organised the meeting looked somewhat shocked and thought that the unions were going to resist Circle activities. However, it was suggested that the full-time official be contacted in order to find out why he should take that view. It was felt that perhaps he should be invited to attend a presentation on the topic and that a similar invitation be made to the full-time officials of the other unions.

This offer was accepted, and the officials of all the unions attended a one-day presentation, together with the senior stewards who had been present at the earlier meeting. About half-way through the afternoon, the full-time official who had originally objected to the concept said: 'the reason why I was against Circles was because one of the companies in my area had introduced Quality Circles and in my view management was using it as a way of manipulating people. But on listening to you I can find nothing I disagree with, and if this company is prepared to introduce it along these lines then as far as I am concerned that is OK.'

That particular company now has one of the fastest growing Quality Circle programmes in the UK and the unions are fully supportive.

These two examples illustrate the importance of ensuring

(a) That the management of the company thoroughly understands Quality Circles and all the considerations before attempting their implementation.

(b) That it operates a policy of total openness with worker representatives and trade unions generally on every aspect of its Quality Circle policy.

(c) That the trade unions on site have an opportunity to co-operate in the development of the concept through the steering committee. This will be discussed further in Chapter 14.

A threat to the union?

Circles represent no threat of any kind to any union interest, and there i absolutely no good reason whatsoever why any trade union should object to their introduction.

Circles are concerned with making more effective use of the existing organisation or the organisation as it may be modified from time to time. They are not an alternative to any of the usual negotiation or bargaining channels, specialist functions, safety committees, or any other activity. Neither do they undermine the influence of workers' representatives.

Circles must recognise the existence and interests of all of these people and groups. They must never by-pass them in any way. Unions and management must be free to negotiate any arrangements they want to, and these negotiations must not be fettered by Quality Circles. Circles must accept the organisation as it is.

For example, suppose that the members of a Quality Circle decide to tackle a problem relating to their work but the solution they find happens to cut across the interests of the union or a safety committee. There would be no point in their presenting such an idea to management because until they can obtain the acceptance of the third party, they have not solved the problem. All they have done is to create another problem for their manager because he will now have to open up discussions with the third party.

When the members of a Circle request a management presentation, it is to talk about their achievements, not to present management with more problems. Consequently, in such situations, the Circle, if it is properly trained, will request a meeting with the third party. If the third party has objections, they will be discussed, and hopefully, a suitable alternative solution will be found. The Circle will then request a management presentation for this new solution, and, all being well, will invite the third party to attend. Apart from the recognition afforded to the third party, in this case the union, it will also convince management of the thorough way in which the problem has been tackled and of the soundness of the solution.

It may be seen from the foregoing discussion that trade unions have a crucial role in Quality Circle activities. It is vitally important that all trade unions in an organisation have every opportunity to discuss Quality Circles with the consultant, with each other, and with management *prior* to the implementation of Quality Circles. It must be recognised that the trade unions should be able to satisfy themselves that the motives of the organisation, and the thoroughness of their preparations have been exhaustively examined before they can be expected to endorse a prospective programme.

Trade unions and Quality Circle steering committees

Trade unions, if they wish, may have an important contribution to make towards the creation of a better working environment based upon the Quality Circle concept.

If Quality Circles really are an opportunity to create a better and more rewarding society for all people then the trade unions should be given the opportunity to participate in their development. They should also receive recognition for that role.

The opportunity for such participating comes at plant level through the steering committee. This is a group of people representing a variety of interests at that plant or location who have volunteered to work together for the success of a Circle programme. The structure and role of the steering committee is fully discussed in Chapter 14, but there is no doubt that Circle programmes which have the active support of the unions on site are considerably more healthy than would otherwise be the case.

TUC guidelines document

The TUC guidelines document on Quality Circles published in April 1981 expressed the concerns of the trade union movement about the growth of Quality Circles, and was the basis of a seminar held at Ashridge Management College where the author and Clive Jenkins of the ASTMS were principal speakers.

Under the heading 'The trade union attitude to Quality Circles', eight observations were made. Items 1 to 8 in the TUC text are not included. These were concerned with description of Quality Circles and their background. Items 9 to 16 are now reproduced with comment by the author.

(9) *Trade Unions have been urging employers for decades to give workers more control over the jobs they do. QC's are a belated recognition of employees' expertise and knowledge and the need to put them to use. At the same time, trade unionists may be understandably sceptical about the merits of the latest in a succession of 'vogue' management techniques.*

Comment Not only is this 'scepticism' understood, it is positively welcomed. The reason why so many so called 'management panaceas' have come and gone over the years is frequently more a result of management misunderstanding of the concept than possible weaknesses in the concept itself.

It is salutary to note that many of the concepts that have been sold as 'the best thing since sliced bread' are very much alive and kicking in Japan, where people appear to have a far more analytical approach to the relative merits of these concepts prior to their introduction.

Hopefully, we have now had our fingers burned sufficiently often to be a little more careful with Circles. Some will have learned their lesson, some unfortunately will not.

(10) *The sophisticated presentation of QCs's by management consultants does not disguise the fact that there is little basically new in the idea of QC's. Many*

companies have already introduced consultative procedures to discuss questions relating to production and quality control which are similar to those connected with Quality Circles. Trade Unionists may therefore not wish to dismantle existing arrangements, where they exist, by introducing QC's.

Comment On this point it is felt that the authors of the TUC guidelines document have some misconception of the true nature of QC's. Quality Circles are not productivity discussion groups or a form of consultation process; they are a form of self-control as explained in the early chapters of the book. Circles do not conflict with the arrangements referred to in Paragraph 10; these should be positively encouraged and hopefully enhanced by the activities of Quality Circles.

(11) *Like any other addition or alteration to working methods, QC's must be subject to existing agreed procedures between management and unions.* **Trade Unions are likely to oppose QC's structures that are imposed unilaterally by management without reference to those procedures.**
(The words in bold type were underlined in the original document.)

Comment DHA would wholeheartedly accept this comment and so would their clients. As has been stated earlier, Circles must accept every established agreement and procedure. They must operate within all the constraints which management and organised labour agree to accept. Circle members accept this by their volunteering to join. This is another reason why everyone should have the opportunity to know precisely what Circles mean *before* being asked to join.

(12) *QC's should not be seen by management as a way of by-passing or competing with existing trade union machinery at the workplace.* **Trade Unionists will be opposed to the introduction of QC's if they challenge in any way existing trade union machinery or practices.**

Comment Again, this is accepted. That is not to say however that such changes cannot be brought about by discussion if it proves to be in the interests of all concerned. No attempt should ever be made by any party to use Quality Circles as a lever in any such discussions.

(13) *Management cannot expect to 'claim' all the productivity and other savings generated by the work of QC's. These, like other elements of workplace productivity, are a matter for established negotiation procedures. The absence of such negotiation will heighten workers' scepticism of management's motives in introducing QC's.*

Comment This observation raises issues which are far too complex to comment on in a few lines. The whole question of reward or 'what do we, or they, get out of it' is fully discussed in Chapter 16.

(14) *Trade Unions will be particularly concerned about the employment implications*

of QC's on, for example, staff in quality control departments as well as employees in other jobs affected by review of work methods.

Comment The authors rightly highlight this important point. Fortunately, it is fair to say that so far no one has lost his job as a result of Quality Circles. If he had, it is fairly certain that the news of such an occurrence would very quickly reach Union HQ with inevitable consequences (Example 1, pp. 155–6). Workpeople know that, and management knows it. If a Circle project happens to reduce the work content of a particular operation, the Circle and management together, and probably also the union, would come to some agreement on how the time might be spent. In one company it was such a situation which led to the greatest Circle achievement. They had saved 32 hours per month in their department through the elimination of a tedious routine. They decided to use the time saved in such a way that it created over £400 000 savings immediately!

(15) *Despite the tightly limited role ascribed to QC's by management consultants, employers must expect trade unions—and possibly QC's themselves—to emphasise the need for broader workers' involvement in other matters affecting quality and competitiveness, such as research and development, marketing and investment. In other words, employers cannot expect trade unionists to see QC's as a substitute for other more far-reaching forms of involvement of the kind set out in the TUC's views on action at company and plant level by EDC's and SWP's.*

Comment Since the publication of the TUC document Quality Circles have emerged in all the areas mentioned above, including accounts departments, warehousing, cleaning, and many other situations. Circles will work anywhere where people work together and share common problems and it does not matter what kind of work it is.

Again, Circles will not conflict with the other forms of involvement. It may be, however, that some of these forms may adopt some of the Circle techniques.

(16) *The TUC has been pressing for the establishment of action teams or factory development committees at company and plant levels to discuss issues associated with the work of EDC's and SWP's such as marketing and investment. If established, such FDC's or Action Teams would clearly devote much time and discussion to aspects of company performance and quality control, the subject areas of QC's. To co-ordinate work on these subjects within the plants or factories, trade unionists would see the establishment of QC's as an extension of the work of FDC's—bodies upon which there would be full union representation.*

Comment Perhaps the co-ordination referred to should be bridged by the FDC and the Quality Circle steering committee rather than by the individual Circles themselves. Since, all being well, the union is represented on the steering committee, this should not present any problems. Certainly, the Circle activists in the company should desire such co-operation and hopefully it would be achieved.

Points of special union interest

Trade union representatives and members who are considering their attitude towards Quality Circles, and that of their local organisation, will naturally want some basis upon which to evaluate their company's approach to Quality Circles. To help in this evaluation, the following ten key points should prove to be of interest.

First of all, it is worth referring to the definition of Circles given on page 1. It must be remembered that the word 'Quality' in the context of Quality Circles has a broader meaning than simply 'product quality' and includes the quality of work life and all other factors relating to Company Wide Quality Control defined in Chapter 2.

1 The term 'voluntary' means exactly what it says. There should be no pressures on anyone to join a Circle and no recriminations if someone decides to opt out. There are now many instances recorded of Circles being formed as a result of the spontaneous demand of people at work.

2 Paid time is usually at the rate at which employees would have been paid had they not attended the Circle meeting, although there are examples now in shift-working departments of Circles that have chosen meeting times outside normal shift hours. In these cases it is essential to have trade union agreement to the meeting arrangements. These will usually have been suggested by the Circle itself. This kind of agreement relates not only to pay, but also to whether the meeting time properly constitutes 'overtime'. Any arrangements made must be compatible with agreements currently in operation.

3 The question of leadership is often raised. Why the supervisor? It is not absolutely essential that the supervisor should be the Circle leader, but he or she should at least be offered first refusal. Circles are not concerned with by-passing anyone and the official leader of the group should have first choice. Again, there are many departures from this 'ideal' situation, and every case should be treated on its merits.

4 The Circle identifies problems although others may add their ideas to the list. The Circle chooses the problem it wants to tackle without coercion, or pressure, from any member of management. Management and others may, on rare occasions, invite a Circle to tackle a specific problem, but the final decision rests with the Circle.

The leader has just one vote like any other member when making the choice of project. In choosing the problem, the Circle should be bound by three simple but effective rules:

(a) It must be 'their' problem, not one from another group's work area.
(b) It must not involve criticism of identifiable individuals. Circles attack problems not people.

(c) *Quality Circles never, repeat never, become involved in matters concerning pay and terms and conditions of employment.* This is one of the most important rules of any Quality Circle programme.

5 All members of the Circle participate in presentations to management. The presentations are always face to face and never in memorandum or report form. Neither are they given by the leader on behalf of the group.

There will be occasions when management cannot give immediate replies, but if ever a Circle's recommendation is rejected, management should be required to give its reasons for rejection in as clear and comprehensive a form as possible.

6 In making recommendations to management, the Circles will probably be claiming to have solved the problems, but the problems have not been solved if there are still trade union objections to the proposals. The Circle must discuss potentially contentious projects with trade union representatives *before* making their presentation. This will ensure that Quality Circle proposals work within the existing machinery and do not conflict with long-standing procedures and arrangements.

7 Quality Circles do not undermine the role of the elected trade union representatives or interfere with their right to raise matters with management. The problems selected and tackled by Circles are generally different from issues relating to industrial relations, and other matters of great concern to trade unions. However, if any overlap exists, the Circle must abide by the rule not to become involved in matters best left to the negotiating machinery.

(Representatives may even use techniques similar to those of Circles in formulating the case they wish to place before management.)

8 It should be established policy that Quality Circles do not receive any direct financial reward other than the payment for their one hour per week meetings. They do not receive percentages of the savings or fixed sum awards. There are a number of reasons for this, but the most important is that everyone in the organisation should benefit equally. If an organisation is attempting to create a situation where all are made to feel that their organisation is the better for their being there, it cannot do it by treating one group differently from another, and some work areas may have a greater potential for big savings than others.

The wages, salaries and standard of living of all employees are a matter for consultation and negotiation between organised labour and management, and Quality Circles as such play no part in this process.

9 Many trade union representatives fear that Quality Circle activities may lead to job losses. This is unlikely. Quality Circles consider problems in their own work and are unlikely to cut their own throats. If management seeks the full benefits from successful Quality Circle programmes, it would be foolish to take advantage of such situations. Quality Circles are not, however, about job losses.

but rather about increased competitiveness, customer satisfaction, problem solving, and improving the working environment. Hopefully, Quality Circles will make a small contribution to creating jobs, not losing them.

10 Finally, there is the function of the steering committee, the membership of which should be drawn from a cross-section of the organisation and include trade union representatives if they wish to join. The committee has a number of functions which will be discussed in Chapter 14.

If the union agrees to participate, it will be able to assist in the formulation of the policies and rules relating to Circle activities. The existence of a properly formulated steering committee will enable the individual problems relating to Circle activities to be resolved in a sensible manner. It also gives the union the opportunity to be identified with a concept which hopefully will change the working environment for the better for all people at work.

Conclusions

A Quality Circle programme that recognises the validity of these ten points as far as employee representatives are concerned, is unlikely to meet insoluble problems. A programme that ignores them is almost certain to fail.

There will always be issues raised, and problems to solve, but if these rules are followed, Quality Circles can offer substantial benefits to everyone, without initiating fear, concern or conflict, and lead to better working conditions.

Quality Circles give workpeople an opportunity to control their own work, and the activities should be enjoyable and beneficial to everyone. In the final analysis, it should be remembered that it is all voluntary; if at any time people cease to enjoy what they are doing, they can stop.

Quality Circle programmes must not be seen as a replacement or alternative for any other activity or practice, but only as an additional means of involving much larger numbers of people in making decisions about matters that are important to them. Each person becomes the manager at his or her own level.

The ideas outlined above will not solve all problems for all people, but they will draw together some of the key elements of Quality Circle programmes for consideration by management and trade unions, and they should emphasise that trade unions are important to Circles and vice versa.

13 Quality Circles, the specialists and non-Circle members

This chapter is about 'everyone else'—in other words all the other people on the payroll who may not necessarily be members of Circles, but who may, nevertheless, be involved in one way or another. These may be classified into two groups.

1 The specialists

2 Non-Circle members

The specialists may be further subdivided into two further sections:

(a) The troubleshooting, problem-solving specialists.

(b) Service functions or other functions whose own activities will influence or be influenced by the work of Circles.

Both (a) and (b) may of course form Circles among themselves if there are enough people in their section, and if they have the desire and will to do so.

The specialists

(1) The troubleshooting specialists

This group will include such specialists as work study personnel, Quality Control, production engineering, O & M, etc. If they are not properly informed about what Quality Circles are, and how Circle development will affect them, they are quite likely to see Quality Circles as a threat. Typically, they will think 'my job is solving problems, why should you teach others to do my job?' Of course, during times of recession, this observation may be especially pertinent. It would be a pity not to dispel such fears before Quality Circles are established because, far from being a threat, Quality Circles, if anything, put more demands on the specialist, not less.

Subsequent follow-up visits by David Hutchins Associates to companies they have trained have shown that the specialists rank amongst the greatest enthusiasts of Quality Circles. This is for two main reasons:

1 The type of problems usually dealt with by Circles are rarely the same

problems that are attractive to the specialist. Consequently there is little conflict of interest.

2   The Circle quickly discover that specialists have access to information and knowledge outside the scope of the Circle, and so they often invite them to join the Circle as consultants, usually for the duration of that project.

Under the Taylor system, specialists are usually regarded by direct employees as 'management'. If the specialists are graduates or perceived by the employees to be deficient in direct experience of their particular activities, employees are likely to be hostile and unco-operative. They will also be deeply suspicious of the motives of the specialists whom they will see as management men only interested in cutting costs and reducing the payroll.

It is surprising how quickly these particular clouds are dispelled when Quality Circles are introduced. As soon as people realise that they are being listened to, that management regards them as sufficiently valuable to give them Quality Circle training time, and that they are recognised as experts in their own jobs, their attitudes change completely. The specialist is then regarded as a potential equal, who happens to possess different skills from their own. Provided that the specialists themselves are prepared to co-operate, a close relation with Quality Circles should quickly develop.

A senior manager in one company with Quality Circles recently commented that one of the most significant changes that had taken place since the commencement of Circles was the relationship between direct employees and the specialists. He said that the specialists were now tending to work in the areas which already had Circles because the people in those sections were more co-operative.

It follows that because the Circles need the specialists to help in their work, the members are more co-operative in helping the specialists in their activities.

(2)   Service functions

In the context of this discussion, service functions include

- All other departments or sections
- People from other work areas
- Managers
- Trade union representatives and committees
- Safety committees
- All upstream and downstream operations
- Outside organisations including both customers and suppliers
- In-house committees, panels and groups
- Other Quality Circles

It has been stated earlier that Quality Circles must accept the organisation as it is. They must respect all other opinions, and the knowledge, experience and feelings of others. Circles must work with these groups and reach solutions that are acceptable to those affected or responsible for work which may be related to the Circle project.

Example It would be pointless for a Quality Circle concerned with a manufacturing problem, to offer management a solution that involved a design change, without first consulting a design specialist. There may be valid reasons, outside the knowledge of the Circle, why such a change may not be advisable. In any case, the Circle will not have solved the problem. It will simply have created another for the manager, who, in addition to other responsibilities, will now be required to take up the matter with design. In many cases, he will not be as familiar with the problems as the Circle members are and may easily underestimate the importance of some factors.

It is far better for the Circle members themselves to meet the specialist at an earlier stage so that they may together arrive at a solution that is acceptable to everyone. Furthermore, such specialists should be invited to attend and participate in the subsequent management presentation, and give further evidence of the thorough nature of their work. This type of co-operation need not be restricted solely to personnel and departments at one location.

A Quality Circle of welders in one UK company had always experienced difficulty in welding one of the long-standing well-established products manufactured by their company. The members decided to tackle these problems as a Quality Circle project. In the process of their activities they asked management if it would be possible for a specialist to give them some advice. As the company did not employ such a specialist, it sought outside assistance, and a consultant was invited to meet the Circle.

When it became known in the factory that this was happening, the production engineers and one or two designers asked if they could sit in on the discussions, and the Circle agreed to this. During the meeting, the consultant was able not only to give the Circle members valuable advice on improving their technique, but also to suggest that the product be redesigned in such a way that the problem was eliminated entirely. The design department agreed to this, and so an important improvement was made, with considerable savings in defect costs.

Some might say that these improvements could have been made without a Quality Circle, and this is true. But the fact is that they were not, and the problem had existed for many years. The real benefit of course was not just the direct savings from the project, but other spin-off benefits which accrued from the greater sense of involvement of that group of welders.

In another example, a Quality Circle, faced with problems involving its packing materials, was given the opportunity of visiting the manufacturers to explain its difficulties to the operators engaged in the manufacture of its materials.

The result of the meeting was the elimination of a problem that had plagued the management of the user company for many years. The quality manager had complained on many previous occasions but nothing had been achieved. After the discussions between the two groups of workers, the operatives at the supplier company said: 'we never realised that this caused real difficulties; we thought management was just getting on at us!'

Non-Circle members

Almost every organisation will find that most departments will contain one or more employees who are not members of the Circle. This will either be due to a lack of interest, or because the department is too large for everyone to be able to join. In such a case it is hoped that it may be possible at some stage to form another Circle. There is no reason why two or more Circles should not be formed in a section.

However, it must be clearly understood by everyone, particularly the Circle members, that they belong to 'their section's Circle' and they are not an elite group. Failure to recognise this is one of the problems that frequently plagues organisations in the early stages of development. It can lead to considerable alienation between the two groups and cause the break up of the Circle.

Causes of alienation between Circle and non-Circle members include:

- Management pressure
- Over-zealous facilitator
- Leader showing favouritism
- Circle not involving others
- Rival factions in the department

Let us now take each in turn:

Management pressure Sometimes management does not fully appreciate the importance of the rule that Circles pick their own problems, and that the one hour per week is the 'Circles hour'.

Interestingly, the Circle is less sensitive to this problem than non-Circle members of the department. They will detect quite quickly that management is 'steering or manipulating' the Circle, and will accuse its members of being 'management favourites'. Generally speaking, it will annoy one person more than others. This person then attempts to 'pick off' a Circle member whom he thinks is sensitive, and tease that member about Circle activities. The first indication of this to an outsider will be one of the Circle members dropping out of the group, followed by another. Usually, the defectors will be reluctant to give reasons for leaving because that would leave them open to further problems with their colleagues.

If the Circle is genuinely left to choose its own problems and is continually made aware of the importance of involving non-Circle colleagues, the problem is unlikely to arise. The problems it selects will be those that everyone would like to see tackled, and all being well, the Circle members should become popular with their non-Circle colleagues as a result.

Over-zealous facilitator The pressure on a newly appointed facilitator must never be underestimated. Those selected will usually be well advanced in their own career and in all probability will have exercised some considerable courage in accepting the appointment. They will be very sensitive to their interpretation of senior management expectations from the Circle's programme.

The worst situation may occur when they think that top management is looking for a quick payback. This will lead to the same type of problem outlined above under 'Management pressure', only this time it will be the facilitator who is manipulating the Circle. Frequently the facilitator does this quite unconsciously. The most likely time for such interference occurs after the brainstorming session, when the Circle members are attempting to select their problem.

After the problem classification stage, it would be easy for the facilitator, particularly with a new Circle, to 'guide' it towards an 'easy' first problem. Unwittingly he may guide it towards a problem that looks as if it has a good payback, or one which has been bugging management. As before, the non-Circle members will be sensitive to such manipulation. It is not a bad idea to allow them to participate in problem selection.

Leader showing favouritism Following the initial introduction of Circles, some non-Circle members may become hypersensitive to the relationship between the supervisor and Circle members. In a few cases, individuals may attempt to evaluate every action of the supervisor to see if favouritism exists. The Circle leader therefore must be extremely careful to avoid the likelihood of such problems and must treat everybody in the department equally, regardless of their attitude towards Circle activities.

Circle not involving others This is usually a training problem and indicates that the facilitator and Circle leader have not taken enough care to ensure that everyone can participate. Many Circles involve non-members by circulating questionnaires to solicit ideas. Publicising Circle activities by displaying worksheets in the department is an excellent way of encouraging outside interest provided that there is little risk of graffiti.

In a number of companies, the Circles make their first presentation to the section before their management presentation. Apart from ensuring that non-members are familiar with the Circle's method of working, it enables them to offer suggestions as to how the presentation might be improved and gives them a sense of involvement.

Rival factions in the department This is a problem outside the scope of Circles directly, and does occasionally, but thankfully rarely, occur. The problem usually boils down to there being two conflicting personalities in the section, each with his or her own loyal supporters. If all the supporters of one person are in the Circle, the others may be alienated. If it is possible, the problem may be avoided by attempting to involve members of each group. Occasionally, fortunately rarely, however, it has prevented a group from being successfully formed.

14 The steering committee

Because of the deep-rooted implications of Quality Circles, it would be impossible to commence a successful programme before all people affected have been given an opportunity to decide for themselves whether they want to become involved. To ensure a positive response at all levels, it would be necessary to give awareness presentations to top management, middle management, trade union representatives, specialists and supervisors. Assuming that the general reaction is favourable, and that there are no major objections, it is then possible to draw up an action plan for the development of a Quality Circle programme.

First of all it will be necessary to determine who will be responsible for this development. Of course, up to this stage responsibility must have already been assumed by someone or some small group. Usually the chief executive, a director or high-level manager will have to make the decision to invite an expert to talk to top management.

After this presentation, one or two other directors or senior managers may have taken an active interest, and so a small team will have been formed. They will plan the next steps. These steps will normally be the awareness presentations to the other groups mentioned above. In some small companies all of these groups may attend a single session together. In other cases several sessions may be necessary. However, following these sessions, all being well, a number of people from different levels and functions are likely to express a keen interest in the subject and to want to play an active part in the subsequent development. These people, together with those already involved, may form what is usually referred to as a 'steering committee'. Some organisations prefer to use the term 'support group', as this term does have certain advantages, although the former term is more common.

Membership of the steering committee therefore, is, like that of Quality Circles themselves, a voluntary involvement. Not all the volunteers will necessarily have put themselves forward, they may have been invited, but as in the case of Circles no one should be forced to join. Perhaps the first point to consider about committees is why it should be preferable to have just one person in charge of the entire programme. For example, some people may think that the facilitator should take all this responsibility. There are several arguments against this.

Firstly, many of the decisions and plans will frequently be made before the facilitator is appointed or the importance of the facilitator's role appreciated. A more important reason, however, is that it is extremely unlikely that there would be any one person who has such intimate knowledge of and familiarity with each department and level of people that he or she could cover successfully all the tasks and work that are to be carried out by the steering committee.

A further consideration is continuity. If the steering committee's responsibilities are vested in one person, it becomes very much a case of putting all the eggs into one basket. That individual, in the execution of his or her duties, would accumulate such a store of knowledge as to become eventually irreplaceable. In other words, the Circle programme would be dependent upon one person and could even become a personality cult. If that person were to leave the company, or suffer some misfortune, the programme might very easily collapse, or at least suffer a major setback. The formation of a good steering committee will prevent all of these risks.

Once these negative reasons for the existence of a steering committee are accepted, there are also some very positive reasons. In Chapter 8 it was stated that most organisations have a very individualistic style of management, and it is necessary to become more consensus inclined for a Circle programme to be ultimately successful.

The steering committee can, if properly constructed, very effectively create the necessary consensus style characteristics essential for the development of a healthy Circle programme.

Who should belong

If the steering committee is reasonably representative of all interests, it will be 'in touch' or 'wired in' to the feelings of all members of staff. It will also induce confidence.

For example, shop floor workers in a factory who are worried about some aspect of Quality Circles may find it difficult to talk to a senior manager, or someone from another section or department. However, if there is someone on the steering committee at their own level, or who they find accessible, then they will have no worries about approaching that person with their observations. Not only is this important from that individual's point of view, it is also valuable to the steering committee itself, because now, they will be more sensitive to the general mood and to people's perspective of the Quality Circle programme.

Union representation

It is also important to give trade unions the opportunity to be represented on the steering committee, not as a form of 'hush money', or obligatory representation, but as an equal member to the others. Union representatives should be approached along the lines that 'we like the idea of Quality Circles and want to form a steering committee. If you also like it, then we would value your membership of the steering committee in order to help build a successful programme'. Union members therefore should be invited into steering committees to make positive contributions, not just to 'keep an eye' on things.

Besides ensuring that policies worked out by the steering committee take account of union views and interests, there are also other advantages. If the unions are not given the opportunity of participating in the development of a Circle's programme, they can hardly be expected to be enthusiastic about it.

In many instances, when employees are approached and asked if they would like to join a Circle they will probably seek the advice of a worker representative before accepting the opportunity. If the worker representative has a jaundiced view of Circles, or has not been informed of what is going on, there is every chance that the advice will be negative.

The modern trade union movement had its origins in the middle of the nineteenth century, when the object was to create better terms and conditions of work. Much has been achieved since those early days, but Taylorism has created a plateau. If Quality Circles provide the opportunity for making a further advance, then it is only appropriate that the trade union movement should have an equal opportunity of sharing in that success. If trade unions adopt a positive attitude towards Quality Circles, and their members identify their union with having helped in the achievement of a better society as a result, it must be in the best interests of everyone.

Membership of the steering committee is the best opportunity for such visible support.

Supervision

In some companies the role of the supervisor, group leader or foreman is more clearly defined than in others. It is just as important that someone from this level should find a place on the steering committee as any other. Some supervisors may be nervous about how Circles will affect their role, and it would be dangerous if the steering committee was not sensitive to these feelings and neglected to have them represented.

Middle management and specialists

This level or group is usually the linchpin of a Circle programme. The attitudes of middle managers both individually and collectively will determine to a large extent the 'flavour' of that company's Quality Circle activities. Middle managers, particularly those who lack confidence, are likely to feel the most exposed by the developing programme. If care is not taken to develop middle managers at the same time as the Circles, some managers may become afraid of the growing confidence of their people. Also, through the acquisition of skills in using the Circles techniques, some managers may become nervous if their people are speaking a language that they themselves do not understand. Key middle managers therefore—those who are more closely associated with other middle managers—can play a vital role in the steering committee activities.

Top management

A steering committee will be largely ineffectual if it does not contain as a member one of the ultimate decision makers at plant level. Someone who can sign cheques. Otherwise the steering committee will lack authority, and all the important decisions will be made by a third party, i.e. top management. It also means that the committee will be required to make representations to top management for decisions to be made and, in all probability, top managers may not appreciate the importance of requests made, simply because they have been less involved.

It is a tremendous boost to everybody's confidence to see the active membership of the steering committee by the chief executive. This is the most impressive manifestation of 'management commitment'.

Summary

- The steering committee should span all functions and all levels.
- It gives continuity, and shows commitment.
- It gives confidence to others through accessibility to members.

The tasks of the steering committee

Because the steering committee evolves in the manner described at the beginning of this chapter, it must not be assumed that all the items mentioned under this heading will necessarily commence after the final membership has been completed. However, it is advisable to review past decisions of the steering committee when new members join. The aim should always be to have the widest possible consensus.

The basic responsibilities of a steering committee can be listed under 16 separate categories. In individual cases others not listed may become apparent.

1 Corporate planning and corporate policy evaluation
2 Quality Circle programmes policy making
3 Policy review

4 Constraints
5 Facilitator support
6 Guidance
7 Continuity
8 Monitoring
9 Presentations
10 Publicity
11 Recognition
12 Reward
13 Assessment
14 Appreciation
15 Liaison
16 Development

Each will be briefly reviewed.

1 Corporate planning and corporate policy

The corporate plan for the company may be evaluated to identify the role of Company-Wide Quality Control. It is suggested that the definition of Company-Wide Quality Control given on page 13 might be used as the basis of such a policy.

The policy statement given in Fig. 9.1 might also be used or modified, and subsequently displayed on a main notice board or in an employee handbook.

2 Quality Circle policy making

Establishing the policy and guidelines for Circle activities will be the most intensive activity of the newly formed steering committee.

Such questions as 'resource allocation' both at plant level and Circle level, 'constraints', 'when Circles hold their meetings', 'where the meetings will take place', are just a few of the items which will require resolution. David Hutchins Associates recommend to their clients that the steering committee should commence its activities in the same way as a Quality Circle and conduct a brainstorming session of all the items which it thinks will be relevant. This usually produces a list of over 100 items. The steering committee then discusses each item in turn. When all of the items have been discussed, agreed, and minuted, the result is a Quality Circles policy statement, covering all aspects of the programme. If copies of this agreement are circulated to all steering committee members, each member will be able to give the same answers to any employee and the agreement will become the foundation of that company's programme. Many of the points which will be raised may be found in the Chapter 18 entitled 'Answers to the 152 questions most frequently asked about Quality Circles'.

3 Policy review

It is unlikely that any initial policy will be absolutely perfect, and issues are bound to arise. These may stem from the steering committee members themselves or from other employees.

Of course, the employees can only influence the programme if the steering committee members are accessible and visible. They must be given the opportunity to know who they are. Many people, particularly in large organisations, know very few people outside their own department. They may have seen them around, or even come into their department, but they will not speak to them unless they know what they do, and where they fit into the organisation generally.

It is a good idea, therefore, for photographs of the steering committee members to be displayed on notice boards, together with their names, their role in the organisation, and where they are to be found.

4 Constraints

It has been stated quite strongly in earlier chapters that Circles must never take on as projects issues relating directly to wages, or terms or conditions of employment. There may be special reasons why a particular company might wish to add further constraints, and this should be considered by the steering committee. It is quite important that any such constraints are clearly understood by potential Circle members *before* they are invited to join a Circle. People are likely to become quite resentful if they are informed afterwards.

5 Facilitator support

The facilitator should always be a member of the steering committee, and will usually be the main source of information. In a larger company with several facilitators, it would be unreasonable for all of them to be represented. Usually, one of them, who in this case could be termed a co-ordinator, will probably be more senior than the others. The co-ordinator would be their steering committee representative and would report back to the other facilitators at a facilitators' meeting.

The steering committee will be the facilitators' main source of support. In companies which have a participative, consensus style of management, this support will not be so important, but in others, particularly those which suffer from strong inter-departmental rivalries, the support of the steering committee may be the difference between success and failure. This is further evidence of the value of having a broadly based steering committee.

6 Guidance

Occasionally, hopefully not too often, the pattern of work flow might threaten the activities of a Circle. For example, a meeting might be suspended in order to meet a shipping requirement. Individual managers will be uncertain when this would be acceptable, and the steering committee will find many instances where it is required to give guidance on such matters. Additionally, the facilitator will also require frequent confirmation on specific points of policy.

When this book was being written, several of the Case Study contributors sought the guidance of their steering committee before agreeing to submit a paper. In some cases, it was necessary for the steering committee to vet the paper in order to give clearance for publication.

7 Continuity

Whilst the majority of companies trained by DHA have very active and involved steering committees, there is nevertheless an awareness, or fear, that in a number of companies the steering committee only pays lip service to the facilitator. Whilst this might appear to be satisfactory in the short term, particularly if the facilitator happens to be a charismatic figure, the committee will suffer ultimately if that facilitator is suddenly lost. A personality cult around the facilitator should never be allowed to develop, and can only be avoided by a visible and active steering committee.

8 Monitoring

The Plan-Do-Check-Act Cycle is no less important in Circle activities than in any other. As the Circle programme develops, each Circle will develop its own innate characteristics, and will be very different from every other Circle.

In the early days of Circles in one company, the facilitator said that at one extreme the Circles were exceeding all expectations, and he felt that if he left them alone entirely he would not have to worry about them. The bulk of the remainder needed some support, but were basically self-sufficient. However, he had one or two Circles that were like cold porridge—if he stopped stirring them, they would settle down.

If some Circles do appear better than others, there may be lessons that can be learned from the more impressive Circles and transferred to others. The same logic applies to Circles in different companies. Monitoring, therefore, can include cross-fertilisation. Steering committee members should be prepared to visit other companies and compare their approaches. In this way, everybody can benefit from everybody else's experience. In DHA, this has been encouraged by the evolution of a 'Circle network'. This is a network of all clients who all receive copies of a periodical entitled *Circle Review*. This magazine carries stories of Circle activities in client companies. The network also includes workshops for facilitators, steering committee members and Circle conventions where presentations are made to an audience of Circle members by Quality Circles from network member companies. This is the basis of Circle development in Japan under the auspices of the Japanese Union of Scientists and Engineers (JUSE).

9 Presentations

The management presentation is the culmination of all of the work carried out by the Circle on its project. If the members have been successful, they will be proud of their achievement and will want to show what they have done.

For the majority of projects, these presentations will be made to the members' own manager, and perhaps to others who are directly affected by their recommendations. Sometimes, however, it is a good idea to allow certain projects to be presented to the steering committee. This has several advantages.

1   The Circle members will be confronted with a number of people they do not normally meet, and the meeting will demonstrate to them the breadth of support that exists in the company.

2   Some steering committee members may not be closely and directly involved in Circle activities, and it gives them an opportunity of seeing for themselves what the Circles are achieving and the enthusiasm generated.

3   It is worth while allowing the early Circle projects to be presented to the steering committee as a whole so that it can see how the programme is developing. DHA have noted that many steering committees have not really 'jelled' until after they have had such an experience.

In one company, the steering committee, which was heavily represented by the personnel department and trade union activists, was seen by several members as an extension of the industrial relations negotiating committees. Instead of being constructive, the members were adopting defensive postures. This resulted in a Quality Circle policy statement which read like a productivity agreement. Fortunately, however, one of the first Circles managed to reach the presentation stage with their first project and this was presented to the steering committee.

This presentation had a profound effect on both management and union members of the steering committee alike. Several of them admitted astonishment that Quality Circles really did operate in the way that they had been told. This resulted in a dramatic change of attitude amongst steering committee members, who subsequently adopted a totally different approach to Circles, with the result that the steering committee has become the focal point of that company's Circle activities. The company concerned is part of a large group of companies and this steering committee has subsequently been a major influence in the establishment of Circles at other sites.

10 Publicity

This topic can be considered under two headings—internal, and external. Internally, the steering committee will consider the importance of publicity both as a means of giving further stimulation to existing Circles by publicising their achievements, and as a means of encouraging others to participate. Externally, the steering committee may see a value in advertising the company's support for Quality Circles as a means of enhancing the Committee's own reputation in the market place.

Internal publicity The internal forms of publicity may include use of notice boards, newsletters and paraphernalia.

Notice boards—These may be used to keep employees informed of the activities of Circles in their area. The photographs of Circle members may be posted, and a description of the Circle projects included. In some companies, a separate position on notice boards has been devoted entirely to Circle news, and members are encouraged to contribute material.

News sheets—There are now a great many companies who publish their own internal news sheets, and these are discussed in a later chapter. The production of a news sheet is hard work, but generally news sheets are regarded as worth while.

Of course, some larger companies have a regular newspaper anyway, but generally, it is not possible to give Circles more than occasional exposure through this medium. Publishing a special newsletter for Circle members gives every Circle a regular opportunity to publicise its own activities and to learn about the achievements of others.

This cross-fertilisation is a vital aspect of Circles' development and it was recognition of this important issue that led DHA to produce the first regular Quality Circle journal in Europe entitled *Circle Review*. This journal regularly carries features of Quality Circle achievements across industry.

External publicity External publicity for Circle activities has now emerged in the West as more and more companies become confident of the permanence of their programmes. In Japan, many organisations see this as an extremely valuable way of demonstrating the care they take to produce good products and reliable service.

11 Recognition

Steering committee members themselves should make every effort possible to take an active interest in Circle activities. This means that in addition to attending the regular steering committee meetings, the members should ask if they can sit in on occasional Circle meetings and presentations. Not only does this give the steering committee members a better insight into the health and vitality of the programme, but also, and most importantly, it demonstrates to the Circles the extent of the committee's interest in their activities.

This personal level of interest is one of the most important forms of recognition for the Circles. It must be emphasised of course that steering committee membership does not imply any extra powers than would otherwise be held, and that all such contacts with Circles should be made through the usual channels. This would usually be via the section head, but it would be as well for such impromptu visits to be made also in co-operation with the facilitator.

12 Reward

No topic has evoked so much discussion of Circle achievements as the subject of reward. It is so important that an entire chapter (Chapter 16) is devoted to it in the next section of the book. All steering committee members should be thoroughly acquainted with the guidelines discussed in that chapter.

Quality Circles can be rewarded for their achievements in many ways, but direct financial rewards should never be given. If this rule is ever violated, the Quality Circle programme will have entered the bargaining arena, and Quality Circles of the kind described in this book will cease to exist. In its place, there may remain a money-swapping trade-off structure which will only survive until it has been submerged by jealousy, envy and disagreement.

Part of management's attraction to Quality Circles is the opportunity it affords to create a sense of corporate identity and corporate loyalty, and for people to feel that their organisation is better for their being there. This cannot be achieved if direct financial rewards are given, but there are many other forms of reward discussed later, which contribute positively to this objective and are extremely attractive to Circle members.

13 Assessment

Just as individual Circles vary, so do Circle programmes. Of the 100 or so locations initially trained by DHA, whilst all have been successful as far as the Circle programmes are concerned, there are nevertheless extreme differences in the vitality of the programmes. The reasons for these differences are many and complex. Undoubtedly the biggest factor is that in periods of recession some Circle programmes may fail simply because the companies themselves cease to exist. However, apart from such dramatic situations, well-designed Circles programmes have proved to be extremely hardy even during times of redundancy.

The factors which most obviously affect the success of a programme include:

Lack of pre-preparation
Low key Steering Committee
Wrong choice of facilitator

Industrial relations tensions
Lack of management support
Trade union suspicions
Inadequate leader/member training
Underestimating the importance of all of the techniques
Insularity—lack of contact with other organisations

These are just a few of the possible causes of disappointment. The complete list could run to several hundred items, many of which appear in Chapter 18: Answers to the questions most frequently asked about Quality Circles.

It is of enormous benefit for a steering committee to establish contact with the steering committees of other companies. This can be achieved by membership of national societies of Quality Circles, or, for those companies which have been trained by David Hutchins Associates, through membership of DHA's International Circle Network of Clients.

14 Appreciation

The steering committee should always be alive to the importance of ensuring that all Circles receive adequate recognition for their achievements. Various departmental managers will differ in their personal recognition of this. Consequently, some Circles will feel more appreciated than others. The steering committee should be aware of this and can help overcome any difficulties by giving some Circles more exposure in news sheets, etc. The aim should always be to keep the whole programme at the same healthy level.

15 Liaison

The Circle programme does not exist in isolation from other company activities, some of which may overlap the work of Circles. In the context of organisational development, it may be necessary for the Quality Circle steering committee to interface with other groups concerned with other concepts such as task force and project group activities in order to produce an integrated programme. Trade unions, for example, may be concerned with the development of FDC's as discussed in Chapter 12.

16 Development

As the programme develops, it will eventually make more and more impact on other activities. The ultimate power of Quality Circles may be realised when Circles become an integral part of company activities—in other words, when everybody can be a member of a Circle. The ultimate aim should be 100% membership, and Quality Circles are simply the way a company manages its people. Before this stage is reached, it will be necessary to establish a formal relationship between functions such as quality control and quality assurance and Quality Circles. All being well, the people in charge of such functions should have realised the importance of Quality Circles in the achievement of their own objectives, and they will be feeding information to the groups. This information will include customer complaints data, articles from Quality journals and anything else which quality control thinks will enhance Circle activities.

This also applies to other functions such as production engineering, work study, accounts, etc. The steering committee can play an extremely important role in the encouragement of such developments.

Summary

It may be seen from the foregoing that the composition and constitution of a steering committee is vital to the success of Quality Circles. It may also appear that such activities may be time-consuming. This is not true. The first few meetings may be lengthy and frequent, but once the policy has been established and the Circle programme commenced, the meetings will become shorter and less frequent. In an on-going programme, the meetings would normally last for about two hours, and occur monthly or bi-monthly.

Those organisations that have already begun Circle programmes but have not yet established steering committees would do well to start such committees immediately. One well-known American company did not do this, and the programme collapsed when the facilitator left. Fortunately, it has since been re-established, but they now have an active steering committee.

15 The facilitator

Prior to the commencement of a Quality Circle programme, it will be necessary to appoint a facilitator. This person will become the hub of the wheel, the centre of gravity of Circle activities. He or she will become a member of the steering committee, and in most instances will be the steering committee's main source of information and advice on Circle activities. Before discussing the appointment, role and activities of the facilitator, it would be pertinent to establish first of all why such a title is used.

Some companies prefer the term 'co-ordinator', others 'promoter' or 'organiser', but all these terms give a wrong impression of the role. The facilitator does all these things. Additionally, the facilitator trains, liaises with others, supports, coaches, advises and consults, and there is no one word which adequately covers all these activities. To facilitate means to 'make easy' and this is really what the facilitator does. Someone once described him 'as the guy with the oil can', which is not a bad description.

The appointment of a facilitator will usually be one of the first positive decisions that a company will make, which will indicate its level of commitment to the programme. Given the potential of a Circle programme, and the profound effect that it will have on an organisation, it is surprising how flippant some companies are when it comes to making the appointment. One can only assume, in most such cases, that top management has either grossly underestimated the whole basis of Quality Circles or, alternatively, has assumed that Circles are some form of perpetual motion requiring little or no help from outside.

Unfortunately, such managements are very quickly disappointed. Having chosen someone with nothing better to do to act as facilitator, they imagine that all the wonderful things they have read about in management magazines about Quality Circles will suddenly appear in their organisation. A few weeks later with disillusionment creeping in from all quarters, such companies realise, too late, that they either appointed the wrong person, or that they have underestimated the time commitment, with the consequence that the facilitator simply isn't facilitating.

Experience has shown that the appointment of a facilitator, together with the establishment of the steering committee are the two most important and influential factors which will determine future success. The facilitator resource is so important in fact that David Hutchins Associates were staggered to read in another text, claimed to be based on experience and published in the UK, the advice that facilitating should be a part-time voluntary commitment to be done in addition to a normal job. Such advice is not only naive but will almost guarantee failure unless applied in the most exceptional circumstances. As a rough and ready rule, a facilitator will need to spend about three hours per week per Circle, particularly in the early stages. This means that a single facilitator can handle a maximum of fifteen Circles satisfactorily given that some of the more mature Circles will need less time than the newer ones. In the early stages, however, the facilitator will need to spend some of the available time at the policy-developing steering committee meetings, familiarising himself with his job, discussing Quality Circles with other managers and generally 'getting the show on the road'.

By definition a 'part-time' facilitator is a part-time something else. In those other activities the facilitator will have a boss. That boss will be more concerned with the facilitator's other responsibilities than the Quality Circle programme. There will be many occasions when the pressure of work in such areas will demand the total commitment of the part-time facilitator, and it is extremely likely that these occasions will happen to coincide with a Quality Circle crisis of some kind. Quality Circles often need considerable hand holding in the early stages and many will suffer from an initial lack of self-confidence. If the facilitator is frequently absent at this early and critical stage, such confidence as has been developed will quickly be dissipated. This is no time suddenly to realise the problem, and then commence a protracted selection procedure for a full-time replacement. It is much better for this to be thought out carefully in advance and proper decisions taken.

Of course, a small company could not justify a full-time facilitator. It probably couldn't afford one even if it were necessary, and it is doubtful whether there would be enough work to fill the time for such an appointment. It is difficult to be specific about the precise size of an organisation that would just be large enough to support a full-time facilitator. This is because there are several factors that need to be considered. As an approximate guide, the size of the company would normally be somewhere in the region of 250–300 employees.

Factors to be considered are:

- Number of levels of command
- Variety of different skills
- Single or multiple location
- Degree of participative style within the organisation
- Labour relations
- Supportive style of management
- Normal day or shift working

f the company is based at a single location and has a short chain of command

and a generally supportive management, then a part-time facilitator may be possible, even if the number of employees is slightly higher than 250–300. However, as has already been suggested, it is important not to underestimate the time spent on Circle facilitation and it would be better to be safe than sorry.

The part-time facilitator

Given that an organisation is unable to justify a full-time facilitator and part-timers are to be appointed, the following points will be helpful.

(1) First of all estimate carefully the expected time per week to be spent on Circle activities and make this a clear commitment by senior management. This allocation must be firmly agreed by:

- Section head for the facilitator's other work
- The steering committee
- The facilitator appointed.

If Circle activities prove to require more time than allocated, this additional requirement should be highlighted by the facilitator so that management may make a decision to increase the budgeted time allowance.

(2) It is better to have two, or preferably three, part-time facilitators than one. If possible they should be selected from different departments. This will have the advantage that Circles will be seen as a company-wide programme and not the extension of a single department's influence.

The main advantage to the Circles is the higher probability that at least one of the facilitators will be available when needed. A further advantage can be obtained by carefully choosing other part-time facilitators as the programme grows. Eventually, every manager will become the facilitator of the Circles in his or her own area, in other words, facilitating Quality Circles has just become the way managers manage their people.

This method can also be applied in larger companies, and will be discussed later. However, it is more difficult and slower than the traditional approach and great care is needed in order for it to succeed.

(3) This is one of the two occasions where the word 'co-ordinator' has some meaning. One facilitator should have higher status than the others, in order to 'co-ordinate' the Circle programme. The other occasion is in a larger company with several full-time facilitators.

The selection of a facilitator

Whilst advertisements for Quality Circles facilitators do appear in the press, the majority of such advertisements are deliberate head-hunting, often for specific individuals, usually from within the same industry. It is doubtful whether an individual new to the company, its culture and its people, could become sufficiently well accepted by people at all levels to fulfil the role satisfactorily. If possible it is much better to make an internal appointment of someone who is liked, trusted and respected by people at all levels. This usually narrows the field somewhat, but the correct choice really will pay dividends.

Bascially, the most important considerations are:

(1) Enthusiasm
(2) Influence
(3) Respect
(4) Experience in company operations
(5) Training skills
(6) Tact
(7) Full-time availability.

1 *Enthusiasm* The person to be selected must 'want to be' a facilitator. Someone who understands what is required and sees it as a challenge. Although the job is a management appointment the candidate must not be coerced into the job or feel that he or she has moved into a backwater.

2 *Influence* Good facilitators will be people who have influence on others. This may be as a result of their status prior to appointment as facilitators, or through their personality. A good facilitator is the kind of person who is not normally brushed aside by an impatient manager, but is likely to be reasoned with in most foreseeable circumstances.

3 *Respect* A good facilitator is somebody who gets on well with people and is not seen as a political threat. Several good facilitators have been selected from amongst senior managers because they are trusted and respected, are approaching retirement and have been in the company for many years. They usually see Quality Circles as a way of re-establishing some old values which they think have been lost, and accept the challenge of helping to re-establish them in their remaining years of service. Because they will be replaced in their other activities sooner or later, it means that at least they will be able to chaperone their replacement whilst developing Quality Circles. One or two companies have even brought senior managers back from early retirement to facilitate the Circle programme.

4 *Experience in company operations* A good choice of facilitator will be someone who knows the organisation well and is familiar with most departments and their work. Somebody who knows where most kinds of information is kept, and who to go to and ask.

Training skills A considerable proportion of a facilitator's time will be spent in training leaders and in working with them in the training of their Circles. Facilitators will also be involved in making presentations to others, and in giving talks to managers and union representatives in other organisations. Occasionally a company may find that the person who is best as a facilitator in all other respects lacks this particular ability. In such cases, many companies have frequently overcome the problem by assigning a training specialist to work closely with the facilitator.

6 *Tact* Inevitably there will be many occasions when the facilitator will want some information or help for a Circle at a time when a crisis of some kind is going on. It is important that the facilitator should be someone who is likely to be tactful and sensitive to the feelings of those under pressure in such situations.

Knowing who to ask and when to ask them is a skill not possessed by everyone, but is essential in a facilitator.

7 *Full-time availability* This has already been discussed earlier but its importance cannot be over emphasised. Even if the directly measurable activities appear not to justify fully the time allocation, an enthusiastic facilitator will easily find jobs to do which will more than pay for themselves later. A good facilitator will use every opportunity to write articles for newsletters and noticeboards, communicate with other facilitators and generally keep up the tempo of the programme. Being visible is vitally important.

In summary a facilitator needs to:

Teach	Support	Consult
Champion	Integrate	Persuade
Lead	Liaise	Use power
Push	Tear apart	
Drive	Listen	

A speaker at a conference was once asked how his company selected the facilitator. He replied that when they had analysed everything the facilitator needed to do, and the kind of person required, they waited until a snowy day then waited until the end of the work shift. When the people left the factory they picked someone who did not make tracks in the fresh snow!

Part-time facilitators in large organisations

Some large organisations have deliberately appointed part-time facilitators even though they are well aware of the time commitment. One large American company developed its programme in this way by introducing facilitator training into its management development programme. It did this initially after i realised that it would eventually have 150 full-time facilitators if it adopted th conventional approach. Now, several years later, every manager is the facilitato of the Circles in his own area, and facilitating Circles is just part of the way h manages his people.

One or two companies in the UK have begun to develop along the same lines. Experience suggests that whilst this may lead ultimately to a more soundly based programme, there is no doubt that initial progress is slower via this route. Great care must be taken to co-ordinate the programme so that all sections and departments adopt a common policy and do not compete with each other.

It is probably better to start with a full-time facilitator and only develop along the lines outlined under this heading after the initial programme has become well established. This will probably take somewhere in the order of two years.

Facilitator job specification

Because the appointment of a facilitator is relatively new, very few organisations will have produced a job specification for the role. The following ideas have now been used, both with and without modification, by a number of client companies of DHA. The specification refers to facilitators in general but in cases where more than one facilitator has been, or is to be, appointed, some points refer principally to the most senior facilitator. The specification is as follows.

(1) Organisation

1 A member of the steering committee and the steering committee's main source of information on Circle activities.

2 Preferably the facilitator will report directly to an executive of sufficiently high status, so that he is not exposed to any interdepartmental political defence mechanisms that may exist.

3 Whilst responsible directly to a senior executive, he will be mainly responsible for carrying out the policy decisions of the steering committee which he both advises and serves.

(2) Communications

1 As stated earlier, to facilitate means to make easy and this is probably the best definition of the facilitator's role. Whilst the following tasks will be helpful to ensure the more obvious aspects of this role, it is important that the facilitator should be able to use his own initiative to ensure the success of the company's Quality Circle programme within the constraints of that company's corporate goals and objectives.

2 He will keep in regular contact with other facilitators in the company both locally and nationally and where possible with facilitators from other organisations.

3 He will be the principal point of on-going contact with the consultants subsequent to the initial training.

4   He will keep abreast of Quality Circle developments nationally, and of the state of the art worldwide wherever possible.

(3)   Training

The facilitator will be principally responsible for training new Circle leaders and working with these leaders in the training of their own Circles. During Circle leader training he may call upon additional training skills, both internally or externally, after consultation with the steering committee.

(4)   Responsibility

1   His role in Circle member training is to support and develop the Circle leader, to build confidence in the Circle leader, and gradually withdraw from direct involvement with the newly formed group as, in his own judgement, it reaches maturity. Subsequently, he keeps in weekly contact with each Circle.

2   His long-term relationship with the Circle is supportive. He is required to ensure the provision of data and help for the Circle, and arranges for consultative advice for the Circle when requested.

3   In order to make sure that the Circle programme develops smoothly, he keeps a close watch on the relationships between Circle members, Circle members and leaders, non-Circle members, management and the trade unions.

(5)   Publicity

1   The level of publicity for Circles both individually and collectively is an important factor in the vitality of a Circle programme. Visibility for Circle activities is an important aspect of recognition, and a good facilitator will always be looking for the best ways of achieving this.

2   In-house magazines, news sheets and items in journals all have a place in Circle development. The facilitator should encourage these activities as much as possible.

3   Management presentations are perhaps the most important form of recognition, and the facilitator should always be prepared to help and advise the Circles at this stage in its activities.

4   Mutual visits to other companies may be worth while from time to time. These are normally organised by the facilitator.

(6)   Threats to a Circle programme

The facilitator should always be on the lookout for signs of trouble. Many problems, if identified early enough, can be dealt with on the spot either by discussion with Circle members or with members and their managers. More deep-rooted problems, or those involving other departments, are sometimes best tackled after consultation with the steering committee, and the facilitator should use his judgement as to when this is necessary.

(7) Programme development

As a Circle programme develops, it will occasionally be necessary to repeat some of the early expositions of the concept to managers, union officials—both internal and external—and occasionally in other situations.

It would be worth while for the facilitator to develop visual aids to make such presentations effectively. If a visual aids department exists within the company, the preparation of well-thought-out OHP transparencies or 35 mm slides, professionally produced, will greatly assist in such presentations.

Summary of Part III

Chapters 8 to 15

1 Quality Circles are intended to strengthen the existing organisation—not create by-passes or alternatives.

2 Quality Circles will help to create a more co-operative work environment, and build bridges between all institutionalised activities.

3 Quality Circles represent no threat to any part of the organisation including the trade unions.

4 Top management must be totally committed to every aspect of the concept if success is to be ensured.

5 Middle or departmental and functional management are the key factors in determining the success of circles within that segment of the operation.

6 The supervisor is usually the Circle leader. Others may lead Circles later when the programme is well established.

7 The support of trade union representatives is extremely valuable, and is consistent with the objective of achieving greater involvement for their members and helping to create a better work environment. Quality Circle programmes should not cut across any legitimate union interest.

8 The specialists in an organisation are vital to Quality Circle projects particularly when their special skills and knowledge are required.

9 Non Circle members should be given the opportunity to become involved wherever possible.

10 The steering committee provides a cross functional supportive framework for circle programme development.

11 The facilitator is the focal point of the programme and in most cases should be a full time appointment.

PART IV **Supporting the programme**

Preface to Part IV

This section of the book is intended to include all the policy considerations that are important to the success of a Circle programme. It is hoped that the guidance given in these chapters will be a major influence on the ultimate success and vitality of Quality Circle activities. All the chapters in previous sections were concerned with laying the foundations and starting a new programme. Whilst this section also contains important considerations for the start-up phase, it also looks ahead to the future.

The first chapter in the section, Chapter 16, is concerned with the appropriation of the benefits derived from successful Circle activities. The 'what's in it for them, or us' questions and includes important considerations which should be thoroughly understood by both management and unions alike before a programme is begun.

The next chapter, 17, entitled 'Vitalising and developing Quality Circle programmes' looks beyond the initial phase. Quality Circle activities once commenced are part of a continuously developing process, which will eventually affect everyone in the organisation.

It is important that the steering committee should not only recognise this but also ensure that each phase in the development is properly supported and planned. It has been suggested in Chapter 4 that the Circles themselves pass through four phases of development, and again this development can be greatly assisted by an enlightened steering committee.

The material in Chapter 17 was separated from the steering committee guidelines mainly because it is also of value to management and trade unions generally to gain an insight into the future.

The final chapter, 18, in this section—'Answers to the most frequently asked questions'—contains over 100 of the most pertinent questions put by people at all levels across a broad spectrum of industry to David Hutchins Associates Consultants over the past five years or so.

These questions have been grouped into those relating to:

- Origins of Quality Circles (p. 211)
- Preparation (p. 214)
- Consultants (p. 217)
- Senior management (p. 219)
- Middle management (p. 221)
- Specialists (p. 222)
- Trade unions (p. 223)
- Steering committees (p. 223)

- The Facilitator (p. 224)
- Circle leaders (p. 224)
- Circle members (p. 225)
- Non-Circle members (p. 227)
- Organisation (p. 228)
- Meetings (p. 229)
- Problem selection (p. 230)
- Presentations (p. 232)
- Measurement (p. 234)
- Motivation and reward (p. 237)
- Other group activities (p. 238)
- General problems (p. 239)
- Company-Wide Quality Control (p. 240)

16 Circle rewards—dividing the spoils

Of all the questions raised at seminars on the topic of Quality Circles, the most emotive are: 'what's in it for us?' or 'what's in it for them?' Interestingly, such questions are almost never an issue once the programme is under way, and the reasons for this will become apparent after assimilating the points covered in this chapter.

When the questions are put in the manner suggested above, one thinks immediately of the benefits that may accrue to Circle members or the interest of trade union activists. However, if the questions are framed differently they can also apply equally to return on investment or 'bottom line' considerations. In this case, they will be: 'what is the benefit to cost ratio?' 'what will it cost?' or 'when will we expect a return?' etc.

It would be a matter of extreme folly for anyone deliberately to evade any of the issues raised by these questions, and every organisation, contemplating the commencement of Quality Circles must produce an extremely clear-cut policy statement covering all aspects of these issues *before* anyone is asked to volunteer for membership. These matters must be fully discussed and agreed with workers' representatives, and time must be allowed for those involved to satisfy themselves of the validity of the rules determined.

This chapter is intended to assist those involved in these considerations.

Cost benefit

Current experience in the UK, the USA and Western Europe suggests that in the early stages the Quality Circles programme should produce a yield somewhere in the order of 3 or 4 to 1 benefit to cost ratio. On the cost side, this would include all of the costs relating to start up, consultancy, facilitator salary and other items identified in Chapter 10. This cost/benefit ratio should improve through the second and third years due to the amortisation of start up costs, together with the continued benefits acrruing from some of the early Circle projects.

It must be stressed that these benefits are only suggested as a reference point. In practice, it is impossible to even guess at the true benefits. In one company, a Quality Circle saved nearly half a million pounds by its first project which was quite simple and took very little time. This achievement would have paid for the entire programme many times over. However, in another company, it may be several months before any great tangible benefit is realised, but it is unlikely that a negative situation will exist for very long. If it does, it is more likely that either the consultancy fees are excessive or that there is some other fundamental flaw in the development.

Many readers may feel that such attention to benefit to cost ratios is alien to the philosophy of Quality Circles, and that a management whose heart is in the right place should want to introduce them regardless of these considerations. At individual Circle level this is true, but taken over all, one must refer back to the original motive for commencing Circles in the first place.

In Chapters 1–3 it was explained that Quality Circles represent an opportunity to develop a more successful organisation by the better utilisation of the resources of its people, and this was to be of benefit both to the individuals and to the organisation as a whole.

Measures of success of course depend to a large extent upon the objectives of the organisation, but cost is always an important consideration. There would be no value in developing the most friendly, happy organisation in the world, if it became insolvent in the process. Therefore, it is unavoidable that a Circle programme, just like any other consideration, must be regarded as an investment, and investments need to show a return. Fortunately, with Quality Circles, the returns are usually so impressive that the cost of a programme is rarely, if ever, a problem. Furthermore, the benefits referred to above are only the results of projects that have produced a tangible benefit.

In addition to these benefits, there will be further gains which, in many cases, will far outweigh the value of the cost-cutting projects. For example, there may be:

Lower labour turnover
Fewer grievances
Higher morale
General improvements to productivity
General improvements to quality

and many problems which will have simply 'disappeared' because people are taking more care. In fact, these are the true benefits to management of a Quality Circle programme, and the cost benefit gains from individual projects should be regarded as a bonus.

Rewards for Circle activities

In terms of cost savings, some Circle achievements may occasionally be quite spectacular. This is readily appreciated by most people in an organisation, and a policy for the appropriation of Circle gains must be formulated before Circle activities commence.

It will probably come as a surprise to many readers that one of the inviolable rules of Quality Circles is that members should never, under any circumstances, be paid directly in cash for any Circle achievement. In fact, one would go so far as to say that should this rule ever be violated, Quality Circles as such would cease to exist in that organisation the moment that such a decision was made.

There are many reasons for this, but the principal one is that direct reward is alien to the entire philosophy of Quality Circles. The object of Circles, as has been emphasised all along, is to create an organisation where all are made to feel that their organisation is better for their being there, and that their contribution is recognised. The aim is to develop a sense of corporate loyalty and corporate identity amongst all employees. This cannot be achieved by treating one group of people differently from another, and no one else is paid directly for solving problems.

That is not to say that Circles and Circle members cannot be rewarded. Indeed, reward is an essential part of human behaviour, but it can take many forms, and direct incentive is only one possibility. Other forms of Circle reward will be discussed later in the chapter, and also in the following chapter.

If an organisation did attempt to make direct payments to Circle members it would find that there are other insurmountable problems, some of which are as follows:

(1) A policy would be required to determine who should be eligible for payment. This could create enormous difficulties. If payment were made to only Circle members, they would immediately be alienated from others, such as non-Circle members and specialists, who might have helped in their work. Such help is unlikely to be forthcoming in the future.

(2) A Circle in one area may be able to save more in one project, just by the sheer value and volume of work flowing through the section, than the entire budget for some other department.

(3) Remembering that the primary aim of Quality Circles is to create a better work environment, and that many of their projects will not normally produce tangible results, assessment could be difficult. Also, it will tend to make Circles concentrate on problems that look as if they will produce a good return, and so Quality Circles will be reduced to a money-swapping trade-off process. The idea of 'self-control' described in Chapter 3 would be lost, and Taylorism would flourish.

(4) The levels of direct incentive would have to be negotiated, with the consequence that Quality Circles would be forced into the industrial relations arena and almost certainly become a negotiating counter for some other non-related objective. Again, the co-operative spirit of the concept would be lost.

Rewards for Circles can be given in several ways:
(1) Recognition
(2) Attendance at conventions, seminars and workshops
(3) Exchange visits to other organisations' operating Circles
(4) Allow Circles to decide how some of the savings may be spent.

Let us now consider each in turn.

(1) *Recognition* Many people grossly underestimate the importance of recognition of achievement as a form of reward. In fact, people get very considerable satisfaction from being listened to, and the Circle presentation to management is the highlight in the whole process for most Circle members.

Many companies operating Quality Circles who are aware of this frequently give their Circles the opportunity to repeat their presentations to others. These presentations may include:

- Other Quality Circles
- Public or semi-public functions
- Steering committee
- 'In-house' Circle conventions
- Presentations at national Circle conventions, such as those organised by Quality Circle Network.

Additionally, special projects may be recorded in news-sheets, articles on noticeboards or magazines such as *Circle Review*.

(2) *Attendance at conventions, seminars and workshops* An extremely powerful form of gratitude for Circle achievements and recognition of the value of their work can be shown by allowing Circles to attend public and semi-public functions. Not only will the Circles find this to be enjoyable and rewarding in itself, it is also consistent with the idea of self-control. The Circles will almost certainly pick up new ideas from the presentations of other Circles, and from the ensuing discussions. Moreover, it means that Circles are being treated like managers who, of course, also benefit from learning at seminars.

(3) *Exchange visits to other organisations operating Circles* This is another of the key forms of reward for Circles in Japan, and is already becoming well established in Europe. Many British companies have an almost formalised relationship with each other for this purpose.

(4) *Allow Circles to decide how some of the savings may be spent* This is the essence of 'self-control'. Nothing could be more impressive as a means of showing trust in a group of workpeople than to allow them to decide for themselves how some of the gains may be utilised. Those managers who might be sceptical of such a revolutionary approach are probably not yet ready to accept the philosophy of Quality Circles. The idea of allowing Circles this degree of responsibility is new to most companies in the West, even those with established Circle programmes. In Japan, however, such practices are almos

universal, but the method of application varies widely, and some differences in approach may be evident in all programmes.

Basically each Circle project is evaluated in much the same way as reward-based suggestion scheme programmes. A proportion of the financial benefits of the project are then allocated back to the Circle. The Circle can then either decide how this money is to be spent immediately or, in many cases, it can let the savings accumulate until a more substantial sum has accrued from several projects.

The Circle will then brainstorm the possible ways in which the money can be spent, and these will probably include:

Better tools and equipment

Ideas for improving the work environment, including even such items as pot plants, carpets, etc.

Better facilities for Circle meetings

Presentation aids such as flip charts, overhead projectors, etc.

Visits away from the factory

Books and training materials

At a recent convention organised by Quality Circle Network the delegates who comprised nearly 90 Quality Circle members and facilitators from a range of British companies voted unanimously that they did not want direct financial rewards, but liked the idea of controlling some of the savings. When asked how they would use the resources, the majority thought better facilities, aids and equipment for Circle activities would be a high priority.

In Japan, Quality Circles frequently use this income for such purposes as parties to introduce new members, as well as to entertain others outside the Circle who may have given assistance.

In one UK company, a Quality Circle, given the opportunity to decide how some of its savings might be used, requested that two table tennis tables be purchased for the works canteen. This was immediately accepted by management. The value of such suggestions is that others in the organisation also benefit, and Quality Circle activities are shown in a favourable light.

Of course it must be emphasised that in many cases the Quality Circle should present its recommendations before spending the money, but this is a matter for the organisation and is unlikely to affect the Circle programme one way or the other.

Quality Circles and reward-based suggestions schemes

It would seem from the foregoing that Quality Circles are in conflict with reward-based suggestion schemes where these are established. Fortunately, this is not so. Suggestion schemes and Quality Circles are fundamentally different, and can live alongside one another quite happily. Interestingly, this is a fact in a very large number of companies. Let us compare the two concepts.

A suggestion scheme is usually operated by placing letter-boxes in convenient locations around the premises. They are often accompanied by publicity materials which encourage people to submit ideas for improvements for which rewards will be given. These rewards are usually calculated on the estimated value of the idea, although some reward is often given even for ideas not accepted. Apart from the time taken by a committee every so often to evaluate the ideas, a suggestion scheme does not cost very much to run. Unlike Quality Circles, people are not specially trained to think up suggestions, nor are they given time to do so.

Quality Circles, on the other hand, receive special training in the problem-solving techniques, and meet for one hour per week in company time. In other words, Quality Circle meetings are an hour of work. It may be a different kind of work, but it is still work. Additionally, the management of the company is making a considerable on-going investment in the programme.

Another important consideration is that Circles only work on one project at a time. If any of the members have ideas about any other topic, there should be nothing to prevent their placing such ideas in the suggestion box in the same way as any other employee.

There should be nothing officially preventing a Circle member from putting ideas into the box relating to the project if he or she so wishes. However, experience has shown that this never happens. At any time, Circle members have the choice of giving their ideas relating to the project they are working on, as their contribution to the Circle, or, if they choose, they can put the idea in the box for their own gratification. Experience again shows that members' loyalty to their group prevents their seeking personal reward. Basically it is a matter of trust. If management is prepared to trust its people, it is unlikely that such trust will be violated.

Integration of Circles with suggestion schemes

Whilst Quality Circles and suggestion schemes are different, that is not to say that they cannot work together. If the idea of Circles having some control of their gains is accepted, then it becomes possible to allow the Circles, if they wish, to place their ideas in the suggestion box with the proviso that any award given will not be taken as a direct cash benefit but may be spent by the Circle in the manner suggested earlier in this chapter.

Summary

Articles have appeared in management magazines expressing disbelief that workers, particularly in Western countries, will produce ideas if they are not to be directly rewarded. The evidence now available from a very large number of organisations totally refutes this view. The carrot and stick theories and the approach of Taylorised management have, through Quality Circles, been totally disproven and rejected.

Given the right environment, people do want to work, do want to improve both themselves and their organisation, and, provided they are given a fair day's pay for a fair day's work, gain considerable satisfaction from recognition of their talents and creativity. This is the main reward of Quality Circles, and the evidence of five years' development in the UK shows that the question 'what's in it for me?' is never asked by active Quality Circles.

17 Vitalising and developing Quality Circle programmes

Perhaps one of the more common causes of failure, or under-realisation of expectations of Quality Circles is the surprising fact that many managers seem to think that Circles represent some form of perpetual motion. Incredibly, they act as though all that is necessary is to light the touch paper and walk away, leaving the Circles to look after themselves.

Far from representing perpetual motion, Quality Circles really do need considerable management attention. The more attention management devotes to Quality Circles, the better will be the results. The development of people has been neglected for so long that there are years of work ahead before their true potential can be realised.

Those hard-pressed managers who may despair on reading this can take heart from the evidence which suggests that many of the problems that make their lives difficult in the normal way will be considerably reduced by the increasingly co-operative spirit that will develop in their department. Consequently, they will be able to devote more time to supportive measures when necessary.

In this chapter, the various ways in which Circles may be supported will be explored. The main theme will be the stimulation and encouragement of Circles during their continuous development. These supportive activities may be separated into two groups—internal and external.

The internal activities are those activities that can be established within the organisation independently of any outside influence. However, a study of Quality Circle activities in Japan shows that tremendous benefits can be gained from giving Quality Circles the opportunity to participate in relevant activities outside their own organisation. These have been developed in Japan to a very sophisticated level through to activities of the Japanese Union of Scientists and Engineers and QC Circle Headquarters. This external support is regarded by the author to be of such critical importance to the survival and development of Quality Circles that the internal and external aspects of support are covered separately in this chapter.

Internal support

In Chapter 5 it was suggested that Quality Circles pass through four phases of development. In this chapter, the supportive measures which may be considered by management, trade unions and steering committees will be related to each phase.

Phase 1—The problem-solving phase

At this early stage, which usually lasts for about one year, Quality Circles will be concerned mainly with improving their skills in the use of the basic techniques, and with developing effective presentations. They will sometimes be quite sensitive at this time, and it is important to ensure that their newly won self-confidence is not shattered by thoughtless remarks from overbearing managers or others.

The supportive measures should primarily be those aimed to give encouragement and confidence, and may include:

- Features and photographs of the newly formed Circles in house journals. This will show the Circle the importance with which their activities are regarded, and is a very positive form of stimulation.
- Repeat presentations. New Circles may be given the opportunity to repeat their presentations to others. This will enable them to 'polish their act' and will lead to even more impressive presentations in the future.
- Participation in competitions, such as Quality awareness campaigns.
- Exchange visits. Towards the end of this initial phase of development, the Circles may be given the opportunity to make outside visits. This will boost their confidence even further, will show recognition, and lead the group into the second phase.

Phase 2—Monitoring and problem solving

There is no clear distinction between this phase and Phase 1, further than the fact that the Circle will exhibit greater self-assurance. When it seems appropriate, and this will be determined by the level of skill achieved in the use of the basic techniques, the Circle should be introduced to control techniques. The use of simple control charts will enable the Circles to monitor and control the levels of some problems, and skill in this ability will lead the group into Phase 3.

Because monitoring and self-control is relatively new to many people outside Japan, there is great value to be obtained from allowing Circles at this stage to witness the presentations of other Circles which have developed this ability.

Phase 3—Innovation: self-improvement and problem solving

The important feature of this phase is that the Circles are becoming innovative. In addition to their problem-solving activities, which will continue for as long as they remain in existence, the Circles will begin to seek ways of making improvements. In other words, they will no longer be satisfied with maintaining the status quo of their departmental performance.

The innovative phase can be a very creative and rewarding phase of Quality Circle development, and will demand a greater involvement with others outside the Circle. In particular, the Circles will seek more help and advice from specialists and specialist departments. They will become involved in experimentation, and take an interest in innovative developments relating to their work.

This can and should be a most rewarding time for the supportive manager. The degree of trust and respect between the manager and the Circle will have grown to such an extent that the manager will become increasingly involved in the Circle activities.

Supportive measures that will be particularly useful at this phase will include all those measures relevant to the earlier phases but will also include:

- Meetings with quality control and other specialist departments to discuss problems of mutual concern.
- Formal feedback to Quality Circles from quality control including:
  Customer complaint data
  Fault analysis
  General Quality information
- Formal feedback from accounts and control departments on:
  Lost time
  Variances
  Standards, etc.
- Feeding Circles with relevant technical data relating to new equipment, sales brochures and innovative articles from journals relating to their work.
- Giving them further access to textbooks and any other materials that may be of interest.

Phase 4—Full self-control

This is the ultimate phase in the development of a Quality Circle. The time lapse between start up and the commencement of this phase will vary considerably depending upon many factors including:

- degree of self-control prior to Circles
- level of education of Circle members
- support of steering committee and facilitator.

Even though a few Circles may reach this stage of development quite quickly it is likely to be several years before this phase is reached on a company-wide scale. It may take at least five years and probably as many as ten for some large companies. It will never be reached without the deliberate and planned support of management consciously working towards this state.

To achieve this goal it is essential that the organisation makes the achievement a corporate objective, and works systematically through each of the phases 1, 2, and 3. It is only when the fourth phase is reached on a corporate scale that the full power of the Quality Circle approach will be realised.

Only then, when this full integration of effort has been achieved, can an organisation justly claim to have successfully introduced Company-Wide Quality Control as defined in Chapter 2. At this stage, the organisation will have fully integrated the activities of Quality Circles with all other functions in the organisation. Circles in one department will be co-operating with Circles elsewhere both on and off site. The Circles will also communicate directly with other organisations as part of their activities.

Additional supportive activities

In addition to the suggestions given earlier, there are many other ways in which an organisation can both stimulate and utilise Quality Circles. Whilst Circles are primarily involved in problem solving, one must never lose sight of the fact that they are also concerned with making work itself more interesting, more rewarding and more enjoyable. Circle meetings should be fun, and comments such as 'I look forward to Circle meetings' should be frequently heard. If Circle meetings are thought to be boring, there is something fundamentally wrong.

Management and steering committees can do much to ensure that Circles are seen to be an exciting concept. For example, the steering committee might perhaps decide to organise a poster competition where Circles are invited to design posters on some selected theme such as:

- Quality awareness
- Cost reduction
- Energy saving, etc.

Occasionally, one or two Circles may be stuck for a problem. This is most likely in situations where the work is particularly simple and monotonous. Such Circles could be given the opportunity to produce posters, instruction sheets or other ideas which may be the result of brainstorming by both the steering committee and the Circles themselves.

Quality month

Another feature of Japanese management is the concept of 'Quality Month'. Fortunately for Japanese companies, November has been designated 'National Quality Month'. During this month national conventions are held for all levels of employee, but in addition to these, individual companies also organise their own internal activities.

As part of a programme for the development of Company-Wide Quality Control, there is great benefit in such a concept. Each company may designate a particular month in the year as its Quality Month. During this month it may hold special conventions where selected Circle presentations are made, run poster competitions, or allow the Circles to come up with their own ideas how Quality Month should be organised.

In order to institute a similar supportive approach David Hutchins Associates have suggested to their clients that they also designate one month in the year as Quality Month and have recommended that March would be a fairly popular choice. It is hoped, therefore, that a 'National Quality Month' will develop in non-Japanese countries along much the same lines as in Japan.

External support—Circle network

The external supportive structure to Quality Circle activities is equal in importance to the internal activities of individual organisations if the true potential of Quality Circles is to be fully realised.

Circle programmes run by the more independent companies which deliberately isolate themselves from others are notably less impressive. There is no doubt whatsoever that mutual visits, exchanges of experience, and the general camaraderie that develops from co-operation between different companies is a significant factor which characterises the more successful companies. From the very outset of DHA's activities in the field of Quality Circles, this interactive spirit has been vigorously encouraged and developed. Commencing initially with facilitator workshops, where trained facilitators were given the opportunity to meet each other at residential workshops, these activities have been extended to embrace the full spectrum of supportive activities into what is now known as 'Circle Network'.

Full membership of this network is restricted to Quality Circle participants from companies and organisations which have undergone a programme of training conducted by one of DHA's senior consultants. Associate membership is open to individuals, groups and organisations who are interested in finding out more about the Quality Circle concept. The main reason for the restriction on membership is to ensure that all members have been trained to the same standard and in the same way.

The particular approach to Quality Circles developed by DHA places the emphasis on a carefully planned programme of the implementation and development of the concept over several years and has led the company to the conclusion that real benefit can only be achieved by restricting full membership to individuals who are starting from the same basis. When members gather at conventions and workshops, they are able to refine their shared skills and broaden their understanding, using techniques understood by all.

Fig 17.1 Circle Network Membership Certificate

Fig 17.2 Circle Review

One of the main aims in allowing Circles to attend conventions is to increase their confidence and enthusiasm. This can only be achieved if all participants have been trained in a similar manner. This is particularly important in the case of fledgling Circles which expect to learn from their peers.

Circle Review

Another feature of 'Circle Network' is the house journal *Circle Review*. This is issued free to all members of 'Circle Network' on a quarterly basis. It contains regular features, stories about Circle activities, and any material which is thought to be helpful in stimulating Circle activities.

National societies of Quality Circles

Awareness of the importance of the Japanese Union of Scientists and Engineers' involvement in the spread of Circles in Japan has led to the development of national supportive movements elsewhere.

United Kingdom

In the United Kingdom a national society entitled 'National Society of Quality Circles' has been formed. Membership is open to any organisation which has an active Quality Circle programme. The society has a regional organisation, produces a regular news-sheet and organises seminars and conventions for its members.

United States

The International Association of Quality Circles (IAQC) was formed in California in the mid-1970s for the propagation of Quality Circles. Since its inception, the organisation has developed a wide range of training courses, organised conventions and published a considerable quantity of materials for the advancement of the concept.

Also, in the USA there is an organisation known as the American Society for Quality Control (ASQC). This organisation whilst taking an interest in Quality Circles is primarily concerned with Quality Control. Internationally ASQC has links with both the Japanese Union of Scientists and Engineers (JUSE) and with the European Organisation for Quality Control (EOQC).

Whilst Quality Circles only form a small part of the activities of ASQC and EOQC at present, it is likely that their importance will increase dramatically when Company-Wide Quality Control begins to emerge from the more well-developed Circle programmes of some larger companies.

18 Answers to the 152 questions most frequently asked about Quality Circles

During the early years of involvement in consultancy and training in Quality Circles, David Hutchins Associates began recording and collating the questions most frequently asked at seminars and in training sessions. The answers are designed to help those concerned with the development of Circles in their own companies. Many of the answers summarise points in the earlier chapters and can be used as quick references to important points. To reduce excessive repetition, reference is sometimes given to the appropriate pages or chapters in the text as an alternative to giving a direct answer in this chapter.

Because it is difficult to list the questions in alphabetical order, they have been grouped into the following categories.

Questions relating to:

- Circle leaders (p. 224)
- Circle members (p. 225)
- Circles: their origin and use (p. 211)
- Company-Wide Quality Control (p. 240)
- Consultants (p. 217)
- Facilitators (p. 224)
- General problems (p. 239)
- Measuring the effects of Quality Circles (p. 234)
- Meetings (p. 229)
- Middle management (p. 221)
- Motivation and reward (p. 237)
- Non-Circle members (p. 227)
- Organisation of Quality Circles (p. 228)
- Other group activities (p. 238)
- Preparation for Quality Circles (p. 214)
- Presentations (p. 232)
- Problem selection (p. 230)
- Senior management (p. 219)
- Specialists (p. 222)
- Steering committees (p. 223)
- Trade unions (p. 223)

Origins of Quality Circles

1 Q. *What is a Quality Circle?*

   A. A Quality Circle is a small group of between 3 and 12 people who do the same, or similar, work voluntarily, meeting regularly for about one hour per week, in paid time, usually under the leadership of their own supervisor, to identify, analyse, and solve some of the problems in their work, presenting recommendations to management and, where possible, implementing the solutions themselves.

2 Q. *How much Japanese culture is involved?*

   A. None. The philosophy of Quality Circles transcends all cultures and has been convincingly proven in widely differing cultures worldwide.

   The concept originated in Japan rather than elsewhere as a result of very special circumstances in the years following the war. See: Appendix: History of Japan's Quality Control Circles.

3 Q. *Why 'Quality' Circles?*

   A. Quality Circles are part, and only part, of 'Company-Wide Quality Control'. 'Quality' means more than just defects as explained in Chapter 2.

4 Q. *Why is Britain slow in adopting Quality Circles?*

   A. Although Britain, and indeed the rest of Europe, have been relatively slow in taking up the concept, the rate of growth since its inception has been at least as impressive as elsewhere. The most likely reason for the original delay is that it is the first concept to be introduced into worldwide management that was not originally developed in one of the formerly recognised industrial nations.

5 Q. *What is the growth rate around the world?*

   A. It is difficult to estimate an accurate answer to this question.

   It appears that the growth rate in any country, or indeed in any individual organisation, is approximately exponential. The data which exists supports this observation in Japan, Korea, Brazil, the United States, and also the UK.

   In 1979 it was claimed that there were over 1 000 000 Circles in Japan, 300 000 in Korea and 30 000 in Brazil.

At that time Circles were relatively new in the United States, and it was estimated that about 150 companies were developing the concept. Since then, the growth has been phenomenal, and in 1982 a figure of 5000 companies was quoted. However, concern has been expressed that the Circle developments in the USA are somewhat divorced from Company-Wide Quality Control and there are some fears as to their long-term survival under these circumstances.

6 Q. *Will QC's help non-Japanese countries to compete?*

A. Yes. That is the main point of the exercise. However, this will only be possible if the entire philosophy is properly understood. See Chapters 2 and 3.

7 Q. *Are there differences between large and small companies?*

A. Only in the selection of the facilitator. See Chapter 16. Apart from that, the only other difference will be the ultimate number of Circles.

8 Q. *Will we just go round in Circles?*

A. No. Quality Circles result in very positive improvements. Whilst Circles are not just concerned with cost reduction problems, nevertheless they will resolve a sufficient number of such problems to more than justify the programme.

9 Q. *Are Quality Circles a voluntary form of scientific management?*

A. Quality Circles represent a voluntary form of participative management leading to self-control. Scientific management will continue to operate the overall systems within which the Circles will operate. See Chapter 3.

10 Q. *Will it work short-term or long-term?*

A. Quality Circles are part of a totally new concept of management. They are therefore neither long nor short term but represent a permanent feature of this form of management.

11 Q. *What is the long-term track record of Circles?*

A. Circles originated in Japan in 1962 and their development is continuing. Even those companies which pioneered the concept are continuing to develop new ideas to increase the effectiveness of the concept. Although Circles have a much shorter history elsewhere, there is no evidence anywhere of a properly introduced and developed programme subsequently resulting in failure.

12 Q. *Is the Circle idea likely to go away like so many other ideas?*

A. It is inconceivable that an organisation would want to suspend Circle activities once the benefits have been realised. It is equally inconceivable that employees would ever want to go back to the old style of working once they had felt the full flavour of Quality Circle style management.

Nippon Steel has claimed that this style of management is estimated to be responsible for around 25% of their profits. It is unlikely that they would want to abandon a concept which had such proven potential.

13 Q. *What if other nations (and other competitors) start Circles?*

A. This is what competition is all about. Either we equal or better the achievements of competitors or we fail. Until a better approach to management appears on the scene, the best protection available is to apply vigorously all the concepts of management that are currently available and offer potential for improvement. Hopefully, this book will make some contribution to that for those who are prepared to accept the Circle concept.

14 Q. *Have Quality Circles come too late?*

A. Better late than never. Fortunately it is always quicker to develop an idea after someone else has done the pioneering work, and so ultimately it may even prove to be an advantage.

15 Q. *Are there any Quality Circles in white-collar areas?*

A. Yes. Quality Circles work anywhere people work together and share common problems. Circles exist in accounts departments, wages, field sales, design, warehousing, distribution, supervision, management, together with traditional production operations.

16 Q. *Can Circles operate in areas of rapidly changing technology?*

A. They can and do. In fact there have proved to be additional advantages resulting from the involvement of operators and others in the development of new methods of working.

17 Q. *Will Circles work with part-time workers?*

A. The main difficulties here include:
   (a) difficulty in reducing even further the 'on-job' hours
   (b) part-timers are sometimes less committed to the organisation.

   However, they also have capabilities worth tapping, and, given the opportunity, many would like to make a greater contribution to the organisation.

   By giving part-time workers this opportunity, they are likely to exhibit greater loyalty in the execution of their tasks.

18 Q. *Are there any 'no-go' areas for Quality Circles?*

A. Yes, there are principally two:
   (1) Circles must never tackle projects relating to pay, conditions, and terms of work
   (2) They must not criticise individuals or departments. Circles tackle problems, not people.

Preparation

19 Q. *How and where do you start a Quality Circle programme?*

A. First of all do nothing, and involve no one, until certain that thorough, sound advice is available from a well-experienced source.

   Secondly, it is essential to ensure the total commitment of top level management prior to any other activity.

   Only then is it time to commence discussions with others, such as senior management, middle management, trade unions etc., prior to the introduction of a pilot programme.

20 Q. *How much does it cost to implement a programme?*

A. Contrary to the unfortunate experiences of some companies, there is no reason whatsoever why the start-up costs at an individual location should be excessive.

   The cost of top quality consultancy and support should not be much more than a year's salary of a typist.

   The other cost considerations will be:
   (1) facilitator's salary
   (2) members attending meetings

(3) time spent by the steering committee
(4) meeting room facilities and equipment
See Chapter 10.

21 Q. *How important is management commitment?*

A. It is essential. Without the total commitment of the most senior management team, failure is certain. See Chapters 10 and 11.

22 Q. *Why should workpeople trust management's motives?*

A. This is a chicken and egg problem, particularly in companies with a poor industrial relations record. The opportunity for worker representatives to join the steering committee is the best way to overcome such problems.

23 Q. *How long does it take to set up a Circle programme?*

A. This will vary greatly from one organisation to another, depending upon circumstances.

As a rule of thumb, it is unlikely that an organisation will be able to form the first Circles in less than three months from the date of the original decision to go ahead, and it will probably be nearer six months for most. For some it will be a year. Speed is not the important factor. The benefits to be gained from a well-prepared programme will far outweigh any advantage gained by jumping too many fences at once. In fact the impatience of some managers has often resulted in some very serious problems. A gardening adage is very relevant at this point. 'Prepare the ground before planting the seed'.

24 Q. *Who gives the tuition?*

A. As soon as the facilitator and initial Circle leaders have been trained, usually by a consultant, they will conduct the subsequent training of the Circle members themselves.

It is not a good idea to use a consultant or training specialist to train Circle members. This should be done by the Circle leader with the help of the facilitator as part of their own development.

However, the initial training of the facilitator, first Circle leaders and steering committee by a *fully experienced specialist with a good track record* is essential to success.

25 Q. *At what levels of the hierarchy do Circles apply?*

A. All. There is no reason why Circles should not be formed at all levels even up to board level.

Most organisations start Circles at direct employee level simply to take advantage of the motivational aspects of the concept. There are some, however, who have started management Circles before they progressed downwards to other levels. Others have commenced task force activities based upon managers and supervisors first, and only commenced Quality Circles after these people have become fully experienced in the concepts.

26 Q. *Is there an optimum company size?*

A. No. Circles have been proved to be beneficial in companies ranging from a mere handful of employees up to the international giants. The mode of operation is identical, and the benefits comparable.

The only problem which is likely to trouble the small company is the difficulty in finding groups larger than three people who do similar work.

27 Q. *Do Circles lose momentum?*

A. They can, but they should not. They sometimes do in situations where management or the facilitator is taking insufficient interest in the group and it begins to lose confidence. The members may hit a snag which they cannot resolve by themselves, and will become demoralised. It is very much the facilitator's job to help them over such crises. This aspect is fully covered in Chapter 17.

28 Q. *Will Quality Circles have teeth?*

A. Quality Circles are not an alternative power force in the organisation. They are formed to make more effective use of the existing organisation and must work with all other groups.

Of course, if they find it difficult to have their ideas implemented or accepted, they will soon lose heart. This is why management commitment is so important. This is the only way in which the Circle actually has 'teeth'. 'Circle power' is really generated from the enthusiasm of the activists which usually proves irresistible.

29 Q. *How do you control a Circle?*

A. A Circle should not need controlling if its members have been trained properly. It is all a question of trust, and given clear guide-lines it is very unlikely that such trust will ever be betrayed.

30 Q. *How do you 'sell' Quality Circles to the shop floor?*

A. It is not really so much a question of selling the concept as of telling the story well. Providing that the concept is clearly described there is usually sufficient support forthcoming to be able to make a start. This is even true in the most unlikely situations where there has previously been considerable hostility to management proposals.

31 Q. *Is there any point in starting Circles if good communications already exist?*

A. This question is best answered by reading Chapters 2, 3 and 11. Basically yes. Such areas are normally the best ones to start in because it should be easy to get the Circles established there. They will then serve as models for others.

32 Q. *Do Circles cause interdepartmental communications problems in the early stages?*

A. Circles should only tackle problems in their own work area, not look over the fence into the affairs of other departments.

33 Q. *Will it work in a class-based society?*

A. Yes, but obviously the most visible manifestations of class within an organisation are always a source of friction. It is difficult to engender loyalty when people are treated differently and made to feel inferior. Hopefully, such organisations will use Quality Circles as a means of reducing these differences and create a better society in the future.

34 Q. *What will Circles mean to our company in the long term?*

A. They will help it to survive, make it more profitable and a better place to work in.

Consultants

35 Q. *Why should we use a consultant?*

A. It is difficult to answer any question in this section without appearing biased, but that would be equally true for non-consultants too.

The advantage of a consultant is that his reputation depends upon doing a good job. That assumes, of course, that the client takes the trouble to check the consultants' claims.

A good consultant is an expert. His life, his work, depend upon his success, and it is a hard road to the top. Quality Circles are a complex topic, and whilst a superficial knowledge of the concept is easily acquired, there are many pitfalls, the solutions to which lie beyond the scope of a single text. An experienced consultant will probably have confronted the same problems before. As has been stated many times in this text, the potential of Circles is such that it would be foolish to risk failure by penny-pinching, particularly when good advice need not be expensive.

36 Q. *How do we find the best consultant?*

A. In the field of consultancy, the best is not necessarily the most expensive in terms of total cost, nor necessarily the cheapest either.

The track record of the consulting organisation is the most important consideration. Ask for a list of satisfied clients, contact as many of them as possible, and compare their comments with those of the clients of other consultants. Under no circumstances should a consultant organisation be selected as a result of its reputation in other fields, or because of its size.

37 Q. *Does our management see Quality Circles the same way as the consultant?*

A. This is another reason why an initial presentation to top management is important. Everyone should have the confidence that they are being told the same story.

38 Q. *Is it necessary for the consultant to be experienced in our particular industry?*

A. No, but obviously it helps if the consultant is familiar with work-related jargon or terminology. All DHA consultants make themselves familiar with the processes and cultures of the organisations they are working in during the training process.

39 Q. *What is the total role of the consultant?*

A. In a sense the consultancy required to assist in the introduction of Quality Circles is not consultancy in its purest sense. It is primarily a training service with consultancy support. A good consultant will train a company to run its own programme rather than come in and do it for them. This should be fully supported with comprehensive training materials for the company's own internal use.

The Consultant should then be contracted to make regular audit visits to review the developments to date, and give advice for future development.

Senior management

40 Q. *How do you make managers listen?*

  A. You cannot. But provided there is management commitment at the top, and there is sufficient support amongst some of the middle managers to get the programme started, others will come around to the idea later. Rome was not built in a day, and some people will take time to become accustomed to the reality of such a revolutionary change. There may be some who will never accept the concept, and this is a problem which senior management will eventually have to face up to. Fortunately it is unlikely to involve more than one or two managers at the most, even in large organisations.

41 Q. *Do Circle programme pose a threat to management?*

  A. Just the opposite. Quality Circles are totally supportive of management. In fact Circles do not pose a threat to anyone. They attack problems in their own work and do not become involved in criticising the activities of others.

42 Q. *Can Quality Circles lead to a change in management attitudes?*

  A. Yes, leading to a far more participative style. This is one of the aims of a Circle programme.

43 Q. *Is management too remote from direct employees?*

  A. In some cases yes, but Quality Circles can help to close the gap. This is first achieved through the presentations by the Circles, but later on a closer involvement will develop.

44 Q. *How do you maintain management commitment?*

  A. Top management must do this for itself. If Circles are achieving results, this is hardly likely to present a problem, particularly if the steering committee is doing its job and keeping management informed of achievements.

45 Q. *Are Quality Circles only an extension of good management?*

  A. Quality-Circles-style management constitutes a new way of thinking. It is consistent with good management, and provided that managers can accept the concept of 'self-control' there is unlikely to be any conflict with other management approaches.

46 Q. *Are Quality Circles 'just another management confidence trick'?*

A. Another? It must be remembered that everything relating to Quality Circles is voluntary and completely open and above board. If people feel that they are being manipulated in any way whatsoever they can always opt out. The fact that this rarely happens shows the trust which develops through a Circle programme.

47 Q. *Does management receive training in Quality Circles?*

A. Yes, but only normally appreciation training except of course where task force activities are also being introduced. The training in depth is usually concentrated on the steering committee, the facilitator, Circle leaders and Circle members in that order.

48 Q. *Will management support Quality Circles?*

A. It must if the programme is to be successful. Circles should not be started in a work area if the support of its manager is in any doubt.

49 Q. *How does management participate?*

A. By ensuring that the facilities are available, that training takes place, that speedy action is taken to implement Circle suggestions by taking an interest in Circle activities, and by learning more about the concept through reading and discussion. Management can be most supportive by deliberately feeding information to the Circles in its area.

50 Q. *Are Circles consisting only of direct employees good enough to solve complex problems, particularly if the members are only semi-literate?*

A. It is surprising to many just how sophisticated Quality Circles can be, even when comprised of the least skilled employees. However, what is more impressive is the fact that many of the most dramatic improvements originate from initially very simple projects.

One fact which has emerged dramatically from Quality Circles is that everyone can benefit from training and everyone, no matter who they are, can make a contribution because in their job they are experts.

51 Q. *Are we solving management's problems?*

A. In a way, yes, but such a question stems from Taylorism (see Chapter 3). In reality, if everyone is to become involved in the organisation, then the problems are everyone's. Management can only solve problems at management level. With Quality Circles everyone becomes a manager at his or her own level.

52 Q. *Do Quality Circles by-pass managers to achieve results?*

A. No. Quality Circles are taught to work within the system, not to create an alternative.

53 Q. *What can Circles do about a manager who is holding a section back?*

A. If this becomes a serious problem, the Circle should discuss it with the facilitator who may be able to deal with it himself. If not, and it is impeding the programme, the facilitator will raise the matter at a steering committee meeting. If it cannot be resolved here, then it becomes a problem for top plant management. See Chapter 15.

54 Q. *Can you have management Circles? To whom do they report?*

A. Yes. It is an excellent idea to form Circles of managers although these are usually referred to as task forces. Apart from the fact that they are often extremely effective, there is the added advantage that such managers become even more familiar with the spirit of the concept and can be more helpful to their own Circles.

It also means that they become more familiar with the language and techniques of Circles, whereas unfamiliarity can sometimes be perceived by some less confident managers as a mild threat.

Such management Circles would normally report to the next most senior manager. If possible the groups should be formed from managers who have a common direct report.

Middle management

55 Q. *Why should we want Quality Circles?*

A. Because it will help to improve the overall performance of the section.

56 Q. *How are Circles any different from 'good supervision'?*

A. This question is a hardy annual. The first Circles will usually be formed by good supervisors. Many managers have subsequently commented that one of the most impressive benefits they have gained from Quality Circles is that their supervisors are now talking like managers. No matter how good a supervisor may be, he or she is always capable of further improvement, and Circles afford a good opportunity for this.

57 Q. *Does a successful Circle programme affect the role of middle managers?*

A. It will affect their role because they will develop a different relationship with their people, but this is a positive factor.

58 Q. *Will Quality Circles improve supervisor/management communication?*

A. This again is one of the great benefits of Quality Circle programmes.

59 Q. *What if there is more than one supervisor in the department?*

A. This does not present a problem. Presumably it is a large work area, and in such cases there is no reason why all supervisors should not have the opportunity of leading a Circle if they wish.

60 Q. *How do you prevent some supervisors from feeling inadequate?*

A. This is a problem which can arise after the initial programme has matured. The first Circle leaders will have been selected from amongst the more confident, but of course that means that eventually the last supervisors to be approached will be the least confident. Added to this will be the fear that they cannot match the achievements of the more mature groups. The only real solution is to devise supervisory training to increase the self-assurance of such supervisors prior to inviting their participation in Quality Circle activities.

Specialists (see Chapter 13)

61 Q. *How do Quality Circles relate to specialist functions?*

A. Circles must be trained to work with the specialists and the specialists must be shown how Quality Circles work. Eventually, the specialists are likely to rank amongst the greatest enthusiasts for the concept, but only if they are involved. See Chapter 14.

62 Q. *How does a Quality Circle programme affect the quality control department?*

A. One of the signs of maturity in a Circle programme is when the quality control department begins to realise that Quality Circles are actually helping to achieve the results they want. It is only when this form of interaction becomes established that an organisation can even begin to think that it is moving towards Company-Wide Quality Control. See Chapter 3.

63 Q. *Will Quality Circles cause conflicts between departments or with specialists?*

A. The training of Quality Circles should ensure that such conflicts will never arise. Circles must work with others not against them. There is no point in Quality Circles making a presentation of an idea to management if there is no chance of its acceptance by another key group. The Circle must obtain such support prior to its presentation.

64 Q. *How relevant are Circles to service industries?*

A. Again Circles will work anywhere where people work together and solve common problems. There are Circles in the gas industry, in electricity, public transport, health and welfare, and in the finance industries.

65 Q. *Should a Quality Control Inspector be in the Circle?*

A. There is nothing wrong in the idea of forming Circles of inspectors or any other kind of employee. The inspector would not normally be a permanent member of other Circles unless invited to do so by the homogeneous group.

Trade unions

All the usual questions relating to trade unions have been dealt with in some detail in Chapter 12 which is devoted to that topic. Given the nature of the questions normally raised and the structure of Chapter 12, it was felt that to answer them again in this chapter would be unnecessarily repetitive.

Steering committees

The following questions relating to the steering committee are all covered in some detail in Chapter 14 which is devoted specially to this topic. These questions, which will not be covered again here, are:

What is the role of the steering committee?
What is the role of the steering committee's chairman?
Are steering committee members volunteers?

Other questions about steering committees include the following.

66 Q. *Who guides or controls Quality Circles?*

A. Circles may be guided but not controlled as such. Within the constraints of the overall programme, Circles should have complete freedom of choice for their activities. Guidance may be given by the steering committee, facilitator, manager or others when requested by the group.

67 Q. *Do steering committee members receive training?*

A. As awareness of the importance of steering committees has grown, so has the realisation of the importance of steering committee training. Such training will make a significant difference to the effectiveness of steering committees.

The facilitator

As with the trade union questions and those relating to the steering committee, the majority of questions raised under this heading have been adequately covered in the text of Chapter 15. Questions which require further amplification include the following.

68 Q. *To whom does the facilitator answer?*

A. Normally to the chief executive. It is definitely an advantage to remove the facilitator from the political arena, which would not be the case if he reported at a lower level.

69 Q. *Does everything 'go through' the facilitator?*

A. Certainly the facilitator should be involved in all major issues, but his role is supportive rather than line functional. It would be wrong to keep information relating to Circles from the facilitator. Therefore, he should at least be informed of all developments.

70 Q. *Who makes sure that Circles stay on course?*

A. Primarily the Circle leader. The facilitator only becomes involved if asked to by the Circle.

71 Q. *How do you prevent duplication of effort in a Circle programme?*

A. The facilitator can be effective in such matters by making sure that everyone is informed of all related activities.

Circle leaders

72 Q. *Does each Circle have its own leader?*

A. Yes. The leader is usually the supervisor or next level up from the

Circle members. Occasionally, a Circle may elect its own leader but only in exceptional circumstances. As has been emphasised earlier, Circles are concerned with making better use of the existing organisation, not with creating an alternative. The supervisor is the appointed leader and should therefore at least have first refusal to lead the group. Should the supervisor not want to do so, and there are no objections to the group finding its own leader, the supervisor must be given every opportunity to be involved and also to attend management presentations. He or she should never be by-passed.

73 Q. *How do you select Circle leaders?*

    A. All leaders must be volunteers, although they may have been invited. The first leaders should be those who already have a good relationship with their workpeople.

74 Q. *What is the role of the Circle leader?*

    A. Refer to Chapter 11.

75 Q. *Is it the supervisor's Circle?*

    A. No. It is a team, and the Circle leader's role is to co-ordinate activities and keep the group together. When the group is in the meeting room, everyone has one vote and no one's opinion is any more or less important than anyone else's.

76 Q. *Can leaders help choose the problems for Circles to tackle?*

    A. As members, yes. But again they have no more influence on the choice of problem than any other member of the team.

77 Q. *What sort of problems face a leader?*

    A. The biggest problems are likely to be the occasional personality clashes which can occur in any group activity. However, experience has shown these to be somewhat rare in Quality Circles, mainly due to the method of working.

Members

78 Q. *Should Circles comprise single or multi-disciplines within a department?*

    A. Whilst multi-discipline Circles do exist and some are successful, such groups also account for a high proportion of Circle failures. Wherever possible homogeneous groups should be the aim.

79 Q. *How are Circle members selected?*

A. Selection is not a good word. Members are volunteers. That is not to say that some may be invited to join. In the event that more people wish to join a Circle than can be accommodated, the alternatives are either to form more than one Circle or to reduce the number by some form of lottery. Deliberate selection is likely to bring accusations of favouritism which will, of course, be very unhelpful.

It is most important to ensure that all Circle and non-Circle members are made fully aware that it is their section's Circle and that all will have the opportunity to become involved if they wish.

80 Q. *What happens if there are insufficient volunteers in a given work area?*

A. Then it is impossible to start a Circle there straight away. Better to start somewhere else but make sure that the employees in the first work area have an opportunity to see what is going on. Perhaps it might be an idea to let them see a presentation by an existing Circle or even invite someone from another organisation to come and talk to them.

It is rare for people to remain permanently unmoved if they have the opportunity to see the enthusiasm of other groups.

81 Q. *What happens if someone wants to leave a Circle?*

A. There should never be any pressure on anyone to remain in a group if they do not wish to. People should be free to join and free to leave. However, someone leaving a Circle should be regarded as a warning sign that all might not be well, and that it would be worth making one or two discreet enquiries.

82 Q. *Are manual workers capable of understanding the techniques used?*

A. Such a question is a sad reflection on the attitudes of a few managers towards their direct employees. When asked to reflect on the hobbies and pastimes of such employees many such managers finally agree that a job does not necessarily relate to intelligence, and in fact Circles made up of totally unskilled members, such as cleaning staff and labourers, have achieved incredible results and have had no difficulty whatsoever in learning and using the techniques. The level of education of most direct employees is more a reflection on our educational systems than it is on the intelligence of the people concerned.

83 Q. *What about the time lost during Circle meetings?*

A. The enthusiasm, greater care, and the projects of the Circles themselves will more than compensate for the loss of time.

Circles will almost always produce more in the one-hour-shorter week, with Circles, than they did previously.

84 Q. *What about fast-moving process work?*

A. Of course, it would not be justifiable to stop a fast-moving process in order to hold Quality Circle meetings.

Management knows this and so do the potential Circle members. In such situations the Circle members will often propose meetings during the lunch break, after shift time, or during a break between operations. If people want to participate, it is surprising how enterprising they can be. People can usually find time for a meeting if they really want to.

85 Q. *Are there problems with mixed ethnic groups?*

A. Quite the contrary. Quality Circles tend to reduce such problems. The author has experience of many such Circles. One calls itself 'Ebony and Ivory' and another, the 'Black and White Minstrels'.

86 Q. *Are there problems with labour turnover in Quality Circles?*

A. Yes. There can be no doubt that stability is a valuable ingredient. Some labour turnover is inevitable, and in such cases it is worth while training the new members to the Circle independently from the group prior to their introduction.

87 Q. *In a large area should membership be rotated?*

A. Definitely no. It is much better to start another Circle. There is no limit to the number of Circles which can be formed, and 100% involvement is the number to aim for.

Non-members

88 Q. *Do Quality Circles split up work forces?*

A. Not if the programme has been properly developed and the Circle properly trained with a good facilitator.

The problem has occurred, and when it has, the most common cause has been due to pressure from management attempting to force a

Circle to select a problem of its choice. This has caused non-Circle members to react.

Generally speaking, Quality Circles tend to build bridges rather than destroy them.

89 Q. *What reaction can be expected from those who do not volunteer initially?*

A. Extremely varied, and it depends upon the historical industrial relations climate. Initial hostility is relatively rare but does exist. Provided that such hostility is not sufficient to discourage the volunteers, it should die away quickly and usually does. There are several cases where hostility has been reversed to the extent that requests have been made to start another Circle in only a matter of two or three weeks after the first Circle has started.

90 Q. *Do non-Circle members accept the recommendations of the Circle?*

A. Yes, if they are given the opportunity to contribute their own ideas and are kept informed of progress by the Circle. In most cases non-Circle members are very co-operative.

91 Q. *Will non-Circle members cover the work during Circle meetings?*

A. Invariably, if they are approached in the right manner. This is particularly true when some Circle projects have proved to make life better at the workplace.

Organisation

92 Q. *How long before a Circle becomes effective?*

A. It depends how effectiveness is being measured. If enthusiasm and morale are considered to be important then the answer is 'immediately'. Usually, the first project is selected within 2 to 4 weeks from commencement and the training constitutes guided experience. This project may be completed within 6 to 8 weeks from the first Circle meeting or it may take 6 months. This is not really important. The most important factor is whether people are enjoying Circle activities and look forward to meetings. If enthusiasm can be maintained the results will show soon enough. As far as the techniques are concerned, it is unlikely that many Circles will be fully skilled in the use of all the techniques in less than six months and the facilitator should always be available to give guidance when required.

93 Q. *How do we overcome the time problem if some members are absent?*

A. Absenteeism from Circles is always a nuisance when it occurs. If it is due to lack of interest then something is fundamentally wrong. Some Circles have deliberately suspended their meetings for 3 to 4 weeks during the peak holiday period. This is not to be recommended as a general solution. Better to suspend the project, but use the meeting time for some related activity. Suspending meetings can become a habit.

94 Q. *How do Circles relate to one another?*

A. Usually extremely well. Circles assisting one another in the collection of data is one sign of a healthy programme.

Meetings

95 Q. *Will Circles just lead to even more unproductive meetings?*

A. No. Circles are extremely productive. In fact, the techniques and the manner in which they are used give every meeting a purpose, and that is to progress towards the eventual solution of the problem. Circles do not keep minutes in the usual way, and do not follow the formal agenda sequence of committee meetings. Therefore, they do not waste a lot of time going through minutes of the last meeting, matters arising and so forth.

96 Q. *Where do Circles meet?*

A. Facilities must be made available and this can become a problem with a rapidly growing programme. Meeting rooms should be free from distractions and noise, and members should be able to keep their materials in a safe place.

97 Q. *What happens if management does not allow a Circle to meet?*

A. Occasionally there will be situations and crises where Circle meetings become inconvenient. Usually the Circle will be aware of the circumstances and if the problem is discussed with its members, they may even decide to hold the meeting outside company time. If a meeting is suspended without adequate explanation, or it happens frequently, the Circle will interpret this as a lack of management support and may discontinue its activities. The steering committee must formulate a policy covering this situation, and should be referred to before any Circle meetings are suspended.

98 Q. *Is one hour per week long enough?*

A. Surprisingly yes. It is amazing how much a Circle can actually achieve in a single hour. Very occasionally, a Circle may need longer for a special reason, but if so it must sell the idea to its manager who will make the final decision.

99 Q. *What problems exist in multi-shift operations?*

A. The Circle concept can be quite flexible in shift work. There are many cases where each shift has its own Circle, there are others where Circles span shifts. Obviously, in the latter case, some agreement must be reached about payment if some Circle members are meeting outside their own shift time, but this is usually reached.

100 Q. *How can you release people for Circle meetings?*

A. Circle meetings usually take place at the least disruptive time in the week. Friday afternoons are often quiet times in some operations. In others, the meetings may take place during the break between operations.

Problem selection

101 Q. *There are so many problems—how can Circles help?*

A. Although a Quality Circle only tackles one problem at a time, there are a great many problems which are only caused by carelessness resulting from a lack of job interest. Many of these problems will simply disappear when Circles are formed. David Hutchins Associates usually refer to this as the 'sprinkling of magic dust'!

102 Q. *How does a Circle select its problems?*

A. It is important that the Circles choose their own problems. That does not mean that problems may not be suggested by others. See Chapter 6.

103 Q. *Who decides if the project is accepted?*

A. If a Circle tackles a project which is known by its managers or others to be undesirable for some reason, the Circle will accept this provided that the reasons are explained to its members. Of course, if this happens frequently they will put a different interpretation on the reasons.

104 Q. *What kind of problems do they select?*

A. Anything which relates to their work and which they believe they can tackle and solve. Waste, delays, incorrect equipment, losses, are all common items. See Chapter 6.

105 Q. *Do Circles solve problems of any importance?*

A. All problems are important if they frustrate the people involved, even though they may sometimes appear trivial to others. Although many projects may save very considerable sums, these must be regarded as a bonus. It must be remembered that the main purpose of Quality Circles is to create a better work environment through which management benefits from a more co-operative work force. The one hour per week is the Circles' hour which may or may not produce benefits for management. Management's pay-off comes in the other 38 or 39 hours of the working week.

106 Q. *How do Circles tackle problems which have outside causes?*

A. They cannot directly, but if they can gain the co-operation of others, they may work together for a mutually acceptable improvement.

107 Q. *Should a time limit be set on problems?*

A. This question shows a fundamental lack of understanding of the concept. It is really no concern of managements how long the project takes. See also Question 105.

108 Q. *What if the Circle cannot solve the problem?*

A. Fortunately this is quite rare. Circles can be very resourceful. If failure seems likely, the Circle may abandon the project, but more usually, the facilitator will suggest that an outside specialist join the group to work with them.

In one case a university professor joined a Circle and stayed with it until the presentation.

109 Q. *Can Circles work in a fast changing jobbing situation?*

A. See also Question 16. Yes. Whilst the product may vary, usually the work locations, procedures, tooling etc., are standardised and there are many problems relating to these. Such work environments frequently offer many opportunities for housekeeping improvements.

110 Q. *What if a change of design affects a patent or outside contractual requirement?*

A. These situations will frequently cause considerable delays in the implementation of accepted suggestions. The reasons for this should be clearly given to the Circle, and these will usually be accepted.

111 Q. *Can Circles affect manning levels?*

A. It is possible but unlikely. It is not unusual for a Quality Circle to work on a project which ultimately results in a reduction in man-hours, but obviously, if a management were to take advantage of this, it is almost certain that the Circle programme would come to an abrupt end. Management knows this and so do the workpeople. Additionally, it must be remembered that the jobs concerned would be those of the Circle members themselves and they would be unlikely to present a suggestion if they feared that management would take that kind of advantage. Normally, if a Circle were to arrive at a solution of that nature, the members would discuss it fully with all their colleagues, and if relevant, with the union, and their presentation to management would almost certainly include a suggestion how the saved time could be effectively utilised.

It must also be remembered that a Circle programme is intended to make a company more competitive and it would be hoped that an effective programme would be more likely to create jobs than to abolish them.

One British company has claimed that it does not believe it would have survived the recession in 1980–2 if it had not been for the activities of its extensive Quality Circle programme.

112 Q. *What happens when they have solved all the problems?*

A. Surprisingly this question is asked seriously and frequently. What an incredible world it would be if there were no problems left to solve! Even if it were possible, it should not interfere with the Circle's activities because by that time the Circle would have progressed from problem solving to problem prevention and on to improvement and developmental activities. There is always something that a Circle can be doing to make improvements.

Presentations

113 Q. *How are presentations made to management?*

A. The Circle presentation is usually made at the completion of a project after the members have verified the validity of their solution. Sometimes however, an interim presentation may be made, if the project is likely to take a long time, or if the Circle needs a management decision before some aspect of the problem can be studied.

The presentation should always be made to the Circle's own manager, although sometimes others may be invited. Subsequently, selected presentations may be repeated to other groups such as the steering committee, other departments or at Circle conventions.

114 Q. *Who gets the recognition?*

A. All the members of the group and anyone who may have contributed ideas or assisted the Circle. All Circle members should be encouraged to participate in the presentation, and ideally those others who have helped should be invited to attend.

115 Q. *Is the presentation the end-product of the project?*

A. Solving the problem and successfully implementing the improvement is the end-product.

The presentation is intended as a means by which management can show its support of the Circle by listening to its story, and giving thanks to Circle members for their efforts. The value of the presentation to the members comes from the natural human need to talk about achievement. Presentations should be fun, and the highlight of Circle activities.

116 Q. *Would the recommendations be written?*

A. Yes. It is always a good idea for all projects to be recorded. This does not require volumes of written explanation. The Wedgwood case study in Chapter 7 is an excellent example of the manner in which Circle presentations may be recorded.

117 Q. *Will too much time be spent on the presentation as opposed to the problem?*

A. The more polished the presentation the better. It makes a good impression and will increase the commitment of all. Bearing in mind that the one hour per week is 'the Circles' hour', it is up to them to judge how much time to allow for their preparation.

118 Q. *Can an individual present his or her own problem or solution to management?*

A. A Quality Circle is a group or team, and it is strongly recommended that all members are encouraged to participate in presentations. Even the most shy members will gain confidence by being encouraged to take an active part.

119 Q. *What happens if the recommendations cost money?*

A. Management has the right to reject a recommendation if it so wishes. Having said that, rejection is quite rare because Circles are usually very thorough in their work and generally produce extremely persuasive arguments in their recommendations.

120 Q. *How much does cost affect the likelihood of management's acceptance of solutions?*

A. Obviously such factors as cost and resources must be evaluated by management in the light of economic circumstances and other plans. If these factors outweigh the benefits from the Circle's project, the recommendations may be rejected. As stated earlier, in such situations it is important that management gives an acceptable explanation for rejecting a project. Fortunately, such rejections are rare.

121 Q. *Will Circles have authority to make changes?*

A. Circles do not have any authority as such. It is up to them to sell an idea to management in their presentation.

122 Q. *Is there an anticlimax after a successful presentation?*

A. Yes. The more successful the project, the more the Circle will be likely to crash afterwards. This is particularly true with new Circles. Usually, however, a little support from the facilitator in the next one or two meetings will carry the Circle into its next project. Momentum will then be restored.

Measurement

123 Q. *How do you measure the results of a Quality Circle programme?*

A. It depends which factors are uppermost in the minds of managers. These include: cost reduction, quality and productivity improvements, waste and energy reductions, increased pride, loyalty and trust, and improvements in morale and general attitudes. See Chapters 9 and 10.

124 Q. *Do Quality Circles require appraisal/monitoring meetings?*

A. This is part of the function of the steering committee. Of course, some Circles will be better organised than others, and it is important to develop a mechanism whereby mutual cross fertilisation between Circles becomes possible.

125 Q. *How cost-effective are Quality Circles?*

A. Some Circles may never make tangible savings. Others will. On balance, the tangible benefits from the cost-saving projects of a number of Circles will more than justify the programme. A minimum of 3:1 benefit to cost is likely in the first year rising to an average of 8 or 10:1 for a more established programme. *Individual Circles should never be compared on the basis of how much they have saved.*

126 Q. *Will Quality Circles influence the cost of the end product?*

A. This must be one of the ultimate objectives, as explained in Chapter 2. One of the main attractions of Circles to their members is the fact that they have the opportunity to help make their organisation more successful.

127 Q. *Do monetary savings ever cause problems?*

A. No, but it is important to read Chapter 16 carefully to understand why.

128 Q. *How do you cover implementation costs?*

A. Apart from the facilitator's salary, the costs of initiating a Circle programme should not be high, and this includes the cost of consultancy. On the basis that you only get what you pay for, consultancy will not be free if it has any value, but at the same time it should not be expensive either. Check the claims of any would-be experts before accepting their services, and be suspicious of anyone who has conducted less than 10–20 complete programmes and is unwilling to invite you to check this with his clients. Your company and your people are too important for you to take chances.

A badly implemented programme may be impossible to resurrect and in the end will cost far more than good advice in the first instance.

129 Q. *How long to break even after initial set up costs have been measured?*

A. It is impossible to say. In some cases the total costs of the first two years might be saved even before the first leaders have completed their training. In others it will take longer, but will usually be less than six months from the initial outlay.

130 Q. *What is the failure rate of Quality Circles?*

A. It depends whether they were properly trained. If the rules of this book are carefully followed and a well-experienced consultant or trainer is used, failures should be very few indeed. In such cases, the total collapse of a programme will be caused by factors outside the influence of the programme. Even the best-trained organisations should expect the occasional loss of an individual Circle, again due to external influences. It would be surprising if such failures amounted to more than one Circle in twenty.

Failures due to badly implemented programmes resulting from bad advice are believed to be almost 100%. Very few self-help programmes have survived for more than one year in the UK.

131 Q. *What are the potential causes of failure?*

A. The most likely causes in order of importance are:
1 Ill-conceived advice
2 Lack of management commitment
3 Deliberate obstruction from within the organisation
4 Poor choice of facilitator
5 Inadequate steering committee

132 Q. *If Circles fail, who is to blame?*

A. The possible reasons are many, varied and potentially complex. Better to seek a review of the programme by an expert and take his advice than start recriminations which will only lead to more entrenched attitudes and a worse situation.

133 Q. *What would be the results of failure?*

A. Of course it depends on how and why the programme failed. Failure can range from sudden and catastrophic failure, due to the withdrawal of support by a key group, to the gentle sinking back into the sand, resulting from lack of interest or support. Either way, there is always the likelihood of loss of face by someone and the need to re-establish the credibility of the concept.

The possibility of failure underlines the importance of sound advice in the early stages.

134 Q. *Do Circles work best in labour intensive industries?*

   A. There may be more difficulties in getting people together for a meeting in some situations, but there is no evidence to suggest that any one industry is either better or worse than any other.

135 Q. *How do Circles ensure that problems do not recur?*

   A. This is one of the advantages that Circles have over other forms of problem solving. Because the problems relate to their own work, they have complete control of the situation. Problem prevention is one of the most powerful signs of maturity in a developing Quality Circle.

Motivation and reward

This was regarded as such an important topic that it was covered almost exhaustively in Chapter 16 and it is recommended that the points highlighted in that chapter are thoroughly digested before a Circle programme is introduced.
One or two questions which were not covered in the chapter include:

136 Q. *Is it possible to create the right environment before implementing Circles?*

   A. Difficulty here will depend upon the industrial history of the organisation. It is essential that all levels of employee involved have a clear idea of what to expect before the programme is commenced. An atmosphere of trust is essential and the formation of a steering committee along the lines described in Chapter 14 will help considerably.

137 Q. *How do you get people interested?*

   A. Only by presenting the concept in an attractive way and by answering all questions openly and honestly. Whilst Rome was not built in one day, it is likely that there will be sufficient volunteers to get started, provided the concept is well explained.

138 Q. *What happens if the project reduces the work content when payment by results schemes are in operation?*

   A. It is important to the smooth running of such schemes that equality of earning power is maintained in the incentive scheme, and that standards of performance are maintained after the introduction of Quality Circles. This is an area for negotiation, but Circles must accept some re-evaluation if the work content of a task is reduced. How such savings are subsequently appropriated is, of course, a topic for consideration by the steering committee.

139 Q. *Would it save money if we stopped piecework?*

A. Whilst direct payment by results schemes are still predominant in some industries such as the clothing and textile industries, they are generally regarded as less than satisfactory and are being replaced in most others.

It is the belief of the author that eventually Quality Circles will produce higher levels of productivity than can ever be achieved by direct payment schemes.

140 Q. *Will Quality Circles work in a piecework environment?*

A. Surprisingly, yes. In the early part of the author's involvement with Quality Circle training it was expected that it might be difficult to implement them here. However, problems have proved to be almost non-existent.

Other group activities

141 Q. *Why Quality Circles rather than other small group activities?*

A. Strictly speaking, although an individual Circle might be described as a 'small group activity', this is not true of the concept as a whole.

Chapters 2 and 3 show how Quality Circles are an integral part of a totally new philosophy of management and do not stand on their own. They therefore cannot be compared with other types of small group activities.

142 Q. *How do Quality Circles differ from 'Briefing Groups', 'Communication Groups', 'Action-Centred Leadership', 'Task Forces', 'Project Groups', 'Job Enlargement and Job Enrichment', etc.?*

A. *(1) Briefing Groups* These are not concerned with solving problems, only with passing down information. They are also referred to as cascade briefing.

(2) Communication Groups Superficially, they may seem similar to Quality Circles but they are only concerned with highlighting problems and not with solving them. They are also referred to as 'grumble shops', 'bitching meetings', 'canteen committees', and so on. These groups are more likely to use the meetings to criticise others than to highlight problems in their own work.

(3) Action-Centred Leadership, Task Forces, Project Groups, etc. Whilst these groups may be involved in problem-solving activities they differ fundamentally from Quality Circles in several ways.

3.1 Management usually selects the membership of these groups which, unlike true Circles, consist of people from different disciplines. Indeed it is the variety of the disciplines represented that constitutes the main usefulness of such groups.

3.2 The problem is selected by management not by the group, as occurs with Circles.

3.3 The group usually disperses after the successful completion of the project although members may be re-formed into different groups for the analysis of other problems.

Circles, on the other hand, are a permanent grouping or team.

(4) Job Enlargement and Job Enrichment These activities do not represent an alternative to Circles. They can take place alongside or within the groups. A certain amount of J.E. will take place as a result of Circles being in existence.

It must be emphasised that none of these activities is in conflict with Quality Circles, and all may exist side by side in the same company. This can lead to an extremely powerful form of organisational development.

General problems

143 Q. *How do we break down 'them and us' attitudes?*

A. Such attitudes may lead to some suspicions when the concept is being presented but since Circles build bridges, their introduction should produce a dramatic improvement in relationships. A properly constructed steering committee will also help to do this. See also Question 33.

144 Q. *Is it necessary to introduce single status canteens etc., before commencing Circles?*

A. The divisions created by selective facilities for refreshments, toilets, car parking, etc., and other conditions of employment far outweigh any conceivable advantages and are best eliminated, whether Circles are to be introduced or not. However, Circles do operate in even the most extreme cases of such environments.

145 Q. *What restriction do strict customer specifications have on Circle activities?*

A. In industries such as defence where tight contractual control is exercised in specification requirements, there will inevitably be some added constraints on the activities of Quality Circles. Provided that the reasons for such restrictions are clearly explained this should not lead to problems. It will also mean that the recommendations of some projects may not be implemented immediately, and again it will be necessary to ensure that Circle members are aware of the reasons for this.

146 Q. *Do the needs of productivity/quality ever give rise to conflicts?*

A. Not if the true meaning of quality is properly understood. From a study of Chapter 2 it will be appreciated that hold-ups, delays, wastage, losses, rework and scrap are all quality problems. If everyone is concentrating on these items, productivity will take care of itself. There is no point in making twice as many items if half of them are rubbish. Much better to make a few more good ones for the same effort. Quality Circle activities make this possible.

147 Q. *How much power does a Circle have?*

A. None save management's desire to show its support by accepting the Circle's ideas. 'Circle Power' is a manifestation of the power of enthusiasm, and that is a very persuasive force. See also Questions 28, 90, 97, 102, 103, 119.

148 Q. *How do you prevent 'over-design' with Circle type activities?*

A. The facilitator can help to prevent such a situation occurring. There is no value either to the Circle or management if they 're-invent the wheel'.

149 Q. *Can Quality Circles work where poor industrial relations exist?*

A. Yes, but this is where failures are most likely to occur. In such situations, the appointment of a high-calibre facilitator is essential. This, together with the construction of a truly representative steering committee with union representation, and the services of a consultant experienced in these situations are also essential if success is to be achieved. Hopefully, the establishment of a good pilot programme will lead to a general improvement in industrial relations, and this would be one of the key objectives in introducing the programme.

Company-Wide Quality Control

150 Q. *Do Circles work in isolation or as an integral part of company activities?*

A. Initially, Circle members will tend to work on projects confined to their own work and will only involve others to a limited extent. As the Circle begins to mature, it will begin to tackle larger projects and will require help and information from others.

This is the essence of Company-Wide Quality Control. Circles should be involved in the achievement of corporate goals in line with the definition given in Chapter 2. The steering committee can play an important part in the development of this objective.

151 Q. *How can Circles be integrated with Quality Control?*

A. To some extent this will happen naturally. The process can be advanced considerably by involving Quality Control in the initial training programme.

152 Q. *How do Quality Circles relate to suppliers and customers?*

A. Circles can often get suppliers to do things that buyers and quality assurance personnel have found to be impossible. It is surprising how much effect the actual users of the materials can have on a recalcitrant supplier.

If a company has introduced a successful Quality Circle programme, why should it not publicise this fact as a means of impressing its market? This is consistent with the overall objective of being more competitive. Why not also impress upon suppliers the virtues of the concept in order to encourage them to follow suit? One must add that care must be taken *not* to use undue influence in this respect. A Circle programme can only be successful if people want to participate, not if they are forced to. This is just as true at senior management level as it is amongst direct employees.

Summary of Part IV

Chapters 16 and 17

1   Circles must be rewarded but not through direct financial benefits. Recognition is an important form of reward. Quality Circle programmes and reward based suggestion schemes are fundamentally different.

2   Quality Circles mature from simple problem solving through monitoring and improvement to the ultimate state of 'self-control'.

3   Newsletters, notice boards and Circle conventions are important methods for helping in Circle development.

4   Societies of Quality Circles now exist in several countries.

5   There are hundreds of questions relevant to Quality Circle programmes. Each organisation should endeavour to determine the questions relevant to its own programme prior to implementation.

PART V The history of Quality Circles

Preface

No text on Quality Circles would be complete if it failed to give an account of their origins and development around the world. This history is not only important to an understanding of the philosophy of the subject but also gives a further insight into the possibilities that this exciting concept affords.

19 Quality Circles in Japan and America

Contrary to some claims made by some sources in the West, Quality Circles originated in Japan and not in the USA. The misunderstanding probably originated from confusion about the true nature of the help given to the Japanese by the USA after World War II. It is true that the United States introduced the concept of Quality Control into Japan, and Chapter 2 of this text explains how Quality Control is an integral part of Company-Wide Quality Control which also includes Quality Circles. But the Americans also introduced Taylorism, and it was the failure of this concept in Japan that led eventually to Quality Circles.

Quality Circles themselves originated in Japan in 1962 as a result of 17 years' development of a new style of management involving Quality Control principles. Japanese education in Quality Control began with seminars intended to increase awareness of the importance of the subject.

The first recorded application of Western-style statistical Quality Control in Japan appeared in the telecommunication industries as part of the plan to restore the entire Japanese telephone and telegraph communication system. During 1946, the Japanese Union of Scientists and Engineers (JUSE) was formed, and began to further the application of Quality Control throughout Japanese industry. This early work was based on American Standards Organisation publications Z1-1, Z1-2 and Z1-3, W. A. Shewhart's *The Control of Quality of the Manufactured Product* (Van Nostrand, 1931), E. S. Pearson's pre-war articles and publications in *Biometrika* and a few other publications which were the only materials available at that time.

The first major Quality Control training programme for the restoration of Japanese industry on a nationwide scale was introduced in 1949 by the Chairman of JUSE, Ichiro Ishikawa, the father of Professor Kaoru Ishikawa. At the same time the Japanese Management Association and the Japanese Standards Organisation independently commenced Quality Control training programmes.

In 1950, the Japanese Government in collaboration with GHQ, American Occupation Forces, invited the American statistical expert W. Edwards Deming to lecture on statistical method in Japan. This was followed by an invitation from JUSE to give a further eight days of Quality Control seminars.

Deming made such an impact on the Japanese that he, together with Joseph

M. Juran, is probably one of the two best-known and celebrated foreigners in modern Japanese industry. Deming greatly broadened the Japanese perspective of Quality Control as a means of becoming more competitive and made them aware of the value of data analysis as a tool for improvement. For this purpose, he introduced a wide range of simple analytical techniques together with the Plan-Do-Check-Act cycle which Japanese refer to as the 'Deming Wheel' (Fig. 19.1).

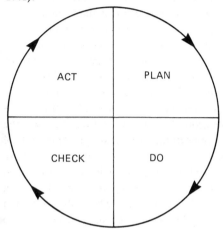

Fig 19.1 The Deming Wheel

Fig 19.2 The Deming Award Medal

The Japanese were so impressed by his techniques that in the following year they established the Deming Prize (Fig. 19.2).

This prize has the same status in Japan as the Queen's Award to Industry has in Britain, but it differs in the sense that it is awarded for Quality achievements, whereas the Queen's Award is based upon export performance and technical achievement. One of the main purposes of the award is to encourage both industry and employees to adopt the techniques expounded by Dr Deming.

A second result of the Deming Seminars was the creation of a National Quality Month, about which more anon.

When the Deming Prize was instituted it was estimated that to rely upon the existing education process as the means by which the Deming ideas could be introduced could take as long as 35 years. Clearly industry could not wait that long. By 1955, the Japanese had begun a massive series of 'self-improvement' programmes on radio and throughout the media.

It was about that time that labour unrest and worker indifference began to emerge as a significant problem in Japan. The Japanese believed the causes were due mainly to having adopted the 'Taylor' system of management (see Chapter 3) from the USA. They concluded that this system was alien to their culture, but initially were concerned mainly with its effect on supervision. They realised the importance of the role of the supervisor and began to concentrate the bulk of this new training effort on foremen and supervisory grades.

In Japan, unlike elsewhere in the world, this training was not conducted in colleges but organised and executed on companies' premises. The training was intended to build up the confidence of group leaders and to teach the Deming techniques. It was realised that an opportunity to make presentations of achievements in problem solving was a valuable form of recognition for those achievements and at the same time, a good way of transferring ideas to others. Consequently, the trained foremen were given the opportunity of making presentations of their achievements at public seminars, to which other foremen were invited. At that time, no other country had developed such an approach to training. By 1960, not only had this concept spread throughout Japan, but, there were already large conventions devoted especially to foremen.

In 1954, Joseph M. Juran was invited to lecture in Japan where he led seminars for both top executives and middle managers. During these seminars he emphasised the concept of 'Management of Quality', which formed the basis of the present Japanese concept 'Company-Wide Quality Control' (CWQC).

Although the basic theory behind CWQC was developed in the United States, no Western organisation has managed to apply it successfully. This is because CWQC is a people-based philosophy which cannot operate in Taylor-based organisations. Fortunately for the Japanese, however, they had already begun to remove the road-blocks of Taylorism, and the development of the supervisor was an important step forward.

Although significant improvements in performance had been achieved in Japan by 1960, management was still faced with serious industrial relations problems. Kaoru Ishikawa suggested that these problems could only be resolved by increasing the job satisfaction of employees. It was then that he suggested the idea of reintroducing the craftsmanship concept along the lines of Chapters 2 and 3 of this book.

Awareness of the importance of Quality Control to the economic success of Japan had reached such proportions by 1960 that the concept of 'Quality Month' was introduced, and November 1960 was designated as the first of these. Nowadays any visitor to Japan in November will become aware of the large number of the Quality conventions and Quality-related functions that take place both nationally and within companies. During the first Quality Month the Q-mark and Q-flags were both formally adopted as the symbol of Quality-related activities.

Fig 19.3 The Q Symbol

In April 1962 the magazine *Gemba to QC* recommended the formation of Quality Circles (known as Quality Control Circles in Japan). At the same time, the editorial committee began organising and propagating the idea, and the concept of Quality Circles proper was born. In May 1962 the first Quality Circle was registered with the QC headquarters of JUSE. This Circle was formed at the Nippon Telephone and Telegraph Corporation. By the end of the year over 35 companies were reported to have commenced QC activities.

Besides recognising the importance of training supervisors, the Japanese quickly realised that presentations to management were an essential part of Quality Control Circle activities, and this idea was incorporated into the concept. They also realised the value of making presentations to a wider audience, and Circles were given the opportunity of making their presentations at public functions. The effect of this was not only to boost the confidence and self-assurance of the Circles still further, but it also became a significant means of introducing them into other organisations.

Once established, the growth of the concept was phenomenal. In November 1962 the first annual Quality Control Conference for foremen was held, and because of the rapid growth of Quality Control Circles, extended sessions were introduced at subsequent conferences to discuss this topic. In May 1963 the first Quality Control Circle Conference was held in Sendai, Northern Japan.

In 1964 the first regional chapters were established in Kanto, Tokai, Houriku and Kuki districts. Later, the entire country was divided into 14 chapters under a nationwide organisation, and each chapter was to hold its own conventions and other activities for members.

The rate of growth continued to increase and by June 1967 there were 10 000 Circles registered with JUSE and many more in existence but not officially recorded. By 1969 the total had risen to an incredible 20 000 Circles registered and in that year the 100th QC Circle Conference was held in Tokyo, and one year later the figure reached 30 000 registrations. By this time the Circle concept had become truly nationwide and formed an integral part of Company-Wide Quality Control (CWQC).

Responsibility for the spread of Quality Circles to non-Chinese character countries is largely attributable to Joseph M. Juran. It was he who recommended that the European Organisation for Quality Control (EOQC) should hold a special session on the subject at its conference in Stockholm, Sweden, in June 1966. After the conference, Juran wrote several articles referring to it, and it was included in his now famous seminars and textbooks.

As stated in the preface to this work, Juran declared in the late 1960s: 'the Quality Circle movement is a tremendous one which no other country seems able to imitate. Through the development of this movement, Japan will be swept to world leadership in Quality'.

Development in Brazil and the United States

Whilst many companies in many countries had attempted to imitate Quality Circles in the 1960s and early 1970s, none had proved successful. This led to several adaptations of the concept, including one famous variant developed by an American, Phil Crosby, known as 'Zero Defects'. Whilst ZD, as it was known, appeared to be successful for a time, and received widespread publicity it eventually disappeared. All these variants failed because they were really only cosmetic adaptations or additions to the entrenched Taylor system of management.

The first real breakthrough came almost simultaneously in Brazil and the United States. Oleg Greshner of Johnson & Johnson in Brazil managed to develop a successful programme based entirely on the Japanese approach with Company-Wide Quality Control as its basis. This programme is well described in the book *The Japanese Approach to Product Quality* edited jointly by Naoto Sasaki and the present author. After Greshner's success, Quality Circles began to spread throughout Brazilian industry and by 1979 it was claimed that 30 000 Quality Circles were active in that country.

In the United States the first recorded success occurred at the Lockheed space missile factory in California. Interest at Lockheed was initiated by a visit to the factory by a Japanese team of Circle leaders in 1972. This was followed by a visit to Japan by a team from Lockheed in order to discover more about the fascinating concept. From this experience, Lockheed adapted Japanese materials to create the first training materials of their kind written in English. These were largely developed by Jefferson F. Beardsley, the Quality Circle Training Co-ordinator, with assistance from his colleague Donald L. Dewar Quality Circle Co-ordinator under the authority of Wayne S. Rieker the Manufacturing Manager.

The first Circles in Lockheed were formed in October 1974 and proved to be incredibly successful, not only in their projects, but in their effect on morale. In less than three years Lockheed claimed that these first Circles had produced a net saving of over $3 million and, like Greshner, a benefit to cost ratio of an estimated 8:1.

Following this initial programme Beardsley, Dewar and Rieker left the company to establish consultancies. Those three practitioners then, independently of each other, began to develop the Circle movement in the United States. The first companies to follow Lockheed included Northrop, Rockwell International, Honeywell, Hughes Aircraft, and Westinghouse Corporation. Towards the end of the decade the success of these companies and the three consultants had reached international proportions.

An international society, the International Association of Quality Circles, had been formed and the number of companies that had commenced Quality Circle programmes was increasing exponentially. By the summer of 1982 it was claimed that there were over 5000 organisations with Quality Circles, including national banks, an airline, the US Airforce, naval dockyards, hospitals, and a wide range of manufacturing organisations.

However, the widespread interest in the concept in the USA and the ensuing publicity attracted other consultants into the field. This unfortunately has led to an alarming dilution of the philosophy, and there are now (1984) fears being expressed by some of the pioneers that the entire field is being undermined by this development.

Another fear, expressed both by the author of this book and by the Japanese, is that in the United States Quality Circles appear to be regarded almost entirely as a behavioural science concept. There seems to be very little recognition of the importance of Company-Wide Quality Control. The author believes that this lack of understanding will prevent the realisation of the true potential of the Quality Circles, and might lead eventually to their disintegration.

In an article on Quality Circles which appeared in the August 1982 edition of *International Management*, Kaoru Ishikawa expressed doubts about the long-term survival of Quality Circles in the West because of the lack of understanding of the importance of Company-Wide Quality Control. This view cannot be expressed too strongly. The Quality Circle conventions, inter-company visits, training seminars, the national activities including 'Quality Month', and the general awareness of the importance of Quality Control are all essential foundations for ultimate success.

20 Developments in the UK and continental Europe—a personal view

The first awareness of Quality Circles came to Europe through the EOQC Conference held in Stockholm in 1966. After this conference nothing much happened for several years. Those who were aware of the concept in those early times, including the present author, did not consider it likely that anything which had been developed in Japan would be adaptable to European society.

For example, in 1969 Harry Drew, the Director General of the Defence Quality Assurance Board, visited Japan with Frank Nixon, a Quality Director from Rolls Royce. Later he wrote to me and said that he returned to the UK full of enthusiasm for the Quality Circle concept but nobody would listen to him. Shortly afterwards Dr Brian Jenney of Birmingham University included Quality Circles in the management syllabus of the educational requirements of the Institute of Quality Assurance. In 1972 a Japanese book entitled *Japan's Quality Control Circles* was published in English by the Asian Productivity Organisation with an introduction by Frank Nixon of Rolls Royce Ltd.

In this introduction Frank Nixon wrote 'Quality Control Circles represent something which is much bigger, much more fundamental to management, than Quality Control as it is understood in most Western countries. The Circles are, basically, an effective means by which the senior managements of a large sector of Japanese industry have succeeded in involving their employees in the aims and the purposes of their enterprises. This involvement, and the special factors which have made the Quality Control movement possible, are underlying reasons for Japan's rapid rate of progress'.

I first introduced an appreciation of Quality Circles into my three-day 'Management of Quality Assurance' seminars in 1972. This was also the time when quality assurance was becoming increasingly demanded as a contractual requirement by large procurement organisations such as the Ministry of Defence, electronics companies and the automotive industry. At this time I became increasingly concerned that these developments, whilst important, appeared to concentrate almost entirely on systems and procedures, and lacked any appreciable attempt to involve people. It was at this point that I took a deeper look at Quality Circles, and it happened to coincide with a visit to the UK by a Japanese Quality specialist Dr Kano. As secretary of one of the regional branches of the Institute of Quality Assurance, I was fortunate to become involved with some of the organisation of his UK tour. It was at this point that I began to realise that there was nothing inherently Japanese in Quality Circles; they represented as much as anything a better way of treating people.

I subsequently began to seek out all available information, and fortunately, in 1978, made the acquaintance of my good friend Professor Naoto Sasaki of Sophia University. When I told him my feelings he replied that he happened to be an acquaintance of Professor Ishikawa, the father figure of Quality Circles in Japan. He said that when he returned to Japan he would inform Professor Ishikawa of my interest.

I later received some correspondence from Professor Ishikawa in which he offered to come to the UK, to give a seminar on the topic. Included with his letter was some material on Quality Circles which gave me a much greater insight into the concept, and it was from this material that I understood clearly the reasons why Taylorism prevents the emergence of effective Circle programmes in our society. The effect of this realisation was electrifying, and from that moment my mind was flooded with the implications.

At that time, as a lecturer in a college of higher education, I had no platform to project these ideas with any impact, and the college was certainly not in a position to finance a speculative function involving an eminent Japanese expert. Such was my enthusiasm that, in co-operation with a private organisation with whom I was involved, a conference was arranged at the Institute of Directors, and held in September 1979 with Professor Ishikawa speaking on the first day. At that time I was totally unaware of developments in the United States or in Western Europe.

In order to do justice to such an eminent visitor, I contacted the Department of Trade, for suggestions as to who might be approached as supporting speakers. My contact then told me that Rolls Royce at Derby were operating a similar programme which they referred to as 'Quality Control Groups', and put me in contact with Jim Rooney at Derby who was responsible for the development of the programme.

Jim invited me up to Derby in June 1979. He showed me the training materials that they had prepared and which were based, to some extent, on a Japanese tape slide entitled 'Quality Control Circles for Foremen', and he gave me the opportunity to talk to group members, a shop steward and several managers. I then asked Jim if he would like to participate in my conference.

Not only did he agree, but he also offered to bring with him a shop steward, Tony Hunt, who was a keen member of one of the groups. Tony received a standing ovation for his presentation. I made a subsequent visit to Rolls Royce at Derby with Jason Crispe of the *Financial Times*, after which an article appeared on August 28th 1979 entitled 'Rolls Royce Shares in the Secrets of Japan's Success'.

During 1978/79 I had worked with Stan Warboys, Quality Manager at Eurotherm Ltd, Worthing, to develop a number of Circles in that factory. The

Eurotherm work resulted from Stan's attendance at a Quality Seminar I had organised in 1977. This was followed by Stan asking me to give a one-day presentation to his supervisors in 1978, at a seafront hotel. These supervisors became extremely enthusiastic, and the Seminars were followed by the establishment of the first Quality Circles. Stan Warboys was also invited to speak at the London conference, and so we were able to follow Professor Ishikawa's presentation of the concept by two real examples of success in British industry. The object of this was to bridge the credibility gap and prove that the concept really can be made to work in our society.

The conference was a huge success, with over 120 delegates from a broad spectrum of industry. These included representatives from Brintons Carpets, British Leyland, British Aerospace, Ford Motor Company, Mullard Ltd, Marks & Spencer, Chloride Ltd, Linotype Ltd, Welworthy, and many other well-known companies. The conference was featured on World Service Radio, and given publicity in a large number of periodicals and newspapers.

Almost immediately after it, I made the acquaintance in London of Jeff Beardsley, the Quality Circle Consultant from the USA referred to earlier. We became instant friends and after long discussions about the concept, training, the pitfalls, and in fact every aspect of the subject, agreed to collaborate with each other. The effect of this was immediate, and the injection of Jeff's experience into my own knowledge gave me the background to offer what has become the backbone of both my and all other David Hutchins Associates training methods and advice. Following these discussions with Jeff Beardsley, I began the training of Brintons Carpets Ltd, at the end of 1979, introducing the ideas which I had learned. This was followed soon afterwards by a similar training programme which included participants from S. R. Gent Ltd, Peter Blond & Co. Ltd, Sussman Ltd, and a Scottish company which did not subsequently take up the concept.

At the London conference Professor Ishikawa said: 'do not expect too much. If you have managed to develop Circles in two companies in one year you will be doing well'. In the event, I had trained 15 companies, with between 6 and 12 Circles in each company. By 1983, and with other consultants Ted Jowett and Brian Tilley joining me, the figure had risen to over 100 locations with active programmes.

During this time other consultants appeared on the scene, each with a different approach and varying levels of ability. Conferences have been organised by the National Economic Development Organisation (NEDO), the Work Research Unit of the Department of Industry and many others.

In 1982 a National Society of Quality Circles was formed, spearheaded mainly by Dick Fletcher of Wedgwood who became its first chairman. Membership of the Society is open to organisations who have active Quality Circles, and its basic intention is to provide a forum for cross-fertilisation and increasing the awareness of others to the concept. It is not a training organisation.

David Hutchins Associates have also developed a Circle Network, membership of which is automatic upon receipt of DHA Quality Circle training. This is supported by a regular newssheet entitled *Circle Review*.

I believe that Quality Circles in the UK and Europe generally are exposed to the same risks as in the USA: namely, that they will fail unless underpinned by Company-Wide Quality Control, and the external infrastructure. This infrastructure does not exist in our society and it was for this reason that Circle Network was formed. It enables those companies that we have trained to obtain the relevant support to ensure the combined growth and development of their programmes.

The development of Circles on the continent of Europe originated in Sweden as a result of the activities of B. Orjan Alexanderson, a well-known speaker at EOQC Conferences.

Apart from Norway, where the awareness of Quality Circles was stimulated by Asbjørn Aune of Trondheim University, it is difficult to pinpoint any particular individual responsible for developments in other European countries. Most countries have some development, with origins mainly in one or other of the sources already mentioned.

We ourselves have worked in many non-English-speaking countries and our experience has further confirmed our conviction that there is nothing cultural in Quality Circles. The concept will work anywhere where people work together and share common work experience. People want to be recognised for their knowledge and talent. If you treat them like human beings they will usually behave like them. Most of our problems stem from treating them otherwise.

In answer to the question 'should we start Quality Circles', one might say, 'what future do we have if we do not?!'

Summary of Part V

Chapters 19 and 20

1 Quality Circles were the result of a national programme of Quality improvement in Japan which commenced after World War II.

2 Two Americans, Drs Deming and Juran, are regarded as being responsible for this development.

3 Dr Juran lectured on the 'Management of Quality' described in his book *Managerial Breakthrough* (see Bibliography) and began the process of management development which ultimately led to Quality Circles of direct employees.

4 Quality Circles are a part and only a part of Company-Wide Quality Control, not a total entity in themselves.

5 Japanese Quality Circles are supported nationally by the Japanese Union of Scientists and Engineers.

6 Quality Circles reached the Western World in 1973 at Lockheed Space Missile Factory in California.

7 Quality Circles were formally introduced into the UK following the conference at the Institute of Directors in 1979.

Highlights of the Quality Circle movement

Events worldwide

Apr	1962	*GEMBA TO QC* (*QC for the Foreman*) begins as a quarterly publication. Formation and registration of Quality Circles are solicited.
May	1962	The first Quality Circle is registered.
Nov	1962	The first Foreman QC Conference is held.
May	1963	The first Quality Circle Conference is held.
Jan	1964	*GEMBA TO QC* is changed into a monthly publication.
Sep	1964	Regional Chapters are organised.
May	1965	Reports on the Quality Circle activities in Japan are presented at the 19th ASQC Convention held in Los Angeles.
Nov	1965	FQC Award is established.
Jun	1966	Special session on Quality Circle activities is organised at the Joint Conference at EOQC and ASOC held in Stockholm.
Feb	1967	QC Basic Course for Foremen starts.
Apr	1968	The first Quality Circle Team (1FQCT) visits USA.
Oct	1969	Many reports on Quality Circle activities are presented at the International Conference on Quality Control (ICQC 1969—Tokyo).
Nov	1970	*Fundamentals of the Quality Circle* is published by Japanese Union of Scientists and Engineers.
Nov	1970	QC correspondence course for foremen starts.
Aug	1971	The 200th Quality Circle Conference is held.

Nov	1971	Quality Circle Grand Prize is established. The first All Japan Quality Circle Conference is held.
Aug	1972	The number of Circles registered reaches 50 000.
Jan	1973	*GEMBA TO QC* is renamed *FQC*.
May	1973	The 300th Quality Circle Conference is held.
Nov	1973	The number of Circles registered reaches 60 000.
Oct	1974	The 400th Quality Circle Conference is held.
Oct	1975	First Quality Circle formed in the United States at the Lockheed Missiles and Space Company.

Highpoints relevant to the United Kingdom

Sep	1979	First UK Conference on Quality Circles entitled, 'The Japanese approach to Product Quality Management' attended by over 100 people. Organised by David Hutchins and held at the Institute of Directors in London.
Feb	1980	International Conference on Quality Circles organised by David Hutchins at Cavendish Conference Centre.
Sep	1980	World Convention on Quality Circles organised by David Hutchins and held at the Waldorf Hotel, London. Speakers from Japan, Norway, Sweden, Brazil, Germany, USA, Australia and UK.
Sep	1981	Second International Convention on Quality Circles, Tokyo. British party organised jointly by David Hutchins Associates and the Institute of Quality Assurance.
Oct	1981	*Circle Review* published by DHA. The first regular newsletter specifically for Quality Circles to be circulated in the UK.
May	1982	Inauguration of the National Society of Quality Circles.
June	1982	'If Japan can, so can we'—two-day conference with Quality Circles making presentations, Cavendish Conference Centre, London.
Oct	1982	First British/Japanese National Quality Circle Convention held at the Skyway Hotel, Heathrow, London.
Mar	1983	First Northern Convention of Network Circle Members Leaders and Facilitators in the UK held at the Post House, Manchester.

Mar	1983	First Southern Convention of Network Circle Members Leaders and Facilitators in the UK held at the Skyway Hotel, Heathrow, London.
May	1983	First National Society for Quality Circles Conference, London.
Mar	1984	First National Convention of Network Circle Members Leaders and Facilitators in the UK held at Stratford-upon-Avon.
May	1984	Second National Society for Quality Circles Conference, London.
Jun	1984	World Quality Congress, Brighton.
Sep	1984	First European Seminar on Quality Circles, Helsinki, Finland.

Highpoints relevant to the United States

June	1966	Dr J. M. Juran address at European Organisation for Quality Control (EOQC) Seminar in Stockholm, Sweden, predicts Japanese success due to Quality Control Circles.
Oct	1974	First US Quality Circles established at Lockheed Space Missile factory in California.
Late	1977	International Association of Quality Circles (IAQC) founded.
	1980	IAQC membership exceeds 1000.
Mar	1982	International resource Development Inc. report indicates 12 424 Circles in US companies.
Mar	1982	IAQC National Conference attracts over 2000.
Oct	1982	IAQC holds first Regional Conference in Memphis.
	1982	New York Stock Exchange Survey shows that 75% of the large manufacturing companies (over 10 000 employees) have Quality Circles. 44% of the total companies with over 500 employees are using Quality Circles.
Apr	1983	IAQC National Convention attracts over 2000 participants.
	1984	Membership of IAQC over 6000 with more than 70 Chapters in US.

Bibliography

Periodical articles (Alphabetical by author then chronological listing, most recent first)

Arbose, J. R., Quality Control Circles: the West adopts Japanese concept, *International Management*, Vol. 35, No. 12, December 1980, pp. 31–2, 36–7, 39.
BIM, What's new in Quality management? *Management Today*, September 1980, pp. 149 & 152.
Beals, R. P., Why Quality Control Circles sometimes fail in the US, *International Management*, November 1982, p. 7.
Berg, H. V., Motivation and Quality principles in practice, *Training and Development Journal* (ASTD), Vol. 24, No. 6, June 1970, pp. 28–31.
Bishop, D. and Gunz, H., Does your management need a Quality Circle? *Director*, Vol. 35, No. 1, July 1982, pp. 26–9.
Brunet, L., Quality Circles: Can they improve QWL? *Quality of Working Life—the Canadian scene*, Vol. 4, No. 2, 1981, pp. 1–2.
Casner-Lotto, J., The Japanese steel industry's version of the Quality Circle, *World of Work Report*, Vol. 7, No. 1, January 1982, pp. 1–3.
Claret, J., Never mind the Quality, *Management Accounting*, May 1981, pp. 24–6.
Cole, R. E., Quality Circle warning voices by US expert on Japanese Circles, *World of Work Report*, Vol. 6, No. 7, July 1981, pp. 49–51.
Cole, R. E., Learning from the Japanese—prospects and pitfalls, *American Management Review*, September 1980.
Cole, R. E., Made in Japan—Quality Control Circles, *Across the Board*, Vol. XVI, No. 11, November 1979, pp. 72–8.
Cole, R. E., Japanese Quality Control Circles: are they exportable to US firms? *World of Work Report*, Vol. 4, No. 6, June 1979, pp. 42–6.
Cornell, L., Quality Circles in the service industries, *Quality Progress*, July 1984.
Dolan, P., Quality Circles, *Industrial Participation*, Spring 1982, pp. 24–6.
Drew, H. E., QC's Motivation by Participation, *Institute of Industrial Management Newscast*, October 1982, p. 6.
Fletcher, R., Quality Circles at Wedgwood, *Industrial Participation*, No. 578 Summer 1982, pp. 2–9.

Gow, E., Would our use of the Japanese 'Quality Circle' bring cost savings? *Management Accounting*, February 1980, p. 18.
Hancock, G., Quality brings sales dividends at Jaguar, *Quality Progress*, May 1984.
Hanley, J., Our experience with Quality Circles, *Quality Progress*, Vol. XIII, No. 2, February 1980, pp. 22–4.
Hartley, J., Converting to Quality Control, *Engineer* (UK), Vol. 255, No. 6589, 8 July 1982, pp. 32–3.
Hartley, J., Through Quality Circles shopfloor creativity turns into hard cash, *Engineer* (UK), Vol. 252, No. 6530, 21 May 1981, pp. 29, 32.
Hollingham, J., Chance to start Quality Control Circles rolling, *Engineer* (UK), Vol. 251, No. 6484, 3 July 1980, p. 33.
Hollingham, J., Round the table thinking to better the job, *Engineer* (UK), Vol. 250, No. 6429, 29 May 1980, pp. 43–6.
Hutchins, D. C., The Application of the Quality Circle concept to reliability engineering, *Quality Assurance*, Vol. 7, No. 3, September 1981, pp. 59–60.
Hutchins, D. C., Ringing the bell with Quality Circles, *BIM Management Review and Digest*, Vol. 8, No. 1, April 1981, pp. 3–7.
Hutchins, D. C., How Quality goes round in Circles, *Management Today*, January 1981, pp. 27–8, 30, 32.
Hutchins, D. C., Why does Britain want Quality Circles? *Production Engineer*, February 1980.
Hutchins, D. C., QC Circles—an introduction, *Industrial and Commercial Training*, Vol. 12, No. 1, January 1980, pp. 8–15.
Hutchins, D. C., Quality Circles in context, *Industrial and Commercial Training*, Vol. 15, No. 3, March 1983, pp. 80–2.
Ingle, S., How to avoid Quality Circle failure in your company, *Training and Development Journal*, Vol. 36, No. 6, June 1982, pp. 54–9.
Ishikawa, K., Father of Quality Control Circles doubts their long-term viability in the West, *International Management*, Vol. 37, No. 8, August 1982, pp. 23–5.
Jones, L., Participative Quality Control—How General Motors adopted a Japanese idea, *Education and Training*, Vol. 19, No. 4, April 1977, pp. 99–104.
Jones, W. G., Quality Circles, *Management* (NZ), June 1982, pp. 69, 70, 72, 74.
Juran, J. M., The QC Circle Phenomena, *Industrial Quality Control*, January 1967.
Juran, J. M., Is Japan cornering the market on product quality? *International Management*, January 1981, pp. 22–5.
Klein, G. D., Implementing Quality Circles: a hard look at some of the realities, *Personnel* (USA) Vol. 58, No. 6, November–December 1981, pp. 11–20.
Konz, S., Quality Circles: Japanese success story, *Industrial Engineer*, October 1979, pp. 24–7.

Metz, E. J., The Verteam Circle, *Training and Development Journal*, Vol. 35, No. 12, December 1981, pp. 78–85.
Metz, E. J., Caution Quality Circles ahead, *Training and Development Journal*, Vol. 35, No. 8, August 1981, pp. 71–6.
Plous, F. K., The Quality Circle concept, growing by leaps and bounds, *World of Work Report*, Vol. 6, No. 4, April 1981, pp. 25–7.
Rendall, E., Quality Circles—a 'third wave' intervention, *Training and Development Journal*, Vol. 35, No. 3, March 1981, pp. 28–31.
Rendall, E. and Maser, M., Using Quality Circles in the Health Service, *Journal of European Industrial Training*, Vol. 4, No. 6, 1980, pp. 12–14.
Sankins, C. and Thompson, A., How QC's involve workers, *Rydge's*, June 1980, pp. 86–8.
Schleicher, W. F., Why QC's don't always work and what to do about it, *Management Review*, 1982, pp. 6–7.
Sussman, N., Quality and people, *Bulletin Clothing and Allied Products ITB*, No. 35, October 1980, p. 3.
Trades Union Congress, Quality Circles, *Industrial Participation*, Autumn 1981.
Vager, E., Examining the Quality Control Circle, *Personnel Journal*, Vol. 58, No. 10, October 1979, pp. 682–4, 704.
Wardle, I., Quality Circles, *AUEW Journal*, Vol. 48, No. 9, September 1981, p. 13.
Wyles, C., Quality Circles: Making better use of shopfloor knowledge, *Works Management*, Vol. 34, No. 10, October 1981, pp. 25, 27, 29, 31.
Wyles, K., How one workforce began to care about Quality, *Works Management*, Vol. 34, No. 4, April 1981, pp. 45, 47, 49, 50.
Yager, E. G., The Quality Control Circle explosion, *Training and Development Journal*, Vol. 35, No. 4, April 1981, pp. 98–9, 101–5.
Yager, E. G., Quality Circles: a tool for the 80s, *Training and Development Journal*, Vol. 34, No. 8, August 1980, pp. 60–2.
Yager, E. G., Examining the Quality Control Circle, *Personnel Journal*, Vol. 58, No. 10, October 1979, pp. 682–4, 708.
York, F., Tenneco implements Quality Circles, *Word and Processing Information Systems*, September 1981, pp. 13, 14.

Periodical Articles (No author—chronological listing, most recent first)

Quality Circles at Jaguar Cars, *Industrial Review and Report*, No. 277, August 1982, pp. 7–10.
Quality Circles: the Lesieur Experiment, *European Industrial Relations Review*, No. 93, October 1981, pp. 16–18.
Honeywell pioneers in the Quality Circles movement, *World of Work Report*, Vol. 6, No. 9, September 1981, pp. 66–8.

Norway: Quality Circles in metallurgical companies, *UIMM Social International*, July 1981, p. 13.
Quality Circles, in particular in the Metal Industry, *UIMM Social International*, June 1981, p. 7.
Norway: establishment of Quality Circles, *UIMM Social International*, June 1981, p. 8.
Productivity and Quality Control: the Japanese experience, Japanese External Trade Organisation, *Now in Japan*, No. 30, 1981.
Preferring to do a good job rather than a bad one, *Production Engineer*, Vol. 59, No. 7/8, July/August 1980, pp. 31–3.
Quality Control Circles Part III, *Productivity*, Vol. 1, No. 3, July 1980, pp. 3, 10.
Quality Control Circles Part II, *Productivity*, Vol. 1, No. 2, July 1980, pp. 5–6.
Productivity and morale sagging? Try the Quality Circle approach, *Personnel*, Vol. 57, No. 3, May/June 1980, pp. 43–5.
The magic of Japan's Quality Circles, *Engineering Today*, Vol. 4, No. 13, April 1980, pp. 26–7.
QC's—Japan's way to better quality, *Production Engineer*, November 1979, p. 35.
An 'uninscrutable' lesson from Japan, *Industrial Management*, October 1979, pp. 16–17, 38.
Quality Control Circles imported from Japan, *Personnel*, Vol. 56, No. 5, September–October 1979, pp. 42–5.
Quality Control Circles: the Human side of Quality Control, Quality of Working Life—the Canadian Scene, Vol. 2, No. 3, 1979, pp. 16–18.

Newspaper articles (Chronological listing, most recent first)

Barber, L., Shop floor Circles aren't so vicious, *Sunday Times*, 17 Oct. 1982.
Lorenz, C., Why Wedgwood went Japanese, *Financial Times*, 28 Jun. 1982.
Austin, R., Quality Circles are well worth looking round, *The Times*, 18 May 1981, p. 16.
Lorenz, C., Giving the Customer pride of place, *Financial Times*, 6 Feb. 1981, p. 11.
Lorenz, C., Why the Quality Revolution must start at the top, *Financial Times*, 4 Feb. 1981, p. 10.
Lorenz, C., The West starts a belated quest for better product quality, *Financial Times*, 3 Feb. 1981, p. 12.
Lorenz, C., The Shopfloor's verdict on Quality Circles, *Financial Times*, 2 Feb. 1981, p. 8.
Lorenz, C., How Europe is tailoring the Japanese design, *Financial Times*, 30 Jan. 1981, p. 17.
Lorenz, C., Weapons for the workers, *Financial Times*, 28 Jan. 1981, p. 10.
Lorenz, C., Full of Eastern promise—but handle with care, *Financial Times*, 27 Jan. 1981, p. 13.

Lorenz, C., Motivation: Japan's new export, *Financial Times*, 26 Jan. 1981, p. 1.
Hill, P., How Japanese workers go round in profitable Circles, *The Times*, 13 Jan. 1981.
Smith, C., Why a Japanese bank began to go round in Circles, *Financial Times*, 13 Aug. 1980.
Lorenz, C., Why Japan wins the Quality race, *Financial Times*, 1 Sep. 1980.
Gooding, K., Ford brings home some Eastern philosophy, *Financial Times*, 9 May 1980, p. 21.
Lorenz, C., What Western managers can learn from Japan's quest for Quality, *Financial Times*, 11 Mar. 1980, Management page.
Young, D., Round in Circles: getting somewhere, *The Times*, 3 Dec. 1979, p. 16.
Crisp, J., How RR is sharing a secret of Japanese success, *Financial Times*, 24 Aug. 1979, Management page.

Books, Booklets, Pamphlets and Papers (Alphabetical author listing)

Aho, T., Quality Circles at Lohja Electronics—experience and examples, *Proceedings of the First European Seminar on Quality Circles*, Helsinki, Finland, September, 1984 (Published by Finnish Society for Quality, Helsinki).
Alexanderson, O., Quality versus Quality Control—cease fire, *Proceedings of the World Quality Congress*, Brighton, UK, June 1984 (Published by British Quality Association, London).
Amsden, D. M. and Amsden, P. T. (eds), *QC Circles: Applications Tools and Theory* (A compilation of papers by Japanese and Western authors plus bibliography), American Society for Quality Control, Milwaukee, 1976.
Asian Productivity Association, *Japan's Quality Circles*, Tokyo, 1977.
Beardsley, J., Training is the heart of the Lockheed Quality Control Circles Program, *American Society for Quality Control (ASQC) 30th Annual Technical Conference Transaction*, 7-9 Jun. 1976.
Codron, J. and Haegeman, M., Quality Circles: a nine days wonder or a long-term energy source, *Proceedings of the World Quality Congress*, Brighton, UK, June 1984 (Published by British Quality Association, London).
Dewar, D. L., *Quality Circles—answers to 100 frequently asked questions*, Quality Circle Institute, Red Bluff, CA, 1979.
Dewar, D. L., Measurement and results of the Lockheed Quality Control Circles Program, *American Society for Quality Control (ASQC) 30th Annual Technical Conference Transaction*, 7-9 Jun. 1976.
Dewar, D. L., *The Quality Circle Guide to Participation Management*, Prentice Hall, 1980.
Egan, J. L., Quality—the Jaguar obsession, *Proceedings of the World Quality Congress*, Brighton, UK, June 1984 (Published by British Quality Association, London).

Engel, P., Japanische Organizationsprinzipien, Verlag Moderne Industrie, Zurich, 1981.
Frisk, J., Experience from Quality Circles in service industry, *Proceedings of the First European Seminar on Quality Circles*, Helsinki, Finland, September 1984 (Published by Finnish Society for Quality, Helsinki).
Goque, J. M., The role of Quality Circles in European industrial culture, *Proceedings of the First European Seminar on Quality Circles*, Helsinki, Finland, September 1984 (Published by Finnish Society for Quality, Helsinki).
Hedmark, S., Quality Circles at Sandvik, *Proceedings of the First European Seminar on Quality Circles*, Helsinki, Finland, September 1984 (Published by Finnish Society for Quality, Helsinki).
Hutchins, D., Quality Circles as part of Company-Wide Quality Control, *Proceedings of the First European Seminar on Quality Circles*, Helsinki, Finland, September 1984 (Published by Finnish Society for Quality, Helsinki).
Hutchins, D., Quality Circles—the management vacuum, *Proceedings of the World Quality Congress*, Brighton, UK, June 1984 (Published by British Quality Association, London).
Ingle, S., *Quality Circles Master Guide*, Prentice Hall, Englewood Cliffs, NJ, 1982.
Institute of Personnel Management, *Practical Participation and Involvement—3: The Individual and the Job*, London, 1982. (Chapter 3, Quality Circles, contains two case studies pp. 80–116.)
Ishikawa, K., *QC Circle Activities* (QC in Japan Series, No. 1), Japanese Union of Scientists and Engineers, Tokyo, 1968.
Ishikawa, K., *Guide to Quality Control* (Details of the tools taught to Japanese Foremen and QC Circles), Asian Productivity Organization, Tokyo, 1976.
Japan Quality Control Circles (Collection of papers by Japanese authors), Asian Productivity Organization, Tokyo, 1972.
Jalonen, A., Quality Circles from a worker's point of view, *Proceedings of the First European Seminar on Quality Circles*, Helsinki, Finland, September 1984 (Published by Finnish Society for Quality, Helsinki).
Japanese Union of Scientists and Engineers, QC Circle Activities in the World, *Engineers*, No. 376, 1980.
Japanese Union of Scientists and Engineers, *International QC Circle Convention Proceedings*, Tokyo, 1981.
Juran, J. M., *Managerial Breakthrough*, McGraw Hill, New York, 1965.
Juran, J. M., *Selected Papers*, (Looseleaf set of 26 papers including 'Product Quality—a prescription for the West' (1981), 'Japanese and Western Quality' (1978), 'The QC Circle Phenomenon' (1966), The Juran Institute, New York.
Juran, J. M., *The Quality Control Handbook*, 3rd edn, McGraw Hill, New York, 1974.
Karvinen, P., The future of Quality Circles in Europe, *Proceedings of the First*

European Seminar on Quality Circles, Helsinki, September 1984 (Published by Finnish Society for Quality, Helsinki).

Keogh, B., Example of a national approach to Quality Circles, *Proceedings of the First European Seminar on Quality Circles*, Helsinki, Finland, September 1984 (Published by the European Organization for Quality Control, Berne, Switzerland).

Lorenz, C. et al., *Learning from the Japanese* (Collection of articles dated 24 Aug. 1979, 6 Feb. 1981 and 1 May 1981) *Financial Times*, London, 1981.

Mohr, W. L. and Mohr, H., *Quality Circles*, Addison Wesley, Reading, Mass., 1983.

Morland, J., *Quality Circles*, Industrial Society, London, 1981.

National Economic Development Office, Printing Machinery Sector Working Party, *Quality Circles: Proceedings of Conference held on 14 Jan. 1981*, London, 1981.

National Economic Development Office, Quality Circles Information Pack, London, 1981.

Nippon Steel Corporation, *Jishu Kanri Activities in Nippon Steel Corporation*, 1980.

Noguchi, J., JUSE's role in Japanese Quality Control, *Proceedings of the World Quality Congress*, Brighton, UK, June 1984 (Published by British Quality Association, London).

Pajunen, T., The present state and trends of Quality Circles in Europe—results of the mapping done by the Quality Circles Committee, *Proceedings of the First European Seminar on Quality Circles*, Helsinki, Finland, September 1984 (Published by Finnish Society for Quality, Helsinki).

Rieker, W. S., QC Circles as Quality motivators: status in the United States, *Proceedings of the World Quality Congress*, Brighton, UK, June 1984 (Published by British Quality Association, London).

Robson, M., *Quality Circles: a Practical Guide*, Gower, Aldershot, 1982.

Rooney, J., *Quality Circles in practice*, Paper presented at BIM and British Management Data Foundation Conference *What's New in Quality Management*, Kensington Close Hotel, London, 3 June 1980.

Sasaki, N. and Hutchins, D. C., *The Japanese Approach to Product Quality*, Pergamon, 1984.

Sesseng, B., Objectives and significance of Quality Circles, *Proceedings of the First European Seminar on Quality Circles*, Helsinki, Finland, September 1984 (Published by Finnish Society for Quality, Helsinki).

Trades Union Congress, *Quality Circles*, London, 1981.

Van der Linden, G., Management and Quality Circles, *Proceedings of the First European Seminar on Quality Circles*, Helsinki, Finland, September 1984 (Published by Finnish Society for Quality).

Bibliographies

Konz, S., Quality Circles: an Annotated Bibliography, *Quality Progress*, Apr. 1981, pp. 30–5.

Work Research Unit, *Information Systems Bibliographies No. 42: Quality Circles*, revised Nov. 1982.

Quality Circle Periodicals

Circle News, Kenwoods, Havant, Hampshire.
Circle Review, David Hutchins Associates, Ascot, Berkshire.
In Stitches, Abbey Hosiery Mills, Nuneaton.
Journal of Quality Technology, American Society for Quality Control, Milwaukee, USA.
La Gazette des Cercles, American Express Centre, Paris, France.
Potting Around, Josiah Wedgwood Ltd, Stoke-on-Trent.
Quality, European Organization for Quality Control, Berne, Switzerland.
Quality Progress, American Society for Quality Control, Milwaukee, USA.
Update, Rieker Management Systems, Los Gatos, California, USA.

Index

The abbreviation 'QC' for Quality Circles is used throughout this index

Analysis
  cause 56
  cause and effect 52–6
  generally 67
  Pareto 50–2
  process 56–7

Brainstorming 45–8, 58, 66–7, 199
Brazil 250–1
British Leyland 124
British Steel 124

Canteen 239
Case studies 70–114
Charts 66
Check list 66
Check sheets 48–50, 67
Circle
  audit 133–4
  authority of 234
  British adoption 211
  constraints 175
  cost–benefit 133, 195–6
  cost-effectiveness 235
  costs 131–2, 235
  criticisms by 214
  definition 31, 211
  development 29, 141–2, 147, 181, 252–5
  difficulties 152–3
  discussion with union 162
  education 32
  equipment 132
  exchange visits 198, 203
  external support for 206–9
  facilities 132
  failures 120–4, 179–80, 236, 240
  golden rules for 136
  growth rate 211
  guidelines 174
  highlights of the movement 257–9
  history 243–51
  implementing solutions 37–8

information for 31, 147, 154, 170
inhibition of members 32
initial stages 30, 139
innovation by 30, 203
integration with Quality Control 241
internal support for 202–6
introduction of 119–90, 217
job creation 162–3
job loss 162–3
leadership 35–6, 143, 145, 161, 224–5
level of members 216
management 221
management level 137
manpower 132
materials 132
members 31–2, 162, 225–7
momentum 216
monitoring 30, 133, 203
morale 133
motivation 237
name 211
national societies 209
network 206–9
non-members 168, 227–8
optimum company size 216
organisation 228–9
origin 246–50
other group activities 238–9
paid time 35, 161
pay questions 162, 214
part-time workers 214
payment of members 162
permanence 212
piecework environment, in 238
policy review 175
policy statement 174
power of 240
preparation and introduction 119–90
problem selection 136, 161, 167–8, 230–2
problem solving 29–38, 69, 203–4, 220
problems tackled by 36–7

Circle (*contd*)
  questions most often asked   210–41
  reception of proposals   58, 68
  recognition   142, 198
  relation to suppliers and customers   241
  relations with others   137, 222–3
  responsibility   142
  rewards   179, 195–200, 237
  self-confidence   142
  self-development   141–2
  size   29, 31–3
  solutions presented to management   37
  successes   120, 211–13
  suggestion schemes   199–200
  supervisor level   137
  support for   170, 202–9
  team-building   142–3
  techniques   43–69, 141
  technological change   213
  'teeth'   216
  terms of employment   163, 214
  track record   212–13
  ultimate object of   136
  utilisation of gains   198–9
  voluntary principle   161, 170, 212
  white-collar   213
  see also Facilitator; Meeting; People;
    Presentation; Programme; Self-control;
    Steering committee; Trade union;
    Training
Communications   25, 187, 217
Company-Wide Quality Control (CWQC)
  concept of   248
  consensus management essential for   122
  definition   13–14, 129
  development of   206
  essence of   241
  generally   240–1
  impossible in West   14, 28, 122, 248
  Japanese definition   13–14, 129
  objective, as   28
  people-based   248
  QC's only part of   211
  role of   174
  USA, in   251
Corporate goals   129–30
Corporate identity   143
Corporate loyalty   143
Corporate plan   128–9
Corporate policy   128–30, 174
Craftsmanship system   22–4
Crosby, P.   10, 250
Culture
  industrial   8
  national   121–2, 124
  organisational   124
  regional   124
Customer satisfaction   10
Customer specifications   239–40

Data
  collection   48–9, 59–68
  types   59
  use for control   62
  variable   63–5
David Hutchins Associates (DHA)   120, 127, 180, 210
Defect locations   65
Definitions
  quality   9–11
  Quality Circle   28, 31, 211
  quality control   12–14
Deming, W.E.   246–8
Drawings of defect locations   65

Education   139
European Organisation for Quality Control   12

Facilitator
  appointment   132, 182
  co-ordination of   175
  job specification for   187–9
  member of steering committee   175
  over-zealous   168
  part-time   184, 186–7
  programme monitoring   133
  qualities required by   185–6
  questions about   224
  responsibility for programmes   170–1
  scope   132
  selection of   184–6
  support for   132, 175
  time needed by   183–4, 186
  title   182
  training   149
  withdrawals   149
Ford, Henry   18

Graphs   66
Groups (other than QC's)   238–9

History of Quality Circles   243–51

Inspection   59–60

Japan
  auditing Circles   133
  background to QC's   9, 246–50
  culture of   122
  definition of Quality Control   13–14
  Deming Prize   247–8
  early 1950s, in   20
  history of Quality Control Circles   20, 243–51
  importance of presentations   249
  labour relations   15, 20
  magazine for foremen   27
  management   20, 22

Japan (*contd*)
  number of QC's 211, 249–50
  origin of QC's 211, 213, 246–8
  post-war reconstruction 9, 15
  Quality Month 205–6, 248–9
  rate of growth of QC's 249–50
  supervisor development in 145
  Taylor system 248
  training 151
  see also Company-Wide Quality Control
Juran, J.M. 248–50

Labour
  manning levels 232
  organisation 17–18
  relations. *See* People

Management
  attitude towards QC's 126
  Circle for 137–8, 221
  Circle solutions presented to 37
  commitment to QC's 130–1, 215–16, 219–22
  consensus 124
  crafts 145
  fear of QC's 124–5
  goals 126
  line or middle 125, 135–44, 172–3, 221–2
  objectives 28, 126
  people development 138
  pressure on QC's 167
  prohibition of Circle meeting 229
  rewards from QC's 126
  response to presentations 57–8, 162, 233–4
  scientific 19–22
  senior 219–21
  statement of objectives 28
  styles 125–7
  systems 15–24
  theory X 125–6
  theory Y 125–6, 139
  top 125, 128–34, 173
Meeting (of Circle)
  attendance 136
  day for 136
  flexibility 230
  paid time, in 35, 161
  place 229
  postponement 136
  productivity of 229
  prohibition by management 229
  regularity of 34
  room 132
  shift work 230
  suspension 134
  time 136, 161, 230
  voluntary nature 33–4
Multi-site operations 134

Non-Circle members 167–9

People
  alienation 138
  boredom 16, 138–41
  development 138–41, 144
  education 139
  flexibility 140–1
  job rotation 140–1
  management role in developing 138–41
  philosophy based upon 15–28
  recognition 139
  responsibility 138–9
  see also training
Presentation
  affecting manning levels 232
  all members participate in 162, 233–4
  always face to face 162
  anti-climax after 234
  attendance at 233
  Circle conventions, to 198, 233
  Circle's own manager, to 233
  climax of Circle's work 57, 198, 233
  cross-fertilisation through 26
  demonstration to others, as 57
  development of supervisor by 27
  face to face 162
  form of 162
  highlight, as 57, 198, 233
  how made 232
  individual, by 237
  interim 233
  involvement in 67, 162, 168, 233–4
  Japanese view of 249
  leader not to give 162
  management response to 57–8, 162, 233–4
  never as report or memorandum 162
  new ideas picked up at 198
  non-members, to 142–3, 168
  other departments, to 233
  other QC's, to 198
  participation in 67, 162, 168, 233–4
  preparation of 67, 232
  public functions, at 26, 198, 249
  recognition obtained through 233
  repeated 198
  section, to 142–3, 168
  selling ideas by 234
  steering committee, to 198, 233
  supervisors, by 26–7
  time spent on 233
  training for 58
  use of visual aids 189
  writing, in 162, 232
Problem solving
  ability of QC's 220
  guide to 69
  phase (of Circles) 30, 203
  progress from 30, 203–4

Problem solving (contd)
  satisfaction from 37
  specialists, by 15–16
  starting point for 'self-control' 29
  Taylorism, under 15–16
Productivity 10–11, 240
Programme (of QC)
  cost 196, 214
  development 189, 202–9
  facilitator's responsibility 188
  investment, as 196
  measurement 234–7
  preparation 214–17
  presentation 189
  threats to 188–9
  use of visual aids 189
Publicity 178, 188, 203

Quality Circle (QC). *See* Circle
Quality 8–11, 240
Quality Control 12–14, 246–50

Resources 131–2
Rivalry 168–9

Sampling 59–61
'Self-control' (of QC's)
  achieving 30, 204–5
  corporate objective, as 208
  education 26
  example 140–1
  full 204–5
  generally 26–7
  information needed for 28
  management style 145–6
  manager's awareness 136
  principle of 29, 138
  responsibility 138
  time-scale 204–5
  training 26
  Western Europe, in 30
Specialists
  conflicts with QC's 223
  enthusiasm for QC's 164, 222
  example of working with Circle 166
  involved in presentation 166
  problems handled by 164–5
  QC's seen as threat to 164, 172–3
  separate from line structure 25
  services used by QC's 32, 153, 165–6, 222
  Taylorism, under 165
  types of 164
Statistical Quality Control (SQC) 13
Steering committee
  contact with other companies 180
  continuity 177
  facilitator 175–6, 187
  function 163
  generally 170–81, 223–4

  initial stages 170–1
  interest in QC's 178–9
  liaison by 180
  membership 171
  middle management on 172–3
  recognition of achievement by 180
  specialists on 173
  supervisor on 172
  tasks 173–4
  top management on 173
  trade unions 157–8, 171–2
Suggestion schemes 199–200
Supervisor
  alternative leader to 36
  Circle for 137
  Circle leader, as 35–6, 143, 145–6, 161
  communication with management 222
  confidence of 36, 222
  development of 26–7, 149
  favouritism by 168
  feelings of inadequacy 222
  improvement of 221
  more than one in department 222
  presentation by 26–7, 162
  role of 24–6
  training 27, 149–51
  unwillingness of 36

Taylor, Frederick 15
Taylorism 15–18, 22–4, 138, 145, 165
Total Quality Control (TQC) 13
Trade union
  agreed procedures 159
  attitude 154–5, 158–61
  co-operation 154, 158, 172
  employment implications 159–60
  examples 155–7
  experience with 154
  FDC's 160
  guidelines 158–60
  hostility 154–5
  key points for 161
  local officials 154–5
  objections 162
  opportunities for 151
  opposition to unilaterally imposed
    structures 159
  policy 154
  questions about 223
  representation on QC's 171–2
  scepticism 158–9
  steering committee and 157–8, 163
  threat to 156–7
  workers' involvement 160
Trades Union Congress 154, 158–60
Training
  additional skills required for 188
  Circle, of 149
  courses 150–1

Training (*contd*)
  DHA, by   120
  facilitator's role   149, 188
  formal   141
  initial   149
  Japan, in   150–1
  key groups, of   120
  leader, by   149, 188
  leader, of   149, 150
  management, of   220
  manager's responsibility   139
  methods   141–2
  needs of department   139
  non-existent   120
  'people-building'   150
  presentation, for   58
  programme   140, 151
  simultaneous   149
  supervisor, by   27
  supervisor, of   149–50
  techniques, in   151

USA
  CWQC in   248
  development of QC's in   250–1
  evolution of Taylorism in   17
  growth rate of QC's in   211–12
  help to Japan   246–8
  national societies   209
  scientific management   19

Visual aids   189

Whitney, Eli   17

Zero Defects (ZD)   250